The Hegel Dictionary

Also available from Continuum

The Derrida Dictionary, Simon Morgan Wortham
The Sartre Dictionary, Gary Cox

Forthcoming
The Deleuze and Guattari Dictionary, Greg Lambert, Gary Genosko, Janell Watson and Eugene B. Young
The Gadamer Dictionary, Chris Lawn and Niall Keane
The Heidegger Dictionary, Daniel O. Dahlstrom
The Husserl Dictionary, Dermot Moran and Joseph Cohen
The Kant Dictionary, Lucas Thorpe
The Marx Dictionary, Ian Fraser and Laurence Wilde
The Nietzsche Dictionary, Greg Moore
The Wittgenstein Dictionary, David Levy

The Hegel Dictionary

Glenn Alexander Magee

Continuum International Publishing Group
The Tower Building, 11 York Road, London SE1 7NX
80 Maiden Lane, Suite 704, New York NY 10038

www.continuumbooks.com

© Glenn Alexander Magee 2010

All rights reserved. No part of this publication may be reproduced or transmitted in any form or by any means, electronic or mechanical, including photocopying, recording, or any information storage or retrieval system, without prior permission in writing from the publishers.

British Library Cataloguing-in-Publication Data
A catalogue record for this book is available from the British Library.

ISBN: HB: 978-1-84706-590-2
        PB: 978-1-84706-591-9

Library of Congress Cataloging-in-Publication Data
Magee, Glenn Alexander, 1966–
  The Hegel dictionary / Glenn Magee.
      p. cm.
  Includes bibliographical references and index.
  ISBN-13: 978-1-84706-590-2
  ISBN-10: 1-84706-590-2
  ISBN-13: 978-1-84706-591-9 (pbk.)
  ISBN-10: 1-84706-591-0 (pbk.)
  1. Hegel, Georg Wilhelm Friedrich, 1770–1831--Dictionaries. I. Title.
  B2901.M34 2010
  193--dc22
                                                              2010010416

Typeset by Kenneth Burnley with Caroline Waldron, Wirral, Cheshire

Contents

Acknowledgements	vii
Abbreviations and Conventions	viii
Introduction	1
The Hegel Dictionary	19
Chronology	263
Suggestions for Further Reading	265
Endnotes	269

To my mother

Acknowledgements

Learning Hegel is not unlike a process of initiation. One has to be taken by the hand and guided by those who have already made the journey through his labyrinthine and often bewildering system. I was fortunate enough to have several excellent guides both as an undergraduate and as a graduate student: Martin J. De Nys, Wayne J. Froman, Thelma Z. Lavine, Donald Phillip Verene and Richard Dien Winfield.

A number of individuals read an earlier draft of *The Hegel Dictionary* and offered advice and constructive criticism. They include Clark Butler, William Desmond, Stephen Houlgate, Gregory R. Johnson, and Donald Phillip Verene.

I must also express my gratitude to the students in my class on Nineteenth Century Philosophy in the fall of 2009. They served as 'test subjects' for many of the formulations given in this volume.

Thanks must also go to my editor at Continuum, Sarah Campbell, who approached me with the idea for this project in the first place.

G. A. M.
New York City
February 2010

Abbreviations and Conventions

A — Addition (additional remarks from student notes on Hegel's lectures, appended to paragraphs in his published writings).

EL — *Encyclopedia Logic*. (Reference is by Hegel's paragraph number; e.g., 'EL § 9'.)

Geraets — *The Encyclopedia Logic*, trans. T. F. Geraets, et al. (Albany: State University of New York Press, 1991).

LHP — *Lectures on the History of Philosophy*, 3 vols, trans. E. S. Haldane (London: Kegan Paul, Trench, Trübner and Co., 1892).

LPR — *Lectures on the Philosophy of Religion*, 3 vols, ed. and trans. Peter C. Hodgson, et al. (Berkeley: University of California Press, 1984).

Miller — *Hegel's Philosophy of Nature*, trans. A. V. Miller (Oxford: Oxford University Press, 1970).
Or
The Phenomenology of Spirit, trans. A. V. Miller (Oxford: Oxford University Press, 1977). Reference is by Miller's page number, not paragraph number (the paragraph numbers in Miller do not exist in Hegel's original and are there simply to provide quick reference to J. N. Findlay's commentary, which forms an appendix to the translation).
Or
The Science of Logic, trans. A.V. Miller (London: George Allen and Unwin, 1969).
The context makes it clear which Miller translation is being referred to.

Nisbet — *Lectures on the Philosophy of World History*, trans. H. B. Nisbet (Cambridge: Cambridge University Press, 1975).
Or

Abbreviations and Conventions

Elements of the Philosophy of Right, ed. Allen W. Wood, trans. H. B. Nisbet (Cambridge Cambridge University Press, 1991). The context makes it clear which is being referred to.

PG   *Phänomenologie des Geistes*, ed. Hans-Friedrich Wessels and Heinrich Clairmont (Hamburg: Felix Meiner, 1988).

PN   Philosophy of Nature. (Reference is by Hegel's paragraph number.)

PR   Philosophy of Right. (Reference is by Hegel's paragraph number.)

PS   Philosophy of Spirit. (Reference is by Hegel's paragraph number.)

VIG   *Die Vernunft in der Geschichte*, ed. Johannes Hoffmeister (Berlin: Akademie Verlag, 1966).

VPR   *Vorlesungen über die Philosophie der Religion*, 3 vols, ed. Walter Jaeschke (Hamburg: Felix Meiner, 1983–7).

Wallace   *Hegel's Philosophy of Mind*, trans. William Wallace (Oxford: Clarendon Press, 1971).

Werke   G. W. F. Hegel: *Werke*, 20 vols, ed. Eva Moldenhauer and Karl Markus Michel (Frankfurt am Main: Suhrkamp, 1986).

WL   *Wissenschaft der Logik*, 3 vols, ed. Hans-Jürgen Gawoll (Hamburg: Felix Meiner, 1986–1992). This includes the 1812 edition of *Das Sein*, but reference to 'WL I' is always to the 1832 edition of *Das Sein*, ed. Hans-Jürgen Gawoll (Hamburg: Felix Meiner, 1990).

Unless otherwise noted, reference to the above books is by page number. I have altered translations here and there, for accuracy.

When referring to specific texts by Hegel, I have italicized their titles. I have *not* italicized the names of the divisions of Hegel's philosophy. For example: 'Volume One of *The Science of Logic* was published in 1812.' But: 'The Logic is the first division of Hegel's system.'

In general I have resisted the practice of capitalizing technical terms in Hegel's philosophy (a procedure carried to extremes in some commentaries, especially in older literature). Since the initial letter of *every* noun in the German language is capitalized, there is no basis for thinking Hegel would have wanted us to refer to Nature, Being, Space, Family, Morality,

Understanding, etc. And virtually every term used by Hegel is employed in a special, technical sense. However, I have adopted the practice of capitalizing certain terms that are of *supreme* importance in Hegel's philosophy, especially those to which he attaches theological significance: e.g., the Absolute, the Concept, Idea, Spirit.

Some of the names of the categories of Hegel's system also serve as titles of major divisions or headings in his works. When I refer to those categories as divisions in Hegel's texts I capitalize them, and put them in quotation marks. For example: 'Hegel divides "Ethical Life" into three major sections: "Family", "Civil Society" and the "State".' However, when I refer to these ideas simply as ideas and not as sections of text, I do not capitalize them: e.g., 'For Hegel, civil society is the antithesis of the family.'

I have included a German translation for most of the terms to which entries are devoted (the exceptions being terms associated with Hegel's philosophy, but not actually used by Hegel; e.g. 'coherence'). German glossaries in scholarly works on Hegel often omit the definite article of nouns. However, given that this is a resource for students I have included these, for the sake of completeness. Where Hegel uses more than one German word to express a concept, I have usually chosen the word he uses most often.

English translations of Hegelian terms found throughout this volume are invariably the ones most commonly utilized today in English translations of Hegel, and in commentaries.

Introduction

The Importance of Hegel

The classical understanding of philosophy – the 'love of wisdom' – is that it is a search for knowledge of the most fundamental things. The wisdom sought by the philosopher will tell us why things are the way they are and, perhaps, what the point of it all is. In short, philosophy seeks to understand *the whole*, and to express knowledge of the whole in a complete account. Accordingly, all the great philosophers are known as 'systematic philosophers' because they attempt to understand *everything*, and to understand how everything hangs together. In short, their philosophies are systematic because they believe the world itself is a system, an inter-related whole. The best classical example of such a philosopher (and the most *apropos* for a discussion of Hegel) is Aristotle, who believed in a scale of nature with God at the top, and everything else striving, in one fashion or another, to imitate God's eternity and perfect self-sufficiency.

Hegel is the modern philosopher of system *par excellence*. The key to understanding his thought is the concept of wholeness, or holism. Hegel attempts to demonstrate that existence itself is an internally differentiated whole in which every element is related to every other – in other words, everything is what it is, in and through its relationship to everything else. One of Hegel's most famous and important statements is that 'the true is the whole'. In other words, the truth about anything is to be found in its relationship to the entirety of existence, of which it is merely a part. Another way to put this is to say that if we are searching for the ultimate meaning or significance of something, it is to be found in the role played by that something in the system of reality itself. But, we might ask, is there a meaning to the whole? The parts may have meaning in relation to the whole, but does the whole itself have any meaning? This is equivalent to the stock question people often associate with philosophy: What is the meaning (or purpose) of existence? (Or, often, 'What is the meaning of life?') Remarkably, Hegel answers this question, in effect, by telling us that the purpose of existence lies in the asking of the question itself.

When we think about it, it is really an odd fact that nature produces beings like us, who have fundamental doubts and concerns about our place in the cosmos, and who, as a consequence, strive to create philosophies. Is it possible that philosophy itself might have some important, metaphysical role to play in the scheme of things? This idea did not really occur to the systematic philosophers who came before Hegel. (One has to look outside the 'mainstream' of the history of philosophy, to the Gnostic, Hermetic, and mystical traditions to find something that approaches this.) Philosophers like Aristotle gave humanity and human reason an exalted place in the scheme of things, but Hegel actually argues, in effect, that philosophy *completes* the scheme of things. For Hegel, human beings are *the self-consciousness of existence itself*. This may seem like an incredible idea, but it is possible to give a very simple and convincing argument for it.

In Hegel's philosophy we find a sophisticated re-thinking of Aristotle's scale of nature. Just as in Aristotle, at the bottom of the scale is non-living matter like rocks and minerals, then plants – which are alive but not truly conscious, and largely immobile – then animals, which are mobile and thus better able to survive, and who are also conscious. Higher still, however, are human beings whose consciousness, unlike the animals, is not caught in a purely immediate, here-and-now focus, but who are also capable of reflection and, most importantly, *self-reflection*. Nevertheless, though our consciousness may be radically different from that of other animals, we are still a type of animal; we are ourselves products of nature. Therefore, when we strive to understand nature in science and philosophy, we can see that in a sense what is happening is that nature is striving to know itself. Existence comes to consciousness of itself through us. For Hegel, this is the key to understanding all of reality. Picture for a moment the scale of nature not as a static hierarchy but as a dynamic process of coming-to-be, constantly bringing forth new life. Lower levels give rise to higher, still more complex ones, and the process continues until it reaches closure: in human beings it turns back on itself, and knows itself as a whole *through* the consciousness of humanity, the highest of its creations. Through humanity, existence achieves closure; it becomes known to itself, aware of itself. The purpose of existence, therefore, is the attainment of this cosmic self-knowledge – and for Hegel we find the 'meaning of life' precisely in

Introduction

our knowledge that we are the vehicle and the consummation of this purpose.

Hegel's manner of arguing for these ideas is just as startlingly original as the ideas themselves. His philosophy begins with a 'phenomenology of spirit' (the title, in fact, of Hegel's first major work), in which he demonstrates that all the different forms of human consciousness surreptitiously aim at an 'absolute knowing' not of this part of reality or that, but of the whole itself. In order to know the whole, however, Hegel argues that we must adopt a philosophical standpoint which is utterly without any determinate presuppositions. We cannot even begin by presupposing that we know what philosophy is, or what we are aiming at in our philosophic work, for then we would skew the result. Hegel's system, therefore, begins with a pure indeterminate 'immediacy', which he defines in short order as being – but a being that is equivalent to nothing! Remarkably, this is how his Logic opens, the first true division of Hegel's philosophical system (*The Phenomenology of Spirit* merely being a preparation for systematic philosophy). The Logic actually develops the concept of the whole itself – the idea of an organic system of elements in which each is what it is in terms of its relationship to all the others. To make his argument, Hegel employs *dialectic*: a new type of reasoning (though with ancient roots) in which ideas contradict and contend with one another dynamically, in a progressive articulation of the whole. The Logic culminates in 'Absolute Idea', a conceptual whole which is what it is not by being related to other concepts, but by being purely and completely self-related. Absolute Idea is literally 'idea of idea'. Thus it is purely self-determined and is the true or absolute whole.

The Logic, however, gives us only the *idea* of wholeness and of this absolute self-determination. In Hegel's Philosophy of Nature he shows how nature itself can only be understood as a kind of material embodiment of the ideas set forth in the Logic. The culmination of this division of Hegel's philosophy lies in 'organic being': the living and literal embodiment (in plants and animals) of Hegel's concept of an organic whole of inter-related moments. Where else do we find a more perfect expression of wholeness than in living bodies? Living things are *systems* of flesh and bone, in which everything is related to everything else, each part is what it is in terms of its function within the whole, and the whole itself is constituted through the interrelation of the parts. However, as I alluded to earlier, Hegel finds animals limited in one crucial way: they lack self-knowledge. They are what they are ultimately only through their relation (in truth, their opposition) to everything else. In short, they do not embody the perfect self-related identity of the Idea, Hegel's paradigm of true wholeness.

Hegel thus passes beyond Philosophy of Nature, to a 'Philosophy of Spirit'. The term 'Spirit' (*Geist*) has been the source of a great deal of confusion. To put it in the simplest possible terms, by Spirit Hegel means human nature, and specifically our unique sort of consciousness. Although we are natural beings, we alone are capable of self-knowledge. This makes us so unique, so different from other animals that it is tempting to think of us (as Aristotle did) as having one foot in the animal and the other in the divine. Self-awareness can come in trivial forms, as when after failing at some task I re-think how I am approaching it and critique my assumptions, or when I take a long hard look at my life and consider whether I'm satisfied with it. In its highest form, however, self-knowledge manifests itself as the attempt by human beings to understand themselves through art, religion and, pre-eminently, philosophy. Hegel calls this 'Absolute Spirit' because it is, in fact, a realization in time and space of Absolute Idea. It is the self-related idea made concrete, actual and living through perfect, philosophical *self-consciousness*. Thus, Hegel's system – his systematic account of reality itself – reaches closure with philosophy, the self-awareness of the infinite whole itself, as achieved by finite human beings.

If we ask what, more specifically, is meant by the 'philosophy' Hegel sees human beings doing, the answer simply takes us back to the beginning of the Logic: philosophy is the account of the whole, capped and completed by an account of the being who accounts for the whole. This conception of the nature of philosophy brings us to another of Hegel's more notorious claims – his belief that his philosophical system consummates the love of wisdom. To put it a different way, Hegel makes it clear that he believes the entire history of philosophy is an account of many brilliant minds groping to express the ideas only he gives full and final form to. Hegel never says this in a way that is personally self-aggrandizing or boastful: he seems to see himself as a vehicle of truth's expression, and he makes it very clear that the articulation of his philosophy was only possible because he could stand in a privileged historical position and survey the labours of the many who had gone before him. Still the idea may seem fantastic – until we recall that virtually all philosophers believe that they have found the truth others

Introduction

struggled (inadequately) to express. Aristotle, for example, begins many of his works with a survey of the thoughts of his predecessors, demonstrating not only why they were wrong but also how in some way they had anticipated some aspect of the correct (Aristotelian) position. Finally, and most important, though all such claims seem grandiose, it should be noted that one of the challenging things about Hegel is that he does in fact do a rather convincing job of showing how his philosophy is, as Martin Heidegger claimed many years later, the climax of the Western metaphysical project. This means that to understand Western philosophy, one must understand Hegel. In a very real sense, Hegel *is* Western philosophy.

For and Against Hegel

One of the disturbing things about Hegel's philosophy is that it is hard to find a way to argue against it. Hegel's system is extraordinarily clever, and within it he has dealt with and often decisively refuted many of the philosophical standpoints from which one might oppose him. To make matters worse, if one accepts the starting point of the system and enters into its argument, one feels oneself being seduced and bewitched by its peculiar logic and sheer grandeur. As Eric Voegelin wrote of Hegel, 'Once you have entered the magic circle the sorcerer has drawn around himself, you are lost.'[1] As a result, those who are intent on resisting seduction have often felt it necessary to get at and to reject the root assumptions of the system itself.

In fact, it can be plausibly argued that all the philosophy that has come after Hegel up to the present day is directly or indirectly reacting to him – either reacting against Hegel (which is usually the case), or developing certain of his insights in new ways. This process began soon after Hegel's death with the division of his followers into 'right wing' and 'left wing' Hegelians. The latter group (also often called the 'young Hegelians') has, for the most part, eclipsed the former, so far as the history of philosophy is concerned. The left-wing Hegelians included Ludwig Feuerbach (1804–1872) who argued that had Hegel truly understood the implications of his own philosophy, he would have seen that he makes man into God. Human beings, Feuerbach argued, have created God by projecting aspects of their own nature into a transcendent ideal.

Concerned over the rise of the left-wing Hegelians, in 1841 authorities in Berlin invited F. W. J. Schelling – Hegel's former friend and mentor – to lecture at the university there. Schelling deeply resented the fact that Hegel had utilized many of his insights, and had become a sharp critic of the Hegelian system. It was hoped that his influence would counteract that of Hegel. This did not really occur, but Schelling had an influence nonetheless. His students included Mikhail Bakunin (the anarchist), Friedrich Engels (later the literary partner of Karl Marx), and the Danish philosopher Søren Kierkegaard. Since Hegel's philosophy is the most elaborate and ambitious of all philosophical systems, some have responded to Hegel by rejecting philosophical system-building altogether. This was the case with Kierkegaard (1813–1855) who saw the Hegelian system as a monstrous intellectual trap which, in its quest for the universal, had completely failed to account for the human individual. His reaction to Hegel sowed the seeds for the modern movement known as Existentialism.

Karl Marx (1818–1883) famously 'stood Hegel on his head' (and shook all the change out of his pockets, one of my professors joked). Misunderstanding Hegel's idealism as something 'otherworldly', he declared that Hegelianism must become *materialistic*. From that materialist turn, and a selective appropriation of Hegelian concepts, he developed the philosophical and economic theory now known as Marxism (or 'scientific socialism'). By the second half of the twentieth century, fully a third of the world lived under regimes inspired by Marxist theory – a decisive refutation (if one were needed) of the claim that philosophy never has an influence! Though Hegel himself, of course, cannot be blamed for the misunderstandings of those influenced by him, or their subsequent actions.

Quite a different case is represented by the positivist movement, best exemplified by the so-called 'Vienna circle' of the 1920s. Harking back to Hume's empiricism, the positivists established their own criterion of meaning: statements are only meaningful if they are 'empirically verifiable'; i.e., if they can be confirmed through some kind of sensory experience (whether aided or unaided), or if they express a logical or mathematical truth. The result was that the positivists declared all statements about metaphysics to be 'meaningless'. One of their chief targets was Hegel – whose philosophy still occupied centre stage in the form of the movement known as 'British Idealism', which included figures such as F. H. Bradley (1846–1924). Since Hegel's Absolute Idea cannot be seen or heard, or detected through any of the means the empirical sciences avail themselves of, the positivists declared all statements about it (and the entirety of Hegel's Logic)

Introduction

to be meaningless. Positivism had a tremendous influence on philosophy in England and America. Though its adherents usually deny it, to this day so-called 'analytic philosophy' carries with it many of the assumptions and attitudes of the positivists (including an antipathy to Hegel), as well as their literary style.

It should be noted that while many of the philosophies I have mentioned thus far are important and thought-provoking in their own right, taken as 'responses' to Hegel they are mostly question-begging: they reject the very possibility of doing what Hegel does, without actually identifying how he has failed to do it. In other words, they do not come to terms with the actual details of Hegel's philosophy and show where the errors lie. Their approach is essentially to sweep Hegel aside, rather than to actually engage him.

While analytic philosophy was taking root in England and America, in Europe Jean-Paul Sartre (1905–1980) and Albert Camus (1913–1960) were developing the philosophy of Existentialism, which would cause a sensation in intellectual circles and have a wide influence after the Second World War. Existentialism is in some ways the antithesis of Hegelianism. Hegel claims to have discovered the meaning of existence itself, whereas Sartre proclaims that 'existence is absurd', i.e., meaningless. Nevertheless, Sartre's *Being and Nothingness* (1943) was heavily influenced by Hegel. In Paris in the 1930s the Russian philosopher Alexandre Kojève (1902–1968) gave a series of lectures on Hegel which exercized an important influence on Sartre and other French philosophers. Though it is not known whether Sartre was actually present for these lectures, many scholars believe nonetheless that Hegelian ideas were communicated to him by Kojève and those he influenced. Kojève's distinctive, neo-Marxian reading of the *Phenomenology of Spirit* also had a major impact on other French intellectuals, among them Maurice Merleau-Ponty (1908–1961), Jacques Lacan (1901–1981) and Georges Bataille (1897–1962). Indeed, it can easily be maintained that a great deal of what is called today 'continental philosophy' traces its lineage, in one way or another, back to Hegel. When continental, post-modernist thinkers like Jean-Francois Lyotard (1924–1998) object to universal claims and 'grand narratives' in philosophy, it is Hegel who is their chief foil, a Hegel mediated to them by Kojève.

Today, Kojève is most famous for his so-called 'end of history' thesis, which he claimed to find in Hegel (a claim disputed by many Hegel scholars). If history is the story of the human struggle for self-knowledge, Kojève maintains that history ends with the advent of Hegel's philosophy, and the spread of the political ideal of man as a free, self-determining being. This idea of the end of history (which Kojève regarded as a mixed blessing) had a huge influence not only on continental philosophy, but on the literature, film, music and drama of the second half of the twentieth century. It has even had an impact on recent geo-political events. Some of the leading intellectuals of the neo-conservative movement, who rose to prominence under President George W. Bush, were directly or indirectly influenced by Kojève. In 1989 the American political scientist Francis Fukuyama popularized Kojève's neo-Hegelianism in a widely-discussed article entitled 'The End of History?' (which became the basis for Fukuyama's 1992 book *The End of History and the Last Man*). 'Neo-cons' like Fukuyama advanced the idea that history had ended with the failure of communism and the victory of liberal democracy. It was, in effect, under the banner of this neo-Kojèvean ideology that the United States toppled the regime of Saddam Hussein, convinced that history (or the end of history) was on their side.

In short, the world we live in has, in one way or another, for better or for worse, been shaped by the philosophy of Hegel.

Using this Book

This volume is primarily intended for undergraduate philosophy students, not professional scholars. It presents explanations of key terms and concepts in Hegel, as well as discussions of other thinkers important for understanding the influences on his thought. Also included are discussions of famous images that appear in Hegel's writings, such as 'the inverted world', 'the owl of Minerva' and 'the cunning of reason'. I have attempted to explain Hegel's ideas in the simplest and plainest language possible, avoiding jargon and presupposing little prior acquaintance with Hegel, or any other figures in the history of philosophy.

In preparing a volume such as this, of course, one must pick and choose which terms or concepts to include, and which to exclude. I based my decisions in this matter in part on what most undergraduate students of Hegel tend to be exposed to in their classes. Typically, students are assigned selections from Hegel's writings, rather than whole works. At the undergraduate level, the texts from which selections are taken are usually *The*

Introduction

Phenomenology of Spirit, *The Philosophy of Right*, and the lecture courses on art, religion and world history (Hegel's introductions to those courses, for example, are often assigned in classes). Thus, the entries in this volume in large measure deal with the ideas in those texts. I have devoted comparatively less attention to the complexities of Hegel's Logic, Philosophy of Nature, and Philosophy of Subjective Spirit, which are seldom taught in undergraduate courses. Nevertheless, the reader will find that many of the most important ideas in these areas of Hegel's system are presented here. The result will, I hope, be helpful to those studying Hegel either in seminars devoted to him, or in survey courses on nineteenth-century philosophy. It is not likely to please specialists, who will no doubt feel that I have glossed over too many complexities.

As is the case with scholarship on any philosopher, Hegelian scholars divide into a number of warring camps. The division is partly along political lines (the so-called 'right wing' and 'left wing' Hegelians) and dates back to the years just after Hegel's death, when his followers and interpreters were trying to come to grips with what he *really* meant. Today, some scholars describe themselves as reading Hegel in a 'non-metaphysical' manner. Much of this approach consists of de-emphasizing the theological side to Hegel. For example, Hegel tells us that his Logic gives us 'the exposition of God as he is in his eternal essence'. Non-metaphysical Hegelians jettison this theological language and interpret the Logic simply as 'a hermeneutic of categories'. I do not find this interpretation convincing, as it requires ignoring too much of what Hegel actually says. I have learned a good deal from the non-metaphysical Hegelians – the most prolific of them, Richard Dien Winfield, was one of my teachers. But I am an unapologetically metaphysical interpreter of Hegel. My own manner of reading Hegel has been greatly influenced by the work of the late Errol E. Harris, whom I consider to be the finest interpreter of Hegel in the English language. (For more on the issue of whether we can treat Hegel as a metaphysician, see the entry on **metaphysics**, p. 147.)

Though Hegel has been one of the major influences on my thinking, only in a qualified sense would I call myself a Hegelian. Therefore, I have no personal interest in interpreting Hegel so as to make him take this or that position. I am concerned solely with an accurate presentation of what Hegel actually said, regardless of whether I am in agreement with it. I should also point out that the entries in this volume do not delve into the scholarly controversies surrounding the interpretation of various ideas in Hegel. I do not wish to suppress such controversies, but a discussion of them is out of place in a volume intended to explain Hegel's ideas to students.

Nevertheless, it should be mentioned that creating a lexicon of Hegel's philosophy presents its own unique philosophical problems. As noted earlier, Hegel believes that existence is an organic whole in which every element is related to every other. Thus, we cannot expect to understand anything in separation from the greater whole of which it is a part. Hegel's philosophical system, in fact, mirrors the holism of reality – each of its ideas can only be understood in terms of its place in the larger whole. How, then, is it possible to create a Hegel lexicon in which concepts are isolated and explained in abstraction from the rest of the philosophy? In Hegelian terms, this ought to be impossible – and indeed it is. That is why key ideas discussed in this volume are always situated in terms of their context within the Hegelian system. This means that of necessity there is a great deal of overlap. The reader will find that the entries are also of very different lengths, with comparatively long discussions devoted to major divisions within the Hegelian system, or major texts by Hegel. Some of the entries in the volume are triadic 'clusters' of concepts: 'being-nothing-becoming', 'quality-quantity-measure', etc. Hegel is notorious for these conceptual triads, and though many of his recent interpreters have been at pains to deny that he makes everything come in threes, a casual glance at any of Hegel's works will show these denials to be somewhat disingenuous. (For more information on this issue, see the entry on **triads**, p. 247.)

This insistence on explaining each Hegelian idea in terms of its place within the system reflects my own manner of teaching Hegel to undergraduates, which I call a 'top-down' approach. I find that students become completely bewildered if we do what Hegel actually seems to want us to do, and begin at the beginning of the system (with the 'pure being' of the Logic) and work through each dialectical transition, slowly constructing the whole. Instead, I begin by presenting my students with the whole itself: a bird's-eye view of the nature of the system, and the major 'point' of Hegel's philosophy (something I did in the first section of this introduction; in terms of texts used in class, the famous Preface to *The Phenomenology of Spirit* is useful in accomplishing this, though difficult to read). I then introduce them to the major divisions within the system – Logic, Philosophy of Nature and

Introduction

Philosophy of Spirit – explaining what each is concerned with and how Hegel makes his transitions from one to the other. I explain key terms and attempt to clear up common confusions. What is the Absolute? What is Spirit? What is Absolute Spirit, and how is it different from Absolute Idea? And so on. Once I have given my students a synoptic view of the whole, I then focus in on some major division of it. For example, one semester I took my students through Hegel's *Philosophy of Right*.

There is no getting around the fact that Hegel is extraordinarily difficult to read. Ideally, he should be approached only after one has become acquainted with a good deal of the history of philosophy, and accustomed to the difficulty of reading philosophical texts. Even then, however, one will find Hegel a terrific challenge. There are several pieces of good news I can offer students, however. First, even advanced graduate students and scholars of Hegel teaching in universities *still* find him difficult. Open any commentary on a Hegelian text and one will find the author admitting at a certain point that he simply cannot understand certain passages in Hegel.

However, reading Hegel does get easier over time. I can vividly recall my first experience with him as an undergraduate, when I hurled a volume of his writings across the room because I simply could not make head or tail of it. Ten years later I was writing a doctoral dissertation on Hegel and teaching him in my classes. In this volume I have quoted particularly lucid passages from Hegel now and then, partly in order to convince students that despite the initial impression of impenetrability that Hegel's texts tend to give us, his statements are often very clear and accessible. The best piece of advice I can give to those trying to read Hegel is to keep reading: if a passage simply does not make sense, keep reading until you encounter one that does. Then go back, if possible, or just go on. Many editions of Hegel's writings contain 'additions' (or, in German, *Zusätze*) culled from the notebooks of students who were present at his lectures, and who attempted to write down what Hegel said verbatim. These are often surprisingly clear and helpful. In general, Hegel was far more clear when speaking to an audience than he was when he set pen to paper. For this reason, Hegel's lecture courses on art, religion, the history of philosophy and world history are much more accessible than the writings he published during his lifetime. (These lecture courses have all been translated and published. See the 'Suggestions for Further Reading', p. 265)

Hegel's Life and Writings: A Brief Overview

Georg Wilhelm Friedrich Hegel was born on 27 August 1770, his birthplace the city of Stuttgart in the Duchy of Württemberg. (At that time Germany was not yet a unified nation-state, and did not become one until 1871.) Hegel's parents were middle class, his father an official in the Royal Treasury, his mother a highly intelligent, cultivated woman who came from a long line of Protestant reformers.[2] Their religious attitude was, broadly speaking, that of Pietism, a Protestant movement that flourished in southern Germany. Pietism emphasized the direct relationship of the individual to God (thus de-emphasizing the role of an intermediary clergy), Bible study and good works. Hegel's parents, however, seemed to have combined their religious piety with an enthusiasm for the ideals of the Enlightenment. This apparent tension between two seemingly opposed orientations – the spiritual and the rational – would be overcome in Hegel's person, and in his philosophy.

In his thirteenth year both Hegel and his mother fell ill. Hegel survived, but his mother did not. It had been her desire that young Georg devote himself to a life of learning, and while his father seems to have been a more practical-minded man, he acceded to his wife's wishes. Hegel was thus enrolled in the Gymnasium Illustre, which was located quite near the Hegel home.[3] In the Gymnasium, young Hegel excelled at a variety of subjects (his favourite being the natural sciences) and graduated first in his class. The private journal Hegel kept during his schoolboy days reveals him to be not only an extraordinarily studious young man, but also gifted with the remarkable 'synthetic' ability that would display itself so dramatically in his mature philosophical writings. Hegel copied out passages from all manner of books into his journal, commenting on them, trying to find the connections between ideas, to achieve a synthesis of knowledge.

When Hegel was eighteen, his father enrolled him in the Protestant seminary at the University of Tübingen. Hegel came to loathe this school, with its extraordinary strictness and ultra-conservative attitudes. He was not interested in reading what his professors wanted him to, and instead read as he pleased. To make matters worse, suddenly the bookish young man became uncharacteristically rebellious – drinking and breaking numerous minor rules. Hegel's room-mate at the seminary was the poet Friedrich Hölderlin, with whom he developed a very close friendship.

Introduction

The year 1789 saw the outbreak of the French Revolution, and Hegel and Hölderlin were consumed with enthusiasm for its ideals of liberty, equality and fraternity. Here we find Enlightenment and Pietist principles coalescing. Millenarianism – the belief in a coming transformation or perfection of the world – had long been a central preoccupation of the Pietists (especially in Württemberg). Hegel and Hölderlin saw in the Revolution the coming of an End Time in which human society would be perfected according to Enlightenment principles. However, both men were Enlightenment enthusiasts of an unusual sort. Unlike many, they did not champion materialism and secularism (often disguised forms of atheism). Instead, they sought some sort of rapprochement between faith and reason – indeed, this was to be one of the central pre-occupations of Hegel's early writings, and it is a major theme in his mature philosophy as well.

In 1790, F. W. J. Schelling arrived at the seminary and shared rooms with Hegel and Hölderlin. Schelling was five years younger than the other two men, but already he showed signs of the precocious genius that was to burst onto the philosophical scene with such force only a few years later. The three became inseparable – united in their enthusiasm for the Revolution, and their antipathy to the seminary. Hegel soon acquired from them a nickname: 'the old man'. In spite of his love of the local taverns, he nevertheless came across as a bit of a fuddy-duddy.

During his time at Tübingen, Hegel read Plato, Schiller, Jacobi, Montesquieu and Herder. The influence of Kant was felt at the seminary through the teaching of Gottlob Storr, who used Kant's theories concerning the inherent limitations of reason to argue that reason must be supplemented by Biblical revelation. Hegel, Schelling and Hölderlin were completely unsympathetic to Storr's position. Nevertheless, the Kantian philosophy did have an impact on them in the person of Carl Immanuel Diez, an older student. Diez melded Kant's philosophy (itself a product of the Enlightenment) with Revolutionary ideals. Hölderlin and Schelling took to this heady mixture immediately, but Hegel was somewhat slow to warm up to Kant. He declined to join a 'Kant Club' formed at the seminary, because he said he was too busy reading Rousseau. Terry Pinkard suggests, with some plausibility, that Hegel was suspicious of the abstract nature of Kantian moral principles, and Kant's apparent failure to grasp that such principles must be grounded in, and concretized by, a living, moral community.[4]

Around this time a controversy had broken out in Europe over the philosophy of Spinoza, largely due to the publication of a work by Friedrich Jacobi in which he quoted Lessing as having praised the philosopher. Spinoza was widely regarded as a pantheist (someone who identifies God with nature), and by others as an atheist. In fact, Spinoza had argued that nature and mind were different attributes of the same divine being. Hegel, Schelling and Hölderlin all found themselves drawn to Spinoza. They thought that perhaps his ideas could be grafted onto the Kantian philosophy and provide them with some way to bridge the intolerable gulf between Kant's realm of 'phenomena' (things as we experience them) and 'noumena' (that which forever transcends our experience). Finding some way to overcome Kant's limitations on knowledge, and to overcome the determinism and mechanism he saw as abiding in the world of experience, became one of the major obsessions of the three friends – an obsession which, in fact, gave birth to post-Kantian idealism in Germany. So taken were the three with Spinoza's doctrine that they adopted a Greek 'pantheist' motto, *hen kai pan* ('one and all' – meaning that the many is one), which Hölderlin inscribed in Hegel's yearbook of 1791.

The students at the seminary were legally obliged to become ministers once their studies had been completed. However, there were few pastoral openings for them and they were thus frequently granted permission to pursue other professions. Hegel had no desire to become a minister (and neither did his friends Hölderlin and Schelling). In 1793, after taking his final exam, Hegel was given permission to take a job as a tutor to the children of the wealthy von Steiger family in Berne, Switzerland. Unfortunately, Hegel found the position oppressive, and he quarrelled with the ultra-conservative Captain von Steiger, a fervent opponent of the French Revolution. However, the household did contain an excellent private library. In his leisure time, Hegel read Grotius, Hobbes, Hume, Leibniz, Locke, Machiavelli, Montesquieu, Shaftesbury, Spinoza, Voltaire and Meister Eckhart. Hegel also now turned to Kant in earnest.

Hegel's job as house tutor gave him little time to himself, but he did manage to publish his first book during this period: a translation (with commentary) of a French Revolutionary screed detailing the oppression of the French-speaking people of the Swiss canton of Vaud, by the German-speaking people of Berne. Hegel published this work anonymously in 1798, after leaving Berne. It would be many years, in fact, before anyone realized

Introduction

it had been produced by Hegel.[5] He also wrote two significant essays during this early period, both concerning themselves with Christianity and its prospects: 'The Life of Jesus', a Kantianized moral interpretation of the Christian teaching, and 'The Positivity of the Christian Religion'. This latter piece developed the ideas of an essay Hegel had written during his last semester at the seminary (the so-called 'Tübingen Essay'). In these essays we find Hegel the seminarian entertaining doubts about whether any 'true religion' was left in Christianity.

Hegel's letters to Hölderlin and Schelling during this time reflect his depression and deep dissatisfaction with his situation in Berne. Hölderlin, who was working in Frankfurt, responded by securing Hegel a post there, as tutor to the Gogel family. And so in 1797 Hegel re-located to Frankfurt, where his situation was much happier. While there, Hölderlin and others introduced him to the writings of J. G. Fichte, who had sought to 'complete' the Kantian philosophy. Fichte's revision of Kant consisted of a thorough-going idealism which attempted to demonstrate that the world itself is the product of an Absolute Ego. (Kant, for his part, repudiated Fichte's system.)

By 1799, however, relations with Hölderlin had become strained. Partly as the result of a love affair gone bad, Hölderlin began showing signs of mental instability – which would later develop into complete insanity. That same year Hegel's father died, leaving a small inheritance which granted him some independence. Once again he sought another position, this time appealing to Schelling. The two men had been out of touch for some time, and though Hegel was still very fond of Schelling, he could not have helped being somewhat envious of the younger man's rapid rise in the philosophic profession. Schelling had already published several important works and had come to be seen as the rising star of German philosophy. Indeed, he had taken Fichte's place at the University of Jena, after the latter was dismissed due to accusations of atheism. Schelling responded generously by inviting Hegel to Jena, and offering him a place to stay. Hegel accepted with relief, and relocated there in 1801.

At the time, Jena had the reputation of being one of the major intellectual centres of Germany. As already mentioned, the controversial Fichte had lectured there. Jena was also the centre of the German Romantic movement. Novalis, Tieck, F. Schlegel, and A. W. Schlegel all lived and worked there. In Jena, Hegel succeeded in getting his degree from

Tübingen counted as a doctorate and began giving classes to university students. He was paid nothing by the university itself (as was the practice then with junior academics), though he could charge students individually for instruction. Also in 1801, Hegel published his first philosophical work: *The Difference Between Fichte's and Schelling's Systems of Philosophy*. Schelling's ideas were heavily influenced by Fichte, though with the addition of a 'philosophy of nature' which interpreted the world as a progressive revelation of God or 'the Absolute', an ideal transcending all of our commonsense categories, including the distinction between subject and object. Hegel's book was basically a defense of Schelling, and did nothing more for Hegel in the minds of the reading public than to create the impression that he was Schelling's follower. This impression was no doubt strengthened by the fact that the two men also co-founded and edited *The Critical Journal of Philosophy*, a short-lived publication primarily intended to disseminate Schelling's philosophy.

Schelling himself left Jena for a post at the University of Würzberg in 1803. His departure seems, to a degree, to have intellectually freed Hegel. From 1803 to1806 he produced a large amount of work, setting out various versions of a new 'system of philosophy'. In the process, Hegel took a good deal of inspiration from Schelling's ideas, but he recast them in a new, more rigorous form, and greatly amplified them. During this period, he also opened himself up to a variety of other influences, some of them quite surprising. For a time he fell under the spell of the German mystic Jacob Boehme (1575–1624), who had also influenced Schelling and various members of the Romantic movement. Boehme is famous for having argued for a dynamic concept of God as progressively embodying himself through the works of nature and humankind. Under Boehme's influence, Hegel produced a number of strange, 'theosophical' texts which puzzle scholars to this day. In 1805, he began work on the book for which he is most famous: *The Phenomenology of Spirit*. Hegel would not have wanted it this way. He conceived the *Phenomenology* as a kind of 'introduction' (or, better still, 'rite of passage') to his actual philosophical system, which came to consist of three components: Logic, Philosophy of Nature and Philosophy of Spirit.

Hegel finished the *Phenomenology* in 1806, just as Napoleon's troops were arriving in Jena. He saw Napoleon as an embodiment of the World Spirit itself, violently overcoming outmoded forms of social order and

Introduction

ushering in a new, more rational age. To add to the chaos, in early 1807 Hegel's landlady gave birth to his illegitimate son, Ludwig. These events combined to convince Hegel of the urgency of leaving Jena as soon as possible (though he would later assume responsibility for Ludwig). He appealed to his old friend Immanuel Niethammer (also a graduate of the seminary) for help finding a post elsewhere. Niethammer came through with a job for Hegel editing a pro-Napoleonic newspaper in Bamberg. Surprisingly, Hegel threw himself into this job with enthusiasm and delighted in Bamberg society, but his happiness there was to be short-lived. Hegel grew tired of the job of editor, especially after the newspaper was investigated by the authorities. So, once more he appealed to Niethammer for help.

This time his friend found him a job as headmaster of a school in Nuremberg. Hegel accepted the position (though, one would imagine, with some reluctance) and moved to Nuremberg in 1808. Once again, Hegel threw himself into his new job with energy, as well as a strong commitment to the ideal of liberal education. He also found time to write his second major work *The Science of Logic* (published in three volumes in 1812, 1813 and 1816). This was Hegel's detailed exposition of the first major division of his philosophy. In addition to all of this, remarkably, Hegel began to build a family of his own: on 15 September 1811, he married Marie Helena Susanna von Tucher, the daughter of an old, aristocratic Nuremberg family. The following year, Marie gave birth to their first child, Susanna, who died scarcely more than a month later. In 1813, however, Hegel's son Karl was born, followed by Immanuel in 1814. Both sons were healthy and died in old age.

Hegel's reputation in the philosophic community had also begun to grow, and finally, in 1816, he was offered a university professorship, at Heidelberg. After moving there, the Hegel family took in Ludwig. Hegel's time in Heidelberg also saw the publication of *The Encyclopedia of the Philosophical Sentences in Outline* (1817). This odd work was a summary of his entire philosophical system in the form of a number of relatively short, numbered paragraphs. Hegel intended the text to be used by his students, and in class he would base his lectures on an amplification of these paragraphs. (The result of this is that in the absence of this amplification the paragraphs themselves are often remarkably obscure – hence most modern additions contain transcripts of notes students made on Hegel's lectures.) Hegel's stay in Heidelberg would also be relatively brief, however, this time for a very happy reason: in 1818 he assumed a professorship in Berlin, a considerable step-up. It was the pinnacle of Hegel's career, and the final period of his life. During his time in Berlin, Hegel became unquestionably the leading philosopher in Germany. People from all walks of life attended his lectures, hanging on his every word (which is surprising considering that he was not known for having a particularly dynamic or accessible lecture style). Hegel also became a fixture of Berlin society. He enjoyed playing cards with friends, attending the opera, and hobnobbing with the aristocracy.

However, in Berlin Hegel also became embroiled in academic and political intrigues. The Prussian government's attempt to root out 'subversives' led to several of Hegel's students and colleagues being charged and arrested. Hegel intervened valiantly on their behalf, and at some risk to himself. Still, in his later years Hegel became more conservative, and increasingly critical of calls for revolutionary change. In 1820 he published his last book, *The Philosophy of Right*, which dealt with moral and political philosophy. He also lectured at length, and several times, on his Philosophy of Religion, declaring that 'philosophy is theology'. He also seems to have developed a renewed interest in mysticism, initiating a friendship with the notorious theosophist Franz von Baader. The two men studied Meister Eckhart together in the winter of 1823–24.

Hegel was such a celebrity in Berlin that in 1826 his birthday celebration was reported in the newspapers, much to the displeasure of the jealous Prussian King. By now in his fifties, Hegel expanded his horizons by travelling to Holland, Vienna and Paris. In Paris, he suffered from acute indigestion – a portent, sadly, of things to come. In the summer of 1831 a cholera epidemic spread to Germany, and the Hegel family (along with many others) fled Berlin, returning only when it seemed the epidemic had passed. On 13 November 1831, however, Hegel became ill and his condition worsened rapidly. Around 5.00 p.m. of the next day, he died. His death was attributed to cholera, though it now seems more likely he died of a gastrointestinal disease. Hegel's funeral on 16 November was a major event in Berlin society. At the time of his death, he had been working on a revision of his *Science of Logic*. Hegel's sons Karl and Immanuel would live long lives, bringing out new editions of their father's works as well as hitherto-unpublished manuscripts. Ludwig, however, predeceased his father while serving in the Dutch army. News of Ludwig's death never reached Hegel, and the family learned of it only later.

—A—

Absolute (n. das Absolute; or adj. absolut)   Hegel's use of the term 'absolute' is the source of a great deal of confusion. Nevertheless, it is the term most commonly associated with his philosophy. Hegel frequently uses it as an adjective, for example in 'Absolute Idea', 'Absolute Knowing', 'Absolute Religion' and 'Absolute Spirit'. He utilizes the substantive 'the Absolute' less frequently.

The term 'absolute' has a long history in German philosophy. Nicholas of Cusa in his *Of Learned Ignorance* (*De Docta Ignorantia*, 1440) used the term *absolutum* to mean God, understood as a being that transcends all finite determinations: the *coincidentia oppositorum* (coincidence of opposites). Schelling's use of 'Absolute' is remarkably similar to Cusa's. For Schelling, the Absolute is the 'indifference point' beyond the distinction of subject and object, or any other distinction. In the famous Preface to *The Phenomenology of Spirit* Hegel rejects this conception of the Absolute, referring to it derisively as 'the night in which all cows are black' (Miller, 9; PG, 13). Hegel means that when the Absolute is conceived simply as the transcendent unity of all things (or as the cancellation of all difference) it really amounts to an idea devoid of all content. It is terribly easy to say 'in this world definite distinctions abide – but in the Absolute all is one.' But what does this really mean?

One might think this would lead Hegel to reject the idea of an Absolute altogether, but he does not. The reason is that Hegel saw the aim of philosophy itself as knowledge of the Absolute, where this is understood, in very broad terms, as the ultimate ground or source of all being. It is this knowledge that was sought right from the beginning of the Western tradition in the Pre-Socratic philosopher Thales who declared that 'water' is the source of all that is. According to Hegel, the trouble with Schelling is not that he has conceived of an Absolute, but that he has misconceived it. (In fact, one might say that from the standpoint of a Hegelian, Hegel's great achievement in the history of philosophy is to have arrived at a proper understanding of the Absolute.)

Hegel retains the idea of the Absolute, and even agrees with Schelling's description of it as somehow overcoming the subject-object distinction. For Hegel, however, the Absolute is *the whole*. The Absolute is not something that transcends existence; it is the whole of existence itself understood as a system in which each part is organically and inseparably related to every other. However, one might ask, how does this conception of the Absolute as 'the whole' show how it is 'the ultimate ground or source of all being'? The answer is simple: Hegel's philosophy attempts to show how the being of each finite thing in existence *just is* its place in the whole, as part of the system of reality itself. The Absolute, however, is not the whole of reality conceived as a static, block universe. Instead, Hegel argues that the Absolute is active and dynamic, continually replenishing or reconstituting itself through the finite beings that make up the infinite whole.

In short, things exist in order that the whole may be complete – for all things are what they are in virtue of their place within the systematic totality of existence. Thus, Hegel believes that he has answered the age-old question 'What is being?' Fundamentally, to be is to be the whole or Absolute, but the finite things of our experience can be said to derive a kind of being from their place within the whole. However, another of the age-old metaphysical questions is 'Why is there anything at all, rather than nothing?', or 'Why does existence exist at all?' Hegel may say that to be is to be a moment or aspect of the whole, but we might ask him why this whole exists in the first place. Hegel does have an answer to this, and it constitutes the most important idea in his philosophy, as well as the true understanding of the specific sense in which the whole is dynamic and active. Very simply, Hegel believes that existence exists in order to achieve consciousness of itself.

Hegel sees all of existence as a kind of 'great chain of being', culminating in the achievement of self-awareness in human beings. Human beings are creatures of nature, but we stand at the apex of nature because we subsume within ourselves the non-living, mineral and chemical world, as well as the vegetative and animal functions (growth, repair, nutrition, sensation, self-motion, etc.). In addition to this, we actualize a function not to be found in lower nature: we are self-aware. Our quest for self-awareness displays itself pre-eminently in our striving to understand ourselves as a species and our place in nature through science and philosophy. Because we are ourselves creatures of nature, we can say that our self-awareness is, in fact, the self-awareness of nature – of all of existence. Thus, in human beings, existence itself reaches a kind of closure or completion: existence rebounds upon itself and knows itself. We can also

Absolute

understand this in terms of the 'overcoming' of the subject-object distinction. In our self-awareness, subject has become object: we subjects become objects to ourselves. At the same time, in our self-awareness object has become subject: our object is in fact the subject – and nature, the objective world itself, has achieved subjectivity through us.

The Absolute, for Hegel, is thus the whole of the objective world understood as a system perpetually giving rise to the conditions necessary for it to confront itself as object, and thus achieve closure. In the *Phenomenology* Hegel tells us that the Absolute is, 'the process of its own becoming, the circle that presupposes its end as its goal, having its end also as its beginning; and only by being worked out to its end, is it actual' (Miller, 10; PG, 14). Further, the Absolute must be conceived in 'the whole wealth of the developed form. Only then is it conceived and expressed as an actuality' (Miller, 11; PG, 15).

Hegel's description of the Absolute begins with his Logic, which offers a kind of skeletal account of the whole itself. It does not discuss the specific members of the systematic whole; instead it is an account of the fundamental ideas or categories that make the whole organic and systematic, and which are being 'realized' or expressed in concrete existence all around us. The system of ideas in the Logic culminates in 'Absolute Idea' – which is absolute because it in a sense 'contains' all the preceding, fundamental ideas. Because there is no further idea that can encompass it, Absolute Idea therefore exhibits one of the classical characteristics of the *absolutum*: it is 'unconditioned' (or uncomprehended) by any finite determinations external to it. Further, the Absolute Idea is conceived by Hegel as a self-related idea. Indeed, it is the idea of idea itself. Nevertheless, Hegel points out that it is *only* an idea: it lacks concrete being or expression.

Hegel's Philosophy of Nature shows how all of nature may be understood as an expression of the categories of the Logic – and as a hierarchy of forms in which the self-relation described abstractly in Absolute Idea is being progressively realized in the flesh. However, true self-relatedness is not achieved in what we think of as the natural world, but only in human thought. Hegel refers to human nature as Spirit and shows how the highest expression of our humanity is what he calls Absolute Spirit: the achievement of self-relatedness as *self-consciousness*, through art, religion and philosophy. Thus, we may say that the Absolute is achieved or consummated through the realization of Absolute Idea in Absolute Spirit, with all non-human, lower nature understood as a dim approximation to Absolute Spirit, and as a set of necessary conditions for its achievement. (The other conditions for the achievement of Absolute Spirit being historical, and cultural.) See also **Absolute Idea**; **Absolute Knowing**; **Absolute Spirit**; **Idea**; **Logic**; **Schelling, F. W. J.**; **nature and Philosophy of Nature**; **Philosophy of Spirit**; **science**; **system**.

absolute freedom and the Terror (die Absolute Freiheit und der Schrecken) In a section of *The Phenomenology of Spirit* titled 'Self-Estranged Spirit' Hegel discusses a type of mentality which finds itself alienated from nature and society, and feels called upon to remake or to perfect both. Hegel is actually engaged in this section in a rather thinly-veiled commentary on modernity. Ultimately, the attitude of self-estranged Spirit becomes thoroughly destructive: insisting that everything must be critiqued, exposed, and made over. Such a standpoint must, Hegel insists, eventually destroy even itself. Here Hegel is offering a critique of the Enlightenment, especially the attitude of the French *philosophes*. The atheism and materialism of this standpoint eventually harden into ideology and become, in fact, a religion-substitute. This worldview finally results in seeing everything in the most mundane possible way, in terms of its utility. In other words, the Enlightenment rejects the idea that things might have any sort of transcendent source, and puts in place of this the idea that things just are their use.

Of course, seeing all things only in terms of their usefulness presupposes an odd metaphysics: the idea that the subject who uses things is absolute. Such an attitude, furthermore, must issue in terrific inhumanity, when we begin to regard other people solely in terms of their utility. It is precisely this mindset that we find in the French Revolution. The Revolution was only possible, Hegel tells us, through a type of Spirit that regards itself as absolutely free of all social and religious connections. It sets itself up as absolute judge of all, and regards everything – including other people – simply as raw material to be made over in the quest for a 'just' world. This seemingly noble absolute freedom actually manifests itself in terrific destruction, while at the same time elevating itself to the status of an embodied universal: Justice itself, or the Spirit of the People.

The result, in the case of the French Revolution, was 'the Terror', which came about more than four years after the onset of the Revolution itself, and lasted from 1793 until 1794. During this period it is estimated that between twenty thousand and forty thousand 'counter-revolutionaries' were put to death, often by guillotine. It is important to understand, however, that Hegel is not engaged here in mere historical commentary. He is discussing the different forms in which human Spirit manifests itself (which is the purpose of *The Phenomenology of Spirit* itself). Though he alludes to specific historical events, the forms of Spirit he describes remain permanent possibilities of human expression. Since Hegel's time there have in fact been many other examples of 'the Terror' (e.g., the Russian Revolution, Mao's 'Cultural Revolution', etc.) and we will no doubt see this pattern again. See also **Enlightenment**; *Phenomenology of Spirit*; **self-estranged Spirit; Spirit**.

Absolute Idea (*die Absolute Idee*)   The Doctrine of the Concept is the third and final major division of Hegel's Logic. In *The Science of Logic*, Hegel describes the Doctrines of Being and Essence as 'Objective Logic', and the Doctrine of the Concept as 'Subjective Logic'. Being and essence may deal with 'the objective', but they are also categories of thought or concepts. In the Doctrine of the Concept, Hegel treats the nature of the concept *as such*. At its conclusion, we arrive at what Hegel calls the Absolute Idea. This is not an idea of some specific idea or other: it is the idea of idea itself, or the concept of concept. Absolute Idea is a purely self-related idea.

This may seem utterly strange at first, but it is easy to see that Absolute Idea is, to speak loosely, the very essence of the Logic itself. The entirety of the Logic is ideas about ideas; thought thinking thought. The Logic begins with 'being': a pure, indeterminate idea which is beyond the subject-object distinction. From this enigmatic starting point, all the other ideas of the Logic flow according to the dialectic. The Logic concludes with Absolute Idea, which is not, like being, *beyond* subject and object, but in a sense the *union* of the two. In other words, the Absolute Idea is idea of itself: as we shall see, it can be seen as a kind of purely conceptual or eidetic (idea-like) representation of self-consciousness, in which the object is the subject, and the subject object. Thus, in the end, the Logic becomes literally and explicitly what it has been all along: thought thinking thought. The initial, empty thought of 'being' finally reveals itself to be the thought of thought itself. For Hegel, 'to be' ultimately means to be Absolute Idea, the 'self-aware' concept.

Hegel conceives Absolute Idea as purely self-determining or self-developing, as opposed to an idea which merely gives way to, or appears in its 'other' (as in the Doctrines of Being and Essence). One might wonder, though, if Absolute Idea does not derive its significance from its relation to the preceding ideas in the Logic. Hegel answers, however, that the entirety of the argument of the Logic is in fact the delineation, or unfolding, of Absolute Idea. Thus, he claims that in a sense all the categories that precede Absolute Idea are 'contained' within it: not as a mere collection of ideas, but as a systematic whole. There are no ideas 'outside' Absolute Idea to which it can be related. Thus, it is what it is purely through its self-differentiation into all the categories of the Logic. Its being is not being in relation to another, but pure being-for-self.

It may seem peculiar to think of the Absolute Idea as 'differentiating itself' into the other categories, since it comes at the very end of the Logic and is their 'result'. Keep in mind, however, that while we must take time to work through the dialectic of the Logic, its categories themselves are not in time and space. Thus, if the entirety of the Logic is the 'definition' of Absolute Idea, then Absolute Idea is logically prior to and, in a sense, 'presupposed by' the very first category, pure being itself. Absolute Idea is the 'result' of the Logic (for us), but it is present from the beginning, behind the scenes.

Given that the Logic is Hegel's account of the fundamental nature of reality, the above certainly makes it sound as if Hegel sees reality as being somehow 'subjective'. In other words, it seems like he is saying that reality just is concepts or ideas (or the Idea). In a way, this is true – but only in a very special sense, as will hopefully become clear when we turn to the relation of Absolute Idea to nature. First, however, some further discussion of the place of Absolute Idea in the Logic is called for.

The Doctrine of the Concept consists of an initial section treating 'Subjectivity', under which Hegel covers, in effect, concepts about concepts (e.g. the forms of traditional logic), followed by a section treating fundamental concepts of 'Objectivity', or ways of regarding the objective world. 'Idea' is the third division of the Concept, and it sublates the material of 'Subjectivity' and 'Objectivity': it is object aware of itself, or subjectivity that has itself as object. Absolute Idea is actually the third (and final) subdivision of what Hegel calls Idea. The first two divisions are 'Life', and 'Cognition and Willing'. The initial transition to life is by means of Hegel's concept of

Absolute Idea

teleology, the final category of 'Objectivity'. Teleology conceives objects as self-differentiating, self-sustaining systems, the paradigm for which is the Logic, which articulates the idea of system or wholeness itself. However, the chief exemplars of such wholes are living organisms. Hence, Hegel refers to life as 'the immediate idea': the Idea that is there, expressed concretely, but not yet aware of itself. Cognition involves inwardizing the objective world; bringing it within consciousness and knowing the world in relation to ourselves. Willing, on the other hand, is not a cognizing of the world but a *doing*: it attempts to make the world over according to our ideals or intentions. In short, both cognition and willing are processes of bringing the object into conformity with the subject. Still, there is no recognition of the underlying *identity* of subject and object. Absolute Idea, however, is the standpoint where the subject recognizes itself in the object explicitly, and Idea is brought face-to-face with Idea. Absolute Idea 'is the Concept of the Idea, for which the Idea as such is the ob-ject, and for which the object is itself – an object in which all determinations have come together' (Geraets, 303; EL § 236).

In concrete terms, we come to recognize the identity of subject and object by seeing the entire conceptual scheme of the Logic – the 'argument' for Absolute Idea – reflected in nature. We come to see all of nature as comprehensible only as a kind of living approximation to Absolute Idea itself, which in fact is only truly realized in Absolute Spirit, in philosophical thought. Hegel's philosophy is not 'subjectivist' in the sense that he regards all of reality as an idea in our minds. However, he does see the concretization or realization of Absolute Idea as the 'goal' or consummation of reality itself. It is thus with Absolute Idea that the Logic closes and Hegel turns to the Philosophy of Nature. The transition between these two parts of Hegel's system is notoriously obscure. However, the preceding essentially sketches out one way of understanding it. To put the matter again, in simpler terms, we can say the following: When all is said and done, Absolute Idea is still *merely idea*. It is not concretely real. The Logic may constitute a formal ontology – a conceptual articulation of the nature of being – but it is still only formal, only idea. Though Absolute Idea represents a system complete unto itself, the system as a whole is deficient because logical or eidetic being is itself deficient. On its own, Logic is formal and one-dimensional. To be fully realized, the Idea must 'express itself' in the world of space and time.

In short – and to put the matter figuratively – for Absolute Idea to become truly Absolute, it cannot abide simply in the realm of ideas: it must become 'embodied'. In Hegel's Philosophy of Nature he uses the categories of the Logic to show that the entire natural world can be understood as, in effect, a series of abortive attempts to manifest in concrete reality the pure self-related self-sufficiency of Absolute Idea. For Hegel, nature culminates in the living organism, which, as a systematic whole, mirrors the holism of the Logic. Nevertheless, animals are not capable of fully or truly embodying Absolute Idea, since they are incapable of self-consciousness. It is in human thought that Hegel finds the true, concrete expression of Absolute Idea, for in human thought (in what Hegel calls Absolute Spirit: art, religion and philosophy) self-consciousness is achieved. Human self-consciousness, for Hegel, is the living expression of the perfect self-relation of Absolute Idea. The Absolute Idea 'strives' for realization in the world, and finds it only in Absolute Spirit – pre-eminently in the self-thinking thought of the philosopher.

It must be emphasized that the above really is a figurative way of putting things. It is a gross misunderstanding to think that Hegel's Logic somehow exists *first* (in time), and *then* comes to expression in nature and human being. In fact, Hegel believes that nature has existed eternally, and is an eternal (though imperfect) expression of Idea. Time only truly figures in the case of human beings, who must undergo a process of development (which we call history) in order to achieve progressively higher forms of Absolute Spirit, and thus a more perfect embodiment of Absolute Idea. Spirit, Hegel says, is the existence or, literally, 'being-there' (*Dasein*) of the Concept (Miller, 443; PN § 376). See also **Absolute Spirit**; **being-for-self**; **Concept, Doctrine of the**; **Idea**; **Logic**; **mechanism, chemism, teleology**; **nature and Philosophy of Nature**.

Absolute Knowing (*das absolute Wissen*) 'Absolute Knowing' is the final subdivision of *The Phenomenology of Spirit*, designated as 'IV (DD)'. In the *Phenomenology* it is made clear that Absolute Knowing is the *telos* or goal of Spirit itself. The first and most basic form of Spirit Hegel deals with is sense-certainty, a naive standpoint in which we believe we can adequately grasp an object through its bare sensory givenness. The dialectical nature of Hegel's philosophy means that the end is, in a sense, a return to the beginning. Absolute Knowing accordingly accomplishes exactly what

Absolute Knowing

sense-certainty cannot: the complete and total grasp of an object. All pre-philosophical attempts at knowing objects fail because objects themselves have their being only in reference to the whole, or the Absolute. It follows that the only true 'object' or individual is the whole itself, considered as an internally-differentiated system. Absolute Knowing thus knows the Absolute – though it is a very peculiar type of knowing indeed. In essence, it is another name for philosophy, and is the third form of what Hegel calls 'Absolute Spirit', the other two forms being art and religion. Absolute Knowing is philosophy in the classical sense of 'knowledge of the whole', which is the wisdom philosophers are loving or seeking.

However, in order to grasp the whole, the separation of subject and object must be overcome in Absolute Knowing. All mundane forms of knowledge are concerned with determinate, finite objects. In other words, they know only *parts* of the whole. Therefore, for Absolute Knowing to succeed in grasping the whole it must prescind from any concern with *specific* objects. Another way to put this is to say that if Absolute Knowing presupposed a particular object as given, its knowing would be deformed by concern with that sort of object and it would fail to grasp the whole. Thus, Absolute Knowing is a knowing without any determinate object. The normal standpoint of knowledge in which there is always a separation between subject and object is simply cancelled in Absolute Knowing. It is, in a sense, 'pure knowing'. What Hegel demonstrates, however, is that this cancellation of subject and object is the vehicle by which we arrive at knowledge of the one *true* object, the whole or Absolute itself.

An analogy may be helpful here. Imagine for a moment that the Absolute and all its moments could be 'transmitted' like a radio or television signal. In the *Phenomenology* we are hunting around the dial for wisdom or the speech of the Absolute, but every channel is occupied by broadcasts that merely pretend to wisdom. One might be inclined to stop at one of these broadcasts and make some sort of beginning with it, re-write its scripts, as it were, if only in our minds, to reach true wisdom. But each turns out to be a 'vast wasteland' in itself. Then we happen to discover a station that is broadcasting nothing at all, for the 'object' of Absolute Knowing is no finite object and thus it is *no thing*. However, it is a very special kind of nothing which, when meditated upon, turns out to be a strange sort of inroad to wisdom.

At the end of the *Phenomenology*, however, we have merely tuned into this station, because the *Phenomenology* does not, for lack of a better term, 'engage in' Absolute Knowing. It merely shows us that all forms of Spirit are approximations to this. Absolute Knowing as an act or activity actually begins in the Logic. There we find philosophy, at its most basic level, to be the generation of categories which are simultaneously subjective thought forms, and objective forms of the being of things. Thus, Absolute Knowing, in transcending the distinction between subject and object is, in fact, *both* subjective and objective (though this is only truly revealed at the end of the Logic). In so far as it constitutes a knowing of thought forms, it is self-knowledge.

There is one important respect, however, in which the simile of the television signal is inadequate: because there is no distinction between form and content, or method and content, in the system, the broadcasts of the Absolute Station and the act of turning to the station are really one: in other words, there is no distinction between Absolute Knowing and an 'object' known in Absolute Knowing. This follows immediately if one simply keeps squarely in mind the fact that the subject-object distinction really is cancelled in Absolute Knowing. There is no 'knower' (or 'knowing') and 'known' here.

We can see from the above that Hegel's Absolute Knowing satisfies another of the classical definitions of philosophy: that it is self-knowledge ('the unexamined life is not worth living', said Socrates). Hegel has demonstrated that in fact there is no distinction between knowledge of the whole, and knowledge of self. Obviously, there can be no knowledge of the self without a knowledge of the whole of which the self is merely a part or a modification – and there can be no knowledge of the whole without awareness of the nature of the self to whom the whole is given. Hegel makes the more radical claim, however, that thought and being are one: the categories of thought are the categories of being. He argues further that all of reality may be understood as having as its consummation the coming into being of a form of thought which can know reality. In other words, Hegel believes that philosophy is the whole knowing itself, and that this is the purpose of all of existence. Thus, Absolute Knowing is not merely the goal or apex of human thought; it is the goal or apex of all that is. See also **Absolute; Absolute Spirit; Logic; *Phenomenology of Spirit*; philosophy and the history of philosophy; sense-certainty; Spirit.**

Absolute Religion   See **Christianity**.

Absolute Spirit (*der absolute Geist*)   Absolute Spirit is the third form of what Hegel calls Spirit. Subjective Spirit deals with the 'psychology' of the individual, including all those aspects of ourselves which are unconscious or preconscious. Objective Spirit is humanity expressing itself in the form of social institutions, such as cultural and governmental forms – though it may not be conscious of the fact that it is doing this. Absolute Spirit, on the other hand, is Spirit come to consciousness of itself; Spirit confronting itself and becoming self-aware.

Hegel holds that there are three basic forms of Absolute Spirit: art, religion and philosophy. All three of these activities are absolutely unique to humanity, and each consists of a way in which humanity confronts itself. In creating a work of art, no matter what it might represent, we are nevertheless expressing our own nature. The artwork is an expression of our perceptions of things – things viewed from our own unique human (or personal) perspective. In religion we attempt to put ourselves into accord with God, which Hegel identifies with the Absolute Idea. Religion does not realize that the Absolute Idea is not and cannot be a transcendent other: it has existence only as embodied by human minds capable of self-knowledge through philosophic thought. Art and religion, further, are alike in that they are both *sensuous*: they employ images, metaphors and plastic media of all kinds in order to find expression. Hegel understands both as groping towards self-knowledge, but unable in the end to truly arrive at it precisely because of the limitations imposed by 'picture-thinking'.

True self-awareness may only be had in the medium of the concept, of thought. This is the realm of philosophy. Even though Hegel believes both art and religion have value in themselves and will never cease as human activities, he also believes that in some sense they are superseded by philosophy. Hegel regards Absolute Spirit and its zenith, philosophy, as the highest expression of humanity, and of the world itself. He believes – as he argues in *The Phenomenology of Spirit* – that all human activities are, in a way, failed attempts to provide what can only be accomplished through Absolute Spirit. Thus, Absolute Spirit is the ultimate goal of all human life, even though most human beings are completely unconscious of this. Further, since humanity is the apex of nature itself, we may say that Absolute Spirit, and specifically philosophy, is the ultimate goal of all that exists.

In his published writings, Hegel presents his tripartite theory of Absolute Spirit first in *The Phenomenology of Spirit*, where Subdivision III (CC) deals with religion and art. Subdivision IV (DD) is entitled 'Absolute Knowing', which is equivalent to philosophy. The presentation of Absolute Spirit is a good deal clearer in *The Encyclopedia of the Philosophical Sciences*, where it occupies the final sections of the Philosophy of Spirit. Hegel never wrote a book on Absolute Spirit, but he did give lecture courses on the Philosophy of Art, Philosophy of Religion and History of Philosophy. These have all been published and constitute a massive explication of the nature of Absolute Spirit. See also **art and Philosophy of Art**; **Encyclopedia of the Philosophical Sciences**; **God**; **Objective Spirit**; **Phenomenology of Spirit**; **philosophy and the history of philosophy**; **picture-thinking**; **religion and Philosophy of Religion**; **Spirit**; **Subjective Spirit**; **theology**.

abstract and concrete (*abstrakt; konkret*) These terms are not 'categories' that appear in the Logic or in any other part of Hegel's system. Instead they are descriptive terms Hegel often employs in his writings, though sometimes with different senses. 'Abstract' generally means, for Hegel, whatever is partial, incomplete, or one-sided. Hegel will often apply this term to certain ideas as they are conceived by the understanding. For example, the understanding insists on the so-called Law of Identity: 'A is A', a thing is what it is. Hegel points out, however, that identity is a meaningless abstraction without the concept of difference. In fact, things are what they are precisely by *not* being all sorts of other things, in myriad ways. The 'concrete', is simply that which is not one-sided but many-sided; not partial or incomplete, but inclusive, or even all-inclusive. Ultimately the only true concrete is the whole, which includes everything.

Hegel's use of 'abstract' and 'concrete' often reverses the commonsensical usage of these terms. Most people regard ideas as abstract, and objects (usually physical objects) as concrete. For Hegel, however, objects are abstract in the sense that they are mere parts of the whole: they are, in themselves, incomplete and partial without the other members of the whole to which they belong. Hegel compounds what, to commonsense, seems like sheer perversity by asserting, furthermore, that the only true concrete is the Idea (or Absolute Idea). Hegel demonstrates in his Logic that the Idea 'contains' all the fundamental thought-determinations of reality within itself. The 'embodiment' of Idea in self-reflective, human thought is,

abstract right

furthermore, asserted by Hegel to be the end or goal of existence itself. All beings, therefore, are what they are in reference to this ultimate whole, the Idea.

To put all of this a different way, Hegel understands the identity of anything to consist in its differences from other things: things are what they are by *not* being others. Hence, if we consider any item in reality in complete isolation from all others it really becomes an unknowable abstraction. Only the whole of reality understood as expression of Idea is complete and concrete, lacking nothing and containing everything. See also **Absolute Idea**; **concrete universal**; **identity and difference**; **Logic**; **understanding**.

abstract right (*das abstrakte Recht*)   Hegel's *Philosophy of Right* is divided into three major sections: 'Abstract Right', 'Morality' and 'Ethical Life'. These represent the principal dialectical moments in which the idea of right (meaning, roughly, justice, or right in the sense of right vs. wrong) develops itself, culminating in a fully adequate theory. At the same time, Hegel tells us that these sections display the human will coming to determine itself in more and more adequate forms.

On one level, abstract right encapsulates the view of right typically held by Enlightenment thinkers like John Locke: right consists in a respect for persons as possessors of property. The most primal way in which human beings express their will (or make it objective) is through claiming that this or that is 'mine'. Accordingly, in abstract right the basic way in which individuals relate to one another is through the exchange of property. The concept of personhood typical of abstract right is frequently described today as 'atomic individualism'. Further, the sort of community that characterizes abstract right is an impoverished one. Relationships between individuals basically fall into two categories: relationships of trade and competition, and intimate or familial relations. The implication of this is that outside of families there is really nothing that binds people together, that creates solidarity, other than self-interest. As a result, under abstract right any kind of overarching social authority or institutions are conceived simply as contrivances serving self-interest. Society under abstract right is viewed as founded upon a contract, and as something created merely for our convenience, to facilitate trade and to protect our 'rights'. Authority in society exists simply to make it easier for individuals to do whatever they want – so long as what they want doesn't interfere with someone else's rights.

Hegel opposes the 'social contract' theory of Hobbes and Locke. He rejects the idea that society is something individuals have freely created. If this were true, we would probably feel that the state is something we have power over (since it is our creation), and that we could, if we desired, simply opt out or change the rules at our pleasure. But Hegel says that this can't be how things are: after all, the state sends men off to fight and die for it. The power of the state, and the needs of society, transcend my individual self-interest. Obviously, it is not in my self-interest to die – yet when called to serve society even at the risk of my own life, I feel that I have a duty to do so. We can thus see that from Hegel's perspective, the way in which abstract right conceives of the relation of the individual to society is defective, and he argues that we must transcend this standpoint in favour of a more adequate one. However, the dialectical mechanism for doing so is revealed through the nature of 'wrong'.

Hegel's discussion of wrong deals with the way in which transgressions against right appear, and how they are dealt with in the system of abstract right. Again, this system is based upon self-interest, and on the right of persons to be 'let alone' (i.e., the so-called 'negative rights'). Such persons make contracts with each other, and – human nature being what it is – there are bound to be individuals who choose to break the rules. The most important sort of wrong that Hegel talks about is crime, which (as he conceives it) always involves some form of *coercion*. When we coerce another individual, Hegel says that we commit a kind of fundamental contradiction. We see ourselves as persons with rights and freedoms, and normally we see others similarly. Yet when we coerce others we behave as if we no longer recognize the nature we share in common with them; we no longer recognize them as rights-bearing individuals. Coercion is thus a kind of denial of reality – a wilful denial of the nature of other human beings. Hegel sees crime and coercion as purely negative and destructive. In recognizing this, however, we are pointed towards something positive: a universal principle of right or justice itself. In seeing certain actions as wrong – as purely negative and in need of putting right – we recognize in fact *that there is a right*. Further, we sense, however dimly, that the character of this principle of right is universal (i.e., that it applies to everyone) and that the criminal has transgressed this. And we see, or soon see, that the criminal's actions require punishment. In fact, Hegel's treatment of punishment is one of the most controversial portions of *The Philosophy of Right*. In a nutshell, Hegel argues that when we punish criminals we are in fact honouring their rational, human nature. The reason for this, quite simply, is that in punishing criminals we do to them what they themselves *would* will, if they were in fact capable of seeing that their crime is a wrong which has to be *righted*.

Still, punishing wrongdoers in the name of right requires impartial judges able to set aside their individual interests or circumstances and to judge according to universal principles. In the world of abstract right, however, we concern ourselves with the rules for purely selfish reasons. Hegel therefore argues that abstract right cannot be self-sufficient because its self-maintenance requires a kind of impartiality which it does not itself engender. Indeed, what is required is a moral standpoint. The world of abstract right provides no guidance at all on *how* to determine what the principles of ethics are, or how to apply them. Abstract right is all about freedom of choice (indeed, such freedom and the 'rights' that go with it are exalted in a society that exhibits the bare form of abstract right). Beyond telling us not to interfere with other people's 'pursuit of happiness', abstract right provides us no guidance in making ethical choices. We are free to be as piggish and immoderate, as uncultivated and unreliable, as rude and unkind as we like – so long as we recognize the freedom of others to be similarly debased. In short, the system of abstract right is morally empty. The dialectic therefore passes beyond abstract right – right considered in its purely external or objective manifestation – to morality, which treats right as it develops itself in the subjective, inner life of the individual. (These two moments, the objective and subjective sides of right, will be reconciled in Ethical Life.) See also **Enlightenment**; **ethical life**; **morality**; **Objective Spirit**; *Philosophy of Right*; **punishment**; **wrong**.

actuality (*die Wirklichkeit*)   The mystic author Meister Eckhart (c. 1260–c. 1328) seems to have been the first to translate the Latin *actualitas* as *Werkelichkeit*, or, in modern German, *Wirklichkeit*. The term *actualitas*, as Eckhart encountered it, was itself a translation of Aristotle's term *energeia*. In Aristotle's philosophy, *energeia* is the opposite of *dunamis*, or potentiality. Something achieves *energeia* when it acts in such a manner as to realize its *dunamis*. For example, human beings have the potential to think rationally. Thus, when human beings think, they are actualizing their potential (and, indeed, realizing their nature, for it is our nature to be thinking animals). This theory of actuality as an *act*, and as a realization of formal possibility, is extremely important for Hegel (indeed, Aristotle was one of the most significant influences on him).

Hegel's Logic can be understood as an ontology – as an attempt to define what being is. Indeed, the Logic begins with 'pure being' as its first category. The dialectic of the Logic begins with an attempt to define pure being, and we find that this attempt requires us to supplement it with further categories. Finally, at the end of the Logic, we reach a category called Absolute Idea, which 'contains' all the preceding categories as moments or aspects, and which can be understood as a fully adequate characterization of being. Absolute Idea is being, but for Hegel it is 'not yet' actual; it is a purely formal reality, or formal possibility.

Like Aristotle, Hegel argues that Idea, to be actual, must be realized in the world, and through the world. Aristotle rejects the Platonic concept of a transcendent world of forms that exist, in some mysterious fashion, parallel to this one. Instead, he holds that forms are to be identified with the functions or 'work' of objects in the world, and are, in effect, eternal possibilities (forms or 'ideas') of action. Similarly, Hegel holds that his Idea is in some sense 'unreal' considered apart from nature, and from human Spirit (which, in Hegel's scheme, ultimately actualizes the Idea in self-reflective thought). Thus, for both Aristotle and Hegel, the actual is the concrete realization of Idea. And for both men, this realization is a dynamic, ever-unfolding act. Hegel holds that the world is eternally actualizing Idea, but that this actualization takes place within time and through change.

Hegel is fond of pointing out how philosophical truths are embedded in the German language. Here we may note that *Wirklichkeit* is related to *wirken*, meaning 'to have an effect' or 'be effective'. Also, *Wirkung* means 'effect'. '*Wirk-*' also occurs as a prefix in a number of words, where it generally connotes action or activity: e.g., *Wirkstoff*, 'agent, active substance'.[6] In the *Phenomenology of Spirit* Hegel speaks of the Absolute as, 'the process of its own becoming, the circle that presupposes its end as its goal, having its end also as its beginning; and only by being worked out to its end, is it actual [*wirklich*]' (Miller, 10; PG, 14). And he tells us that the Absolute must be conceived in 'the whole wealth of the developed form. Only then is it conceived and expressed as an actuality [*als Wirkliches*]'

Actual Soul   35

(Miller, 11; PG, 15). In *The Philosophy of Right* Hegel states that 'What is rational is actual [*wirklich*]; and what is actual is rational' (Nisbet, 20). This well-known quotation simply means that reason or the Idea has concretized itself in what is actual; and what is actual is a concretization of the Idea. In his lectures, Hegel expressed this same thought as 'What is actual becomes rational, and the rational becomes actual.'[7]

The above represents a general account of what, in Hegel's philosophy, is understood to be truly 'actual' or real. In the Doctrine of Essence of the Logic, 'Actuality' has a narrower, more restricted meaning. The categories of Essence involve a dichotomy between 'inner' and 'outer' (or inner 'essence' and outer 'show', or appearance). This dichotomy is overcome in 'Actuality', the third and final major division of the Doctrine of Essence. Again, an analogy to Aristotle is useful. In Aristotelian actuality, a thing can be understood to 'become its own essence', since actuality consists of something acting or working in such a way as to realize or actualize its own form. The Hegelian category of actuality overcomes the inner-outer dichotomy through being a whole which is nothing other than its parts considered in organic relation to one another. (In other words, the whole is nothing over and above 'the sum of its parts', because in this case the parts form an organic unity.) Thus, actuality anticipates Absolute Idea, but lacks the self-relatedness of Absolute Idea. We might thus say that for Hegel *true* actuality (as opposed to the partial actuality encountered in Essence) must consist in the whole being for-itself, or aware of itself. However, as discussed earlier, this is not even truly achieved in the Absolute Idea, but only in Spirit. See also **Absolute Idea**; **Aristotle**; **being, nothing, becoming**; **Essence, Doctrine of**; **Logic**.

Actual Soul (*die wirkliche Seele*)   'Actual Soul' is the concluding section of the 'Anthropology' portion of Hegel's treatment of Subjective Spirit, and constitutes the third to 'Natural Soul' and 'Feeling Soul'. 'Soul' is Hegel's term for Spirit at its lowest, most primitive level. It is, in effect, the 'animal' part in us, and Hegel refers to it as 'the sleep of Spirit'. In the development of human personality, the lower levels of consciousness must be brought under the sway of the higher levels and, to a great extent, mastered. If this does not take place, the individual remains at an animalistic, subhuman level and the higher forms of Spirit (including self-aware reason in all its forms) cannot emerge. Had you, the reader, not brought the baser levels of your being under your conscious control (and achieved thereby a kind of 'self-possession') it would be impossible for you to read and comprehend this book. Hegel claims that it is primarily through the development of *habit* that the 'natural' part of the self is tamed. Habit frees the higher levels of the mind for other activities, including philosophy and science. Through the mastery of the body, we transcend the merely natural aspect of ourselves. This natural aspect becomes, as it were, an 'other' to us: something to be conquered and controlled (much as the human race conquers and controls the natural world). This achievement constitutes the development of actual soul, a necessary condition for the unfolding of the higher levels of Spirit. See also **anthropology; feeling soul; habit; natural soul; Philosophy of Spirit; Spirit; Subjective Spirit.**

aesthetics See **art** and **Philosophy of Art.**

animal See **organics.**

animal magnetism (*der animalische Magnetismus*) In Hegel's writings and lectures on Subjective Spirit he discusses the phenomenon of animal magnetism, or mesmerism, at length. Franz Anton Mesmer (1734–1815) was a physician practicing medicine in Paris who found that passing magnets or magnetized materials over his patients not only seemed to improve their conditions, but sometimes put them into a trance. In time, Mesmer found that he could dispense with magnets and produce the same effects merely by passing his hands over his patients. He theorized that these phenomena depended upon the presence of a fluid force which he called 'animal magnetism'. While in such trance states, individuals often seemed capable of psychic or paranormal powers, such as telepathy and clairvoyance. These phenomena were widely discussed in Hegel's time, and captured the interest of many philosophers and intellectuals, including Schelling and Schopenhauer.

Hegel's treatment of animal magnetism constitutes one of the most extensive discussions of any topic in the Philosophy of Spirit. Briefly, he argues that in paranormal states the 'feeling' part of the soul temporarily usurps the higher-level, 'mental' functions. In a sense, one identifies one's self – again, temporarily – with the most primordial part of the soul. In this identity with the feeling soul ordinary spatio-temporal distinctions are

appearance

overcome, and along with them the distinctness of individuals. As a result, Hegel theorizes, phenomena like clairvoyance and mind reading become real possibilities. He states that we can never understand animal magnetism as long as we assume an atomistic or mechanistic model of the universe, and treat beings as related merely externally. However, Hegel makes it very clear that he regards such paranormal states as an aberration of Spirit, not as an elevation of it.

Hegel's interest in animal magnetism seems strange to us today. However, there are significant reasons why he believed that paranormal phenomena are important for philosophy – and we need not believe that such phenomena exist in order to understand his point. Hegel explicitly states that the ability of his philosophy to explain the paranormal is an important proof of its explanatory power. Further, since Hegel believes that *only* speculative philosophy can explain such matters, this constitutes – for him – proof of the bankruptcy of science and philosophy done from the standpoint of the understanding. See also **feeling soul**; **relation**; **speculation**; **Subjective Spirit**; **understanding**.

anthropology (*die Anthropologie*)   When Hegel's system makes its transition from the Philosophy of Nature to the Philosophy of Spirit, it is to Subjective Spirit that it initially turns. Subjective Spirit deals with the 'psychology' of the individual, including all those aspects of our selves which are unconscious or preconscious, as well as such matters as perception, will, imagination, memory, and the passions. Hegel divides Subjective Spirit into three sections: 'Anthropology', 'Phenomenology' and 'Psychology'. Anthropology, Hegel tells us, deals with Spirit still implicit, 'Spirit in nature'. Anthropology, in other words, deals with that aspect of us that is still mired in nature and is not a function of the conscious mind. It is, as it were, the 'natural self', and Hegel calls it 'the soul'. Hegel refers to soul as the 'sleep of Spirit'; the raw material out of which character is formed. It contains depths that very often go unfathomed by the conscious mind. Hegel further subdivides his treatment of soul into 'Natural Soul', 'Feeling Soul' and 'Actual Soul'. See also **actual soul**; **feeling soul**; **natural soul**; **Philosophy of Spirit**; **Subjective Spirit**.

appearance (*die Erscheinung*)   Appearance is a key concept in the second major division of Hegel's Logic, the Doctrine of Essence. At the beginning of the Doctrine of Essence we are invited to consider the determinate forms of being (covered in the preceding division of the text) as *mere appearance*, beyond which might exist a mysterious inner essence. The distinction here is in fact one of 'appearance vs. reality': the inner essence is true reality, in contrast to the deceptive and insubstantial appearances. Certain philosophers and mystics have taken precisely this approach – denying reality to the world of objects all about us, and asserting instead that the real is something that completely transcends appearances, as well as our language. In other words, they have said that the essence of things is ineffable.

Hegel rejects this approach, holding that there are insuperable difficulties with it. Since appearances are *there*, appearing to us, Hegel argues that the only basis for saying they are somehow 'unreal' would be to show that their existence depends upon essence. To do that, however, one would have to be able to show some *positive* relation between essence and appearance. But the theory just discussed conceives appearance and essence as externally related – the appearances are a deceptive show; a knowable (or sensible) not-being contrasted to a being that is ultimately unknowable. Furthermore, if essence is conceived as unknowable, if we can really say nothing about it, then it is conceived purely negatively, as not-appearance. But this makes of essence an empty, contentless abstraction: in fact, it makes essence a non-being.

Thus, Hegel rejects such attempts at setting up a dichotomy between appearance and reality. Nevertheless, ultimately he does endorse a much more sophisticated version of the appearance-reality distinction, one in which the two are understood to be internally related. Hegel completely rejects the traditional philosophical denigration of appearance. What is it, he asks, that appears in appearance? Hegel answers: the being of a thing; what it truly is. Appearance is the showing-forth, the displaying of what something is. Appearance must be this manifestation, or what is it appearance *of*? And essence must manifest, or what is it? Essence without appearance is a nullity. To adapt the familiar Aristotelian example, the essence of the oak may be in the acorn, but the oak tree is its appearance: the realization of essence.

Hegel's treatment of appearance and essence can be understood as two-tiered. On one level, we can say that the myriad appearances of each thing – the many ways in which it displays itself – are all manifestations of what it

Aristotle

is, its essence. On a deeper level, however, we can say that *the things themselves* are appearances of the Absolute. The Absolute is not some mysterious 'beyond': it is the whole of reality itself conceived as a system in which each part is organically related to every other. Hegel attempts to show how the being of each finite thing *just is* its place in the whole; a part of the system of reality itself. Thus, each thing may be understood to be an 'appearance' of the Absolute. This does not mean, however, that Hegel reverts to the position that the Absolute is the truth that abides beyond 'mere appearance'. Without these finite things through which the Absolute displays itself, there would be no Absolute. See also **Absolute**; **Aristotle**; **Essence, Doctrine of**; **Kant, Immanuel**; **whole, the**.

Aristotle (384–322 BC) Hegel's discussion of Aristotle in his *Lectures on the History of Philosophy* is about three times longer than any of his discussions of subsequent thinkers. Next to Kant, Aristotle is arguably the most important philosophical influence on him. Indeed, it would not be implausible to argue that in certain ways Hegel's philosophy is a kind of post-Kantian transformation of Aristotelian ideas. The Aristotle–Hegel relationship has been the subject of much scholarly discussion, and what follows merely scratches the surface.

Plato held that spatio-temporal, sensible objects are merely imperfect 'copies' of eternal, immaterial patterns called forms (*eide*; or 'ideas', in older translations of Plato). For example, an individual dog is a flawed copy of the form of 'dogness'. Sensibles were said by Plato to 'participate in' or 'partake of' their forms. Aristotle accepts the existence of eternal patterns in nature, but accuses Plato of resorting to mere poetic metaphor in his doctrine of participation, as well as in his characterizations of forms themselves. Aristotle's revision of Plato involves understanding a form not as something fixed and static, existing apart from nature, but rather as the characteristic 'work' or action of a thing. In other words, a thing *is* what it does, or how it behaves: its nature is its work or activity. For Aristotle, when a thing acts or behaves in accordance with its nature it is *actualizing* its form – and this is the case regardless of whether the thing in question is living or not living. The significance of this doctrine is that Aristotle has, in a sense, made forms immanent in nature, rather than transcendent as Plato had held. In short, it is Aristotle's view that forms are, in a sense, 'realized' in nature through the actions of material bodies. Aristotle remains an idealist, like Plato, only his idealism finds 'idea' (form) immanent in nature itself – and he holds that nature is only intelligible as the realization of idea.

Nevertheless, for Aristotle, every material thing actualizes its formal being only partially and imperfectly. The reason for this is that matter and form are opposites, and matter always, in one way or another, is an obstacle to the perfect realization of form. For example, Aristotle would analyze a deformity such as a club foot as an instance of a material body being quite imperfectly suited to expressing (or, we might say, receiving) form. If there is any such thing as a *pure* actuality, therefore, it would have to be purely formal and without any matter at all. This may seem like an impossibility, but Aristotle argues that such a pure actuality *must* exist in order ultimately to explain why we find things in nature striving to actualize their forms. In fact, Aristotle claims, all things are unconsciously striving to imitate this pure actuality.

But what would such a pure actuality really be like? If it has no body, but is nevertheless in act (and again, all actuality for Aristotle is act), then it could only be a mind that thinks. Further, Aristotle reasons that if this mind is non-material, it can have no parts; no division within itself. Thus there can be no distinction in it between its thinking and *what* it thinks. The only kind of thinking in which there is no such distinction would be self-thinking, or self-awareness, in which the object of consciousness is in fact the subject (and vice versa). In short, pure actuality would be a self-knowing mind. Aristotle calls this mind 'God', and also the 'Unmoved Mover': God itself is unaffected by anything, yet it moves all else since every being in nature 'strives' to replicate its perfect eternity and self-sufficiency. Aristotle understands all of nature as a hierarchy or scale in which 'higher' beings are those that come closest to imitating God. Since it is only human beings who are truly capable of self-awareness, humans are the highest of all terrestrial beings (and the philosophers, who put 'know thyself' into practice as a science, are, in a way, the most human of humans).

Turning now to Hegel, it may easily be seen that his response to Kant is structurally similar to Aristotle's response to Plato. Hegel asserts, contra Kant, that *phenomena* (appearances) do not cut us off from reality (things-in-themselves) – just as Aristotle responds to Plato by claiming that sensibles do not cut us off from forms. Instead, for both Aristotle and Hegel, appearance is just the expression or unfolding of reality itself. According to Hegel, considered in itself the Absolute Idea of the Logic

art and Philosophy of Art

(equivalent to Plato's Form of the One/Good) is merely ghostly and irreal. It only achieves actuality by becoming manifest through the world of nature. Thus, in both Aristotle and Hegel we find a rejection of the idea that the world that appears to our senses somehow cuts us off from truth or from what is real. Instead, nature is seen as the flowering of truth and being. Furthermore, like Aristotle, Hegel sees nature as a scale in which true self-relation or self-consciousness is being approximated at every level. For Hegel, however, self-consciousness is fully and truly manifested in human Spirit (especially the Absolute Spirit of art, religion and philosophy). Hegel thus immanentizes Aristotle's transcendent God, insisting that God in fact is actualized through human Spirit itself. Though this seems like a radical revision of Aristotle, one might argue that Hegel has only made Aristotle more Aristotelian. The opposition of the disembodied Unmoved Mover to the world that only imperfectly approximates it is a vestige, it seems, of Platonism. Hegel insists, however, that actuality – *all* actuality – is only actualized in and through nature, and human nature. Hegel asserts, further, that human Spirit develops and comes to realize itself through history. Aristotle, by contrast, treats human beings much as he treats every other being in nature: as an eternal, unchanging species. Aristotle has little to say about the historical development of humanity.

One can thus see that despite significant differences, there are striking structural similarities between the central metaphysical ideas of Aristotle, and those of Hegel. Hegel seems to have been fully aware of these. There are also many other similarities between the two thinkers. For example, Hegel's *Philosophy of Right* insists that ethics is a political inquiry – that it has little meaning apart from a social context that serves to concretize moral rules and hone the judgement of moral agents. In fact, this is one of the more famous claims made by Aristotle in his *Nicomachean Ethics*.

G. R. G. Mure's classic *An Introduction to Hegel*, devotes its first few chapters to a summary of Aristotle, using him as a means to explain Hegel to beginners (see Appendix B: Suggestions for Further Reading). See also **Absolute Idea**; **actuality**; **appearance**; **God**; **Kant, Immanuel**; **nature and Philosophy of Nature**; **philosophy and the history of philosophy**.

art and Philosophy of Art (*die Kunst; die Philosophie der Kunst*) Along with religion and philosophy, art is one of the forms taken by what Hegel calls Absolute Spirit: Spirit (or human being) confronting or knowing itself. In all the forms of Absolute Spirit, the subject makes itself into an object, or the object becomes the subject. In the artwork, the ideas and intentions of Spirit are expressed or embodied in various materials. For example, the artist conceives an idea for a sculpture, then realizes that idea objectively by transforming a block of marble. The result is that through the artwork, humanity *confronts itself* through something objective. (It is not necessary, by the way, that the artist – or the spectator – be aware that this is the meaning or purpose of the artwork.) To put things the other way round, in the artwork the objective has become *subject-like*: the objective has ceased to be purely objective, because it has received the stamp of the subject. For Hegel, the Absolute Idea, which overcomes the dichotomy between subject and object, is 'embodied' in each of the forms of Absolute Spirit. Thus, Hegel claims that in art, and our contemplation of art, the Idea is embodied in sensuous form – through shapes, images, sounds, etc.

Hegel derived much of his view of the nature of art from Schelling, who accorded art and the 'philosophy of art' a good deal more importance than Hegel does. In Schelling's early system, art is a sensuous appearance of the Absolute (the 'indifference point' beyond subject and object) and the philosophy of art is the 'keystone' that connects transcendental idealism and philosophy of nature. Hegel, by contrast, sees religion, and especially philosophy (as he conceives it), as more significant and adequate approaches to the Absolute.

In Hegel's Lectures on Aesthetics, he discusses the different forms of art and their historical development. He distinguishes between different art forms in terms of how well the conceptual 'content' of the artwork and its material medium are harmonized. In great art, a complete or perfect harmony is present. For Hegel, there are three major forms of art: the symbolic, the classical and the romantic.

In symbolic art, the meaning of the artwork is so abstract that it cannot find adequate expression in material form. As a result, the artwork is inscrutable, and confronts us as a riddle. Hegel gives the monumental architecture of the Egyptians as an example of this. In classical art, such as the sculpture of the Greeks, there is a perfect marriage of content and form. In Greek sculpture, Spirit achieves greater awareness of itself through the representation of the human form. In romantic art – principally the poetry, painting and music of the Christian world – we find the artist struggling to

'bacchanalian revel, the'

express the infinity of Spirit. The attempt is inevitably a failure, for no material medium can be truly adequate to Spirit's self-expression. Thus, we pass to the attempt to confront Spirit through an 'immaterial' form. In short, we pass from art to religion. See also **Absolute Idea; Absolute Spirit; classical art; philosophy and the history of philosophy; religion and Philosophy of Religion; romantic art; Schelling, F. W. J.; symbolic art.**

attraction and repulsion   See **repulsion and attraction**.

Aufhebung   See **sublation**.

— B —

'bacchanalian revel, the' (*der bacchantische Taumel*)   Hegel writes in the preface to *The Phenomenology of Spirit*, 'Appearance is the arising and passing away which itself does not arise or pass away, but is in-itself, and constitutes the actuality and movement of the life of truth. The true is thus the Bacchanalian revel in which no member is not drunk; yet because each member collapses as soon as he drops out, the revel is just as much transparent and simple repose' (Miller, 27; PG, 35). This is one of the most famous images in all of Hegel, an allusion to the drunken orgies in honour of the god of wine, Bacchus (the Roman equivalent of the Greek Dionysus). Philosophers have often understood 'appearance' to separate us from a more fundamental truth which does not itself appear: for example, Kant's distinction between *phenomena* (appearances) and things as they are in themselves, or Plato's distinction between forms and sensibles. Hegel holds, however, that truth displays itself in appearance. No single one of the appearances – no single one of the many things that show themselves to us – conveys the whole truth. The truth, in fact, is the whole, as Hegel states in an earlier passage in the Preface. In the 'bacchanalian revel', each celebrant has a specific character, but all are united by drunkenness or, we might say, imbued with the spirit of Bacchus. In the same way, each of the appearances is a partial, incomplete showing of the truth. In the revel, each member displays himself then 'drops out' and falls down unconscious, thus temporarily losing his individual identity in oneness with the god. Similarly, each stage of the Hegelian dialectic stands for a time, but then reveals itself to be partial or incomplete; to derive its being (or meaning) only in relation to the Absolute. See also **Absolute**; appearance; dialectic; **Kant, Immanuel**; *Phenomenology of Spirit*; sublation; truth.

'beautiful soul, the' (*die schöne Seele*)   In subdivision '(BB) Spirit' of *The Phenomenology of Spirit*, Hegel presents us with one of the most famous and often-cited images in his philosophy, that of 'the beautiful soul'. Hegel derives this image from a character in Goethe's novel *Wilhelm Meisters Lehrjahre*. The context in the *Phenomenology* is Hegel's discussion of morality (a subject he covers in greater detail and much more systematically in the later *Philosophy of Right*). Hegel's discussion of the 'Moral World-View' and 'Dissemblance' (*die Verstellung*) amounts largely to a re-statement and critique of Kantian ethics and its insistence on autonomy; on the human agent 'giving a law to itself' and following that law, or duty, for its own sake. From there, Hegel turns to 'Conscience' (*das Gewissen*) a kind of practical wisdom that does not involve the generation of moral rules. A certain universality is to be found in the claims of personal conscience, since I affirm that what is *right* for me should be affirmed as such by others. Hegel points out, however, that all these forms of moral consciousness are inherently subjective and have the potential to be cleverly twisted in order to suit the purposes of the actor.

Conscience may, however, take a different turn. Instead of producing the man who manages disingenuously to convince himself that whatever he does is justified, it may lead to the beautiful soul. This is the sort of man who may be so wary of the possibility of self-deception, and of the unintended consequences of action, that he refrains from taking any action, or from taking a stand at all. It is as if the beautiful soul fears that its purity may be tainted by actually doing anything. There is one thing, however, that the beautiful soul does not shrink from, and that is passing judgement on those who do take action. The beautiful soul is the self-righteous critic who is proud of never actually doing anything; proud of having retained his purity of heart. He tends to indulge in escapist fantasies and, Hegel tells us, may eventually go off the deep end and succumb to

Being, Doctrine of

madness or consumption (*Schwindsucht*, an older term for tuberculosis). In the argument of the *Phenomenology*, the beautiful soul is overcome in religious consciousness, a different sort of moral standpoint in which oppositions between individuals disappear. In short, it is at this point that the dialectic of the *Phenomenology* transitions to Absolute Spirit. See also **Kant, Immanuel**; **morality**; *Phenomenology of Spirit*; *Philosophy of Right*.

becoming   See **being, nothing, becoming**.

Being, Doctrine of (*die Lehre vom Sein*)   The Doctrine of Being is the first of the three major divisions of Hegel's Logic. The way to the Logic has been prepared by *The Phenomenology of Spirit*, at the conclusion of which we arrive at 'Absolute Knowing'. What Absolute Knowing knows, ultimately, is Absolute Idea, which specifies itself in pure thought into the system of categories that is the Logic. But since this knowing transcends subject and object, it cannot begin with a discussion of anything in particular. Hegel argues emphatically that if philosophy begins by assuming *any* sort of determinate thought or object at all as true or as given, then it cannot fulfill its claim to be an absolute, presuppositionless science. Thus, the starting point of the Logic is a pure indeterminacy (for all intents and purposes identical to Absolute Knowing). What can we say about this indeterminacy, Hegel asks? We can say only that *it is*. The Logic thus begins with 'pure being' as the first of its categories, and the dialectic takes off from there.

The Doctrine of Being ranges over all of the most basic concepts involved when we deal with objects in their *immediacy*: i.e., how they present themselves to simple, unreflective awareness. In the *Encyclopedia Logic*, Hegel explains that being involves thought 'In its immediacy – the doctrine of the Concept in-itself' (Geraets, 133; EL § 83). Hegel begins with the pure immediacy of being and shows, dialectically, how it goes over into its opposite, and how this is reconciled by a further concept, and so forth. In this way, Hegel derives all the categories of the first division of the Logic. When one goes through the system of concepts that is the Doctrine of Being (a system which, as we shall see, cannot stand on its own) one finds many of the thought-forms from earlier philosophers recapitulated – especially the Pre-Socratics. However, Hegel does not simply take these concepts over from the history of philosophy. Instead, in Hegel's view, these categories actually *develop themselves*, one from another, through the dialectic. Hegel would argue, in fact, that the reason why this section of the Logic bears such a similarity to Pre-Socratic ideas is that the entire history of philosophy is an imperfect and partial 'recollection' of the categories to which he gives full, systematic form.

The Doctrine of Being as a whole, however, is flawed because our focus on the givenness or immediacy of objects is itself unstable and incomplete (a point which Hegel also argues very effectively early on in *The Phenomenology of Spirit*). Objects are not exhausted by their surface appearance, and the attempt to understand them necessarily goes beyond (or beneath) the surface. This is, in effect, what is realized in the transition from the Doctrine of Being to the Doctrine of Essence (which is itself superseded by the Doctrine of the Concept).

The Doctrine of Being is divided into three subdivisions: 'Quality', 'Quantity' and 'Measure'. The basic idea here is that objects appear to us as possessing qualities of various kinds, but always in some quantity or degree. (For example, two objects are red; but one is 'redder' than the other, or, perhaps, one is red all over and the other is not.) However, qualities may not exist in just any quantity. (For example, a dog cannot be twenty stories tall and still be considered merely 'a dog'.) Thus, a standard of measure must come into play. Ultimately, however, the dialectic compels us to pass beyond measure, and the immediacy of things entirely, to consider whether it might be in terms of some hidden 'substrate' that the truth of things may be known. What is introduced here is, in effect, a distinction between 'appearance' and 'essence', and thus the dialectic passes beyond Being to the Doctrine of Essence. See also **Absolute Knowing; being, nothing, becoming; Concept, Doctrine of the; Essence, Doctrine of; Idea; logic; measureless;** *Phenomenology of Spirit***; quality, quantity, measure.**

being-for-self (*das Fürsichsein*)   'Being-for-self' is the final subdivision of 'Quality', in the Doctrine of Being in Hegel's Logic. Earlier, Hegel establishes that a being is determinate in *not* being another. Thus, it appears to have its being *for another*. But Hegel goes on to contrast this sort of finite being, which is merely the negation of another, to one which possesses its determinate character in virtue of its internal self-differentiation. In other words, rather than being what it is merely in contrast to

being, nothing, becoming

others, it is what it is in virtue of contrasts (or distinctions) *within* itself. Being-for-self is 'the infinite determinacy that contains distinction within itself as sublated' (Geraets, 153; EL § 96 A). It can easily be seen that most things have their being in both ways: my body, for example, is what it is in not being other bodies, but also in being a complex, articulated system of distinct, complementary parts. In being-for-self Hegel is anticipating (as he does throughout the Logic) the Concept, or concrete universal – or, more simply, the whole: a being which is absolute because it subsumes *all* finite determinations within itself, and thus does not derive its being from its opposition to anything outside itself. See also **Absolute; Being, Doctrine of; concrete universal; determinate being; Logic; quality, quantity, measure; whole, the**.

being, nothing, becoming (*das Sein, das Nichts, das Werden*)
Being or 'pure being' (*das reine Sein*) is the name Hegel chooses for the pure indeterminacy with which the *Logic* opens. The standpoint at the beginning of the Logic is prepared by the *Phenomenology of Spirit*, which ends with Absolute Knowing – a type of knowing that does away with the distinction between subject and object. What Absolute Knowing knows, therefore, is nothing determinate and specific: it simply *is*. Since Thales, philosophers have sought to know what being is. Hegel points out, however, that as a category being is entirely empty. To say that something *is* indicates nothing specific about it whatsoever. What, then, is being? In fact, it is no thing at all. And so Hegel claims, famously, that being seems to be indistinguishable from nothing (or 'not-being' – in *The Science of Logic* Hegel allows that 'not-being' conveys what he means by nothing). Nevertheless, the mind insists on distinguishing them. It seems commonsense, after all, that being is something quite different from nothing – in fact, its opposite. If we again think through their opposition, however, we regenerate the same paradox: thinking being we realize that it is an empty nothing; but thinking nothing we insist it is not-being, being's opposite.

It is easy to see how the mind could become caught in this paradox and oscillate back and forth between being and nothing. Indeed, this oscillation between the two is precisely what Hegel terms becoming, the third, reconciling member of the triad. Becoming is the movement from being to nothing, or vice versa. Hegel states in the *Encyclopedia Logic*: 'If we speak of the concept of being, this can only consist in becoming, for as being it is the empty nothing, but as the latter it is empty being. So, in being we have nothing, and in nothing being; but this being which abides with itself in nothing is becoming' (Geraets, 144; EL § 88 A). This is still rather obscure, but we can puzzle out the relation of becoming to being-nothing in the following way: For A to become X is for something that was not X to come to be X. For A to become not-X means for A to be X, then to come to not be X.

This dialectical triad is not only the first in the *Logic*, it serves as the basic paradigm for all others in the system. This means that while the text begins with being, this category is really never left behind: the entire Doctrine of Being, one third of the Logic, is an exposition of the nature of being. However, one can also argue plausibly that the entire Logic is an ontology: an account of being-as-such. See also **Absolute Knowing; Being, Doctrine of; dialectic; Logic; *Phenomenology of Spirit*; sublation.**

being-there   See Determinate Being

Boehme, Jacob (1575–1624)   Hegel devotes considerable space in his *Lectures on the History of Philosophy* to an unlikely figure – the German mystic Jacob Boehme. Hegel mentions Boehme in only a few other places, but the subject of Boehme's influence on him has been much-discussed, and is a controversial issue among scholars. Some assert that he had a positive influence on Hegel's philosophy (though, perhaps, only early on), while others believe that Hegel was sharply critical of Boehme right from the beginning. In the *Lectures*, Hegel refers to Boehme as the *philosophicus teutonicus* (the Teutonic, or Germanic, Philosopher), and juxtaposes him to Francis Bacon as one of the two representatives of 'Modern Philosophy in its First Statement'.

Boehme was a shoemaker in Goerlitz, Lusatia, on the borders of Bohemia. In 1600 he had a mystical vision in which, for about fifteen minutes, he felt able to intuit the essences or 'signatures' of all things. Boehme wrote nothing for years, then produced *Aurora* (*Morgenröthe im Aufgang*) in 1612, his first attempt to explain the revelation he had received years earlier. *Aurora* is largely a work of theosophy; an attempt not only to know the nature of God, but to attain divine wisdom itself.

Boehme conceives God as an active, evolving being; not as a God that exists whole and complete apart from creation. In fact, Boehme believes

Boehme, Jacob

that God develops or realizes himself through creation, and that considered separately from creation God is 'not yet' God. It is out of a desire to confront himself or to achieve self-consciousness that God expresses himself as nature. In one of his later works, Boehme wrote 'No thing can be revealed to itself without opposition'. In other words, in order for God to become the truly realized God he must oppose an 'other' to himself, through which he comes to be. This process of God expressing himself in creation and achieving self-awareness reaches completion with man.

There is an obvious similarity between these ideas and Hegel's philosophic system, and it is for precisely this reason that many have asserted that Boehme positively influenced Hegel. The scholarly debate on this point more or less centres on whether Boehme is in fact the source of these ideas, or whether Hegel conceived them independently. (The problem is not settled by pointing out that much the same ideas are to be found in Schelling, since Schelling also read Boehme, but it is not clear when Schelling first encountered him.)

Hegel's treatment of Boehme in the *Lectures* is long, involved, and written in a respectful tone. However, he ends by noting that Boehme's thought is flawed in that it is expressed entirely in idiosyncratic images. Boehme explains his ideas in a highly cryptic form, and portrays the stages of creation in terms of a bizarre system involving seven 'source spirits' (*Quellgeister*). These are given such names as Sour (*Herb*), Sweet (*Süss*), Bitter (*Bitter*), etc. In the years 1804–05, while apparently under the influence of Boehme, Hegel composed a 'myth' concerning Lucifer. In this text, Hegel describes God externalizing himself in nature, then becoming 'wrathful' over it and, through this, achieving self-awareness. God's wrath becomes the spirit of Lucifer, which reflects God back to himself. Hegel described his own myth critically as 'the intuitions of barbarians' precisely because of its picture-thinking. However, the tone and terminology of this myth resurface in the 'Revealed Religion' section of the *Phenomenology of Spirit* (1807). Hegel writes there of the 'first-born Son of Light' (who is Lucifer), 'who fell because he withdrew into himself or became self-centered, but that in his place another was at once created' (Miller, 468; PG, 504). Also in 1804–05, Hegel produced another 'theosophical work' referred to by scholars as 'the divine triangle fragment.' Hegel's early biographer Karl Rosenkranz (who quotes at length from the now-lost fragment) claims that the text was influenced by Boehme.

Hegel seems to have maintained an interest in Boehme throughout his lifetime. In 1811, a former student named Peter Gabriel van Ghert (1782–1852) sent Hegel Boehme's collected works as a gift, to which Hegel responded with a warm letter praising Boehme. Hegel's revision of the 'Doctrine of Being' section of the *Science of Logic*, one of the last projects he worked on before his death, alters one passage in order to credit certain ideas to Boehme. See also **Christianity**; **God**; **mysticism**; **picture-thinking**; **Schelling, F. W. J.**; **theology**; **Spinoza, Benedict**.

— C —

chemism   See **mechanism, chemism, teleology**.

Christianity (*das Christentum*)   Hegel is notorious for having regarded Christianity as the 'absolute religion'. Furthermore, he has in mind Christianity specifically in its Protestant form.

Hegel tells us that the content of both religion and philosophy is identical – both concern themselves with God. 'God is the one and only object of philosophy' (LPR I, 84; VPR I, 3). Religion understands its subject matter in terms of images, metaphors and stories (what Hegel calls 'picture-thinking'), whereas philosophy understands God in purely conceptual, rational terms. God, according to Hegel, is the same thing that he calls the Absolute or Absolute Idea, which he defines as the self-knowing thought that is the consummation of existence itself. Religion typically understands the divine as absolutely transcending this world. However, Hegel argues that Absolute Idea truly exists only as 'embodied' by self-aware human beings (Absolute Spirit).

In the *Lectures on the Philosophy of Religion*, Hegel refers to religions as 'sprouting up fortuitously, like the flowers and creations of nature, as foreshadowings, images, representations, without [our] knowing where they come from or where they are going to' (LPR I, 196; VPR I, 106). All religions approach the truth, but Hegel believes that some come closer to it than others. In the *Lectures* Hegel presents a kind of taxonomy of religions past

Christianity   51

and present, which he altered a great deal over the years. This material is grouped by Hegel under the heading 'Determinate Religion' (i.e., determinate forms taken by the religious impulse). This section is then followed by 'Absolute Religion', which refers exclusively to Christianity. Hegel states elsewhere that 'God has revealed Himself through the Christian religion; i.e., he has granted mankind the possibility of recognizing his nature, so that he is no longer an impenetrable mystery' (Nisbet, 40; VIG, 45).

Hegel's privileging of Christianity might be dismissed as pure and simple bias on his part: Hegel was, after all, raised as a Protestant Christian and educated in a seminary. However, philosophy requires that we come to terms with the reasons thinkers give for their positions. Speculation about the biases or ulterior motives of philosophers is no substitute for this and tends to lead to the fallacy of *ad hominem* (attacking the person – rather than the person's arguments).

All religions are essentially ways of relating humanity to the whole of existence, but Hegel argues that in Christianity this idea or essence of religion becomes the religion itself. In other words, in Christianity the relation of the human to the divine becomes the central element of the religion, through the person of Jesus Christ, who is man become mysteriously one with God. Hegel sees in Christianity a kind of allegory depicting the central truths of his own philosophy. God, the eternal *logos* (Idea), creates an other: nature. He then creates humanity, whom he exalts above all things in nature. Human beings are natural creatures, but they are capable of understanding creation itself, and of attempting to raise themselves up to its source through religious worship. At the appropriate point in history, once human beings have become ready to receive the ultimate truth, God appears among men as Jesus Christ. In one person, human and divine, finite and infinite are brought together. It takes philosophy, however, to reveal the inner meaning of this revelation: that the end of creation, and the realization of the being of God, lies in Spirit. It takes philosophy (as philosophy of religion or theology) to explain that 'the word [*logos*] made flesh' is the Idea come to concretization, and that the real message of Christianity is that what is true of Christ is true of us all: we are all Absolute Spirit.

Hegel treats Christianity in his earliest writings. In his essay 'The Life of Jesus' (1795) Hegel argued that the original teachings of Jesus, properly understood, are an expression of Kantian morality. The implication here is that much else that has come to be understood as 'Christian doctrine' is extraneous to the true Christian teaching. This approach is elaborated and developed further in Hegel's essays 'The Positivity of the Christian Religion' (1795) and 'The Spirit of Christianity and its Fate' (1798–99). ('Positivity' refers to those aspects of the religion decreed by authority and tradition, as opposed to those which flow from the subjectivity of a people.) In *The Phenomenology of Spirit* (1807), Hegel's discussion of religion is divided into three major sections: Natural Religion, the Religion of Art and Revealed Religion, and he identifies the latter with Christianity. In all of the forms of religion the dichotomy between finite and infinite, human and divine, remains intact. Nevertheless, Hegel sees religion as working for its own dissolution since, at every step, it seeks to overcome the divide between God and man. Man 'yearns' after God (as in the *Phenomenology*'s 'unhappy consciousness'), prays to God, seeks God's favour, tries to represent God in art, etc. The goal of this process is man actually reaching God; God and man becoming one, in some sense. Hegel does not promise this or spell out how it can be accomplished. Instead, he believes it has already been accomplished, through Christianity and the teaching of the Incarnation of God in Jesus Christ.

In the 'Revealed Religion' section of the *Phenomenology*, Hegel presents speculative interpretations of traditional Christian doctrines. The most famous of these is his treatment of the Trinity, which he alludes to in numerous other texts. Indeed, it would be plausible to say that Hegel's understanding of the Trinity is central to why he sees Christianity as the Absolute Religion. The Trinity, for Hegel, is a kind of mythic representation of the three moments of speculative philosophy. Christianity therefore comes remarkably close to realizing the truths of philosophy, though it does not grasp the full import of what it teaches. Only speculative philosophy can do that, in the form of Philosophy of Religion. (Though it might be added that certain mystical forms of Christianity do come remarkably close to revealing the 'inner truth' of the religion in a manner that often seems 'proto-Hegelian' – a fact that Hegel himself recognized.)

We find this treatment of religion's relation to philosophy, and of Christianity as the absolute religion, elaborated in the *Encyclopedia of the Philosophical Sciences*. These ideas find their fullest expression, however, in Hegel's *Lectures on the Philosophy of Religion* (which he delivered four times from 1821 to 1831, and which were published posthumously). As noted earlier, the lectures are partly devoted to offering a taxonomy of religions, showing in effect how each is only an imperfect approximation to Christianity. However, Hegel's knowledge of many religions (especially those of the East) was very inadequate, due to the comparatively rudimentary state of scholarship in his time. To his credit, he continually revised his account as new information became available. Hegel's treatment of Christianity vis-à-vis other religions has frequently been criticized. Some critics charge that his understanding of Christianity itself is flawed. Others argue that many of the 'speculative' features that he credits to Christianity can be found in other, non-Christian sources, e.g., the philosophies and religions of India.

Hegel holds that true philosophy is not hostile to religious belief. In fact, he argues that religion is in and of itself absolute truth. He states that 'religion is precisely the true content but in the form of picture-thinking, and philosophy is not the first to offer the substantive truth. Humanity has not had to await philosophy in order to receive for the first time the consciousness or cognition of truth' (LPR I, 251; VPR I, 159). Also, in a certain sense philosophy depends upon religion, because the philosopher first encounters the content of absolute truth in religion. In fact, Hegel holds that before Christianity appeared philosophy could not have presented absolute truth in a fully adequate or complete form. Famously, Hegel remarks that 'philosophy *is* theology, and [one's] occupation with philosophy – or rather *in* philosophy – is of itself the service of God' (LPR I, 84; VPR I, 4).

Still, because it is only philosophy that can understand the *meaning* of religious myth and dogma, it can also be maintained that philosophy stands on a higher level than religion. It is able to articulate the truth in a way religion never can, because of religion's reliance on picture-thinking. Hegel believes, however, that encountering the truth through philosophy alone is not enough: human beings also need to encounter it in 'sensuous form'. Therefore, religion is intrinsically valuable and necessary, and religious belief and religious practice will never cease to exist as human activities. See also **Absolute**; **Absolute Spirit**; **God**; **mysticism**; **picture-thinking**; **religion and Philosophy of Religion**; **theology**; **Trinity**.

civil society (*die bürgerliche Gesellschaft*) In *The Philosophy of Right*, Hegel discusses 'Ethical Life': his account of how ethics is founded upon social institutions and practices, not abstract rules. Ethical life has three dialectical moments: family, civil society and the state. Love unites the members of the family, who learn, in a very basic way, to subordinate their individual desires to the good of the whole. Eventually, children leave the protective cocoon of the family and enter what Hegel calls civil society, its antithesis. This is, in the main, the dog-eat-dog business world of the middle class, in which relations are divisive, and anything but loving. People in civil society relate to each other primarily as traders, and the division of labour dictates where individuals belong.

Hegel divides civil society into what he calls the 'estates' (*die Stände*). The 'Substantial Estate' consists of farmers. The 'Estate of Trade and Industry' involves those engaged in manufacturing and mercantilism. Finally, the 'Universal Estate' refers to individuals who work for the interests of civil society itself, such as civil servants. There are a number of factors that determine which estate one may find oneself in, including birth. For example, if one's father is a farmer and owner of his own land, it is very likely one will also pursue that occupation.

However, civil society is also a sphere in which there is room for the exercize of the arbitrary will: within certain limits, one may decide to enter whichever estate one chooses. For Hegel, this is a very important choice. Realizing myself as a human being in the social world and coming to exercize freedom means taking on determinations of various kinds, and acquiring a determinate sphere in which to exercize my freedom. In civil society we must choose to determine ourselves. The result is that although I limit myself and become *just* a farmer, or *just* a merchant, in identifying myself thusly all the various options open to these ways of life become mine. By contrast, if I simply choose to drift along and become nothing in particular, I have none of the options (and none of the perquisites) open to those who have freely determined themselves according to one of the forms society makes available to us. Hegel writes that 'the individual in his particularity may see himself as the universal and believe that he would be lowering himself if he became a member of an estate. This is the false notion that, if something attains an existence which is necessary to it, it is thereby limiting and surrendering itself' (Nisbet, 239; PR § 207 A). For Hegel, to be means to be something *determinate*.

Membership in the estates is one aspect of ethical development, made possible largely by an institution Hegel calls the corporation (*die Korporation*).

civil society

Corporations are guilds, unions and professional associations that unite those in a certain occupation and serve to advance their interests and well-being. (It is important to note that this has nothing to do with a 'corporation' in our sense of the term, which refers to a large, profit-making company regarded as a collective, legal person.) Each corporation typically has its own 'code of ethics' – such as the Hippocratic Oath of physicians, or the manufacturer's commitment to certain standards of craftsmanship. Membership of the corporations encourages co-operation and fellow-feeling; it allows one to feel a certain kinship with others in civil society. Through his participation in civil society, the individual comes to see that society itself and its economic arrangement are conditions for the possibility of his freedom. Civil society therefore pushes him in the direction of behaving in a co-operative, public-spirited manner. Once again, ethical development involves seeing oneself as part of a larger whole. Nevertheless, within the sphere of civil society this public spiritedness is still largely motivated by self-interest. (For example, the maxim that 'honesty is the best policy' nicely reflects the ethics of civil society: it does not assert that honesty is morally obligatory, it merely states that honesty is the prudent or profitable 'policy' to adopt.)

Under 'Administration of Justice', Hegel covers the aspect of Civil Society that has to do with the protection of property. In this section Hegel discusses a number of basic legal precepts that are now taken to be universal standards of justice. For example, the idea that everyone is equal before the law. Hegel also stresses that the law must be codified: it must be written down and publicly accessible. Further, legal proceedings must be made public. Hegel goes on to discuss the function of police, and of the role of the corporations in the administration of justice. He believes that to a certain extent professional associations must police themselves (for example, as the Royal College of Physicians and American Medical Association do today). Hegel assigns to the police many functions that are surprising: 'The police should provide for street-lighting, bridge-building, the pricing of daily necessities, and public health' (Nisbet, 262; PR § 236 A). Clearly, Hegel conceives 'the police' in a different sense than we are accustomed to, as a broad-based public authority. Hegel opposes what we would call the 'welfare state', arguing that when people become dependent on government assistance they are robbed of their dignity and lose their sense of shame.

Individuals come to develop a sense of public spiritedness in civil society, through its various guilds, unions and professional organizations. As we have seen, however, in civil society ethical sentiments are largely motivated by self-interest. Therefore, Hegel argues that there must be something in society that binds people together irrespective of individual self-interest. This role is played by the state, the third moment of ethical life. See also **ethical life; family; freedom;** *Philosophy of Right*; **state.**

classical art (*die klassische Kunst*) Hegel's Philosophy of Art discusses the different forms of art and their historical development. Hegel distinguishes between different art forms in terms of how well the conceptual 'content' of the artwork and its material medium are harmonized. In great art, a complete or perfect harmony is present. For Hegel, there are three major forms of art: the symbolic, the classical and the romantic.

In symbolic art, the meaning of the artwork is so abstract that it cannot find adequate expression in material form. Spirit is struggling to express itself in the symbolic artwork, but it does so in a way that is indefinite and mysterious. The move from symbolic art to classical is, essentially, the move beyond the expression of strange, indefinite ideas, to the expression of concrete, human individuality. In classical art, a perfect harmony is achieved between content and form. Hegel's chief example here is the sculpture of the ancient Greeks, in which the human form at its most beautiful takes centre stage, and is used even to represent the form of the gods. These artworks exemplify what Hegel takes to be the truly self-conscious Spirit of the Greeks. In fact, Hegel holds that classical art is art in its most perfect form. This often confuses students of Hegel, who expect him to identify the third and final 'stage' of art as the highest or most adequate. Nevertheless, classical art cannot ultimately satisfy Spirit's desire to confront itself because art *as such* cannot fully satisfy Spirit – something which is dramatically illustrated by the third case Hegel deals with, the ultimately 'tragic' character of romantic art. See also **Absolute Spirit; art and Philosophy of Art; religion of art; romantic art; symbolic art.**

coherence It has often been claimed in recent years that Hegel held a 'coherence theory of truth'. In fact, Hegel never describes his concept of truth in this manner, and the coherence theory is associated with thinkers

coherence

and movements far removed from Hegel and Hegelianism. (For example, the logical positivists Carl Hempel and Otto Neurath both advocated a version of the coherence theory.)

The coherence theory of truth stands in sharp contrast to the more commonsensical 'correspondence theory', which holds that a statement is true if and only if it 'corresponds' to facts of reality. For example, the statement 'Snow is white' is true, according to the correspondence theory if, and only if, snow *really is* white. To confirm the truth of a claim, in other words, we check to see if it matches up to the facts. This sounds simple enough and, within certain contexts, it is a perfectly reasonable approach to truth. However, it is open to a number of objections. Correspondence seems to presuppose our ability to separate ourselves from the conceptual scheme with which we operate and to assess objective 'facts' which transcend that scheme. But what constitutes a fact? And is it even possible (or conceivable) for us to peer out from behind our concepts and behold 'facts' directly? One might respond to the correspondence theory by saying that when we judge a statement or theory to be true, in reality it is usually because it fits with what we already know, or think we know. Such a suggestion gives us the 'coherence theory' in germinal form.

Coherence theories generally understand truth to involve the 'fit' of a statement or theory within an entire body of knowledge. This suggests the image of our knowledge as not just a collection of claims and concepts, but as a system in which concepts are mutually supporting and confirming. In turn, this suggests that truth may ultimately be a property not of isolated concepts or assertions, but of whole systems. It is with this claim that we approach something that does indeed look like what Hegel himself said about truth, given that in the Preface to *The Phenomenology of Spirit* he states that 'the true is the whole' (Miller, 11; PG, 15). In brief, the 'truth' of something for Hegel is in fact its place within the total system of reality (though unlike today's philosophers Hegel is interested less in the truth of statements or reports than in the truth – or meaning – of concepts and objects).

The coherence theory is closely associated with the neo-Hegelian movement known as British Idealism, which was influential from the mid-nineteenth century into the early twentieth century. British Idealists such as F. H. Bradley (1846–1924) offered Hegel-inspired coherence theories of truth. This movement influenced many, including the American philosopher Brand Blanshard (1892–1987), who offered a coherence theory of truth in his early work *The Nature of Thought* (1939). See also **Absolute Idea; dialectic; sublation; truth; whole, the**.

commonsense (*der gesunder Menschenverstand*, literally 'sound human understanding') Hegel sometimes uses the term 'commonsense', generally to refer to an unsophisticated form of what he calls 'the understanding'. The understanding is characterized by a type of shallow thinking that fails to think beyond the ordinary conceptions of things, especially when these are expressed as conceptual oppositions. For example, the understanding insists that identity excludes difference, that being excludes nothing, and that the infinite excludes the finite. Commonsense not only thinks in terms of various 'either-ors', it also has a tendency to yank certain ideas out of the larger context from which they derive their meaning and to hold them up as unchallengeable absolutes. Speculative philosophy's 'way of despair' involves transcending the level of commonsense. See also **dialectic; reflection; speculation; understanding; 'way of despair'**.

Concept, Doctrine of the (*die Lehre vom Begriff*) In *The Science of Logic*, Hegel designates the Doctrines of Being and Essence 'Objective Logic', and the Doctrine of the Concept 'Subjective Logic'. Nevertheless, though the categories of being and essence deal with 'the objective' they are also categories of thought; they are concepts. Indeed, in the Logic the distinction between thought and being (or reality) is overcome, and its concepts are just as much categories of thought as they are of the real. In the Doctrine of the Concept – in Subjective Logic – Hegel treats not this concept or that, but the nature of the Concept *as such*. (Older translations often render *der Begriff* as 'the Notion'.)

In the dialectic of being, each category is supplanted by one which is wholly other. In essence, categories 'appear' in their opposites (for instance, 'matter' is part of the idea of 'form' itself). Hegel demonstrates how the dialectic of Objective Logic is incomplete on its own and must be supplemented – or, better yet, sublated – by Subjective Logic, in which concepts are related to themselves. Another way to put this is to say that in the Doctrine of the Concept, thought reflects for the first time consciously and explicitly on thought itself, and all the preceding categories are understood to have their meaning and significance precisely in being

Concept, Doctrine of the

comprehended by a self-aware thought. The Concept is thought 'In its being-returned-into-itself [*Zurückgekehrtsein in sich selbst*] and its developed being-with-itself [*Beisichsein*] – the Concept in-and for-itself' (Geraets, 133; EL § 83). The dialectic of Hegel's Logic demonstrates how the pure thought-categories of being and essence pass over into the categories of the Concept; how the Concept reveals, again, the higher-level (or deeper-level) unity of being and essence. Accordingly, the Doctrine of the Concept is devoted to *concepts of concepts*, and culminates in what Hegel calls the Absolute Idea, a purely self-related category: the idea of idea, or concept of concept itself.

Hegel will go on to argue, however, that what transpires in the realm of idea also plays itself out in the world. Nature, Hegel claims, can only be understood as a scale of forms approximating to self-related thought: the concrete embodiment of the Concept. The Concept, in short, is the *telos*, the goal or end of nature itself. In fact, however, this goal is consummated only in human beings, who alone are capable of true self-consciousness. Indeed, they are capable of comprehending the Logic, and since the Logic lays bare the formal structure of reality, we can say that through humanity, reality comes to consciousness of itself and reaches a kind of closure. The truth of reality itself, therefore, is the Concept. (This is the sense in which Hegel is an 'idealist'.)

Hegel opens the Doctrine of the Concept with a radical re-thinking of the traditional categories of logic. He begins with a consideration of the most basic forms in which we speak about concepts: universals, particulars and individuals. Hegel next turns to the different forms of judgement and the syllogism. He treats the judgement forms as members of a self-specifying whole, each of them approaching a kind of ultimate judgement. This reflects the basic fact that for Hegel 'the true is the whole'. His treatment of the syllogism is similar, again seeing it as an attempt to express the whole – and his own philosophy, therefore, as a kind of syllogism. All of these matters are covered in the first subdivision of the Concept, 'Subjectivity', which represents one form in which thought thinks itself. In every case, Hegel's treatment of these traditional logical categories displays his usual speculative brilliance, but the complexities of his discussion cannot be canvassed in a brief account such as this.

In the succeeding subdivision, 'Objectivity', Hegel deals with concepts which represent our most basic ways of understanding objects, and objects in their inter-relations. Specifically, Hegel discusses three forms in which we understand the objective world: mechanism, chemism and teleology. Teleology describes, in the most abstract terms possible, a self-differentiating, self-sustaining whole which is, in effect, the objectified Concept or concrete universal. Thus, in the idea of teleology, thought confronts itself in yet another way, and reveals the true end of objectivity: thought discovering itself objectified within the world. These three concepts of objectivity are homologous with Being, Essence and Concept, and they prefigure the division Mechanics, Physics, Organics in the Philosophy of Nature.

In the third division of the Concept, 'Idea', we find the distinction between subjectivity and objectivity overcome. Idea is object aware of itself, or, subjectivity that has itself as object. The entirety of the Logic has served as the argument for Idea. At every stage, Hegel has essentially been articulating the idea of wholeness or system. Each dialectical transition is possible because a category asserts itself as a 'provisional definition' of the whole (or Absolute) but each is seen to be a merely partial or one-sided presentation of it. It is because we have an implicit awareness of the whole at each stage that we are able to pass beyond these limited standpoints. Ultimately, the whole is not truly whole, or complete, unless it *conceives of itself*. This is precisely what happens in Idea: the system arrives at a point where it turns back upon itself. To repeat, Absolute Idea is literally idea of idea, or 'thought thinking itself', to borrow Aristotle's description of God (which is, in fact, quoted by Hegel in this context). With Absolute Idea, therefore, the system reaches closure and becomes self-grounding. Nothing fundamental has been omitted from it; in a sense it even contains an account of itself.

At the end of the Logic, Hegel has traversed the entire realm of fundamental ideas. Again, however, they are merely ideas, and Hegel describes the Logic as a 'realm of shadows'. For Idea to become actual, it must be 'embodied'. And, in fact, we do find it embodied all around us. The ideas of the Logic are the forms we think in terms of, but they are also 'objective ideas' that we find expressed in nature. Hegel's system thus passes from Logic to Philosophy of Nature, his attempt to understand nature as a coherent system which 'expresses' the fundamental ideas of the Logic. See also **Absolute Idea**; **Being, Doctrine of**; **Essence, Doctrine of**; **Idea**; **idealism**; **judgement**; **Logic**; **mechanism, chemism, teleology**; **sublation**; **syllogism**.

concrete universal, the

concrete universal, the (*das konkrete Allgemeine*) Universals are normally understood to be abstractions, related externally to the objects which exemplify them. Consider, for example, the relation of the universal 'man' (or 'manness') to men. Virtually all philosophers would grant that these are two very different sorts of thing – a universal and its exemplars – with Plato going so far as to say that the universal is another sort of being entirely, existing in a different plane of reality.

Hegel, however, sees serious problems with the way in which other philosophers have conceived of the relation of universals and particulars. For one thing, in addition to seeing the universal as separate from its particulars, philosophers have also spoken of universals as 'in' things, as their 'essence' (e.g., the 'manness' in men). But how can we square these two ways of considering universals and particulars? One of them sees universals as transcending particulars, the other sees them as immanent within particulars. In truth, the tension between these two contradictory ways of conceiving things (insoluble for the understanding) sets the stage for their dialectical overcoming. Hegel's resolution of the problem lies in his doctrine of the concrete universal, which is quite simply the universal that 'contains' or comprises its particular instances. For Hegel, universals and particulars are not absolutely separate beings, nor are universals 'within' particulars. Rather, particulars are, in a sense, 'within' universals: the universal has no reality apart from the concrete instances that are its self-differentiation or specification.

To employ for a moment the distinction between whole and parts (discussed by Hegel in the Logic's Doctrine of Essence), we may understand the particulars as 'parts' of the universal, which is the whole. The parts are within the whole constituting, in fact, its reality – but the whole is also immanent in all the parts, constituting their 'essence'. To take a very mundane example: apart from individual dogs, 'dogness' (the universal) has no reality, no concrete expression. Each dog is understood to be an individual manifestation of what dogness is – dogness, again, come to concrete expression in a unique way. It is as if dogness is unfolding all the aspects of itself in our world through the continual coming-into-being of each and every unique Lassie, Rover and Spot. However, though each of these animals is a unique individual, they are united in having the universal immanent within them. The whole is a whole only in and through the parts, but the parts are only parts in so far as they belong within the whole.

Each of the parts, furthermore, may be considered a 'provisional version' of the whole, revealing some but not all of its aspects or possibilities. Thus, Lassie may be an exemplary dog in many ways, but she does not express all that is dogness. She is particularly adept, say, at herding but not at hunting, an aspect of dogness better exemplified by Rover. In short, species (living and non-living) are continually revealing the whole through the coming-into-being of individuals – each of which reveals the whole, however, in a finite and imperfect manner. (Hegel's treatment of these issues displays his deep debt to Aristotle, and to Aristotle's rethinking of the Platonic understanding of the 'participation' of particular things in universals.)

The paradigm of the universal–particular relationship, and of the concrete universal, is set forth by Hegel in his Logic. Each of the categories of the Logic is a 'provisional definition' of the final category, Absolute Idea. Each is a kind of dim reflection of Absolute Idea, which is understood to be the whole itself, 'containing' all the preceding categories as, in effect, its 'particular instances'. The Absolute Idea is thus *the* concrete universal as such; the paradigm for all other universals. See also **Absolute Idea**; **Aristotle**; **Logic**; **relation**; **understanding**; **universal, particular and individual**; **whole, the**; **whole and parts**.

consciousness (*das Bewußtsein*)   'Consciousness' is the first major subdivision of *The Phenomenology of Spirit*. Essentially, what Hegel covers here is the ordinary, pre-reflective awareness of the world, taken as if it were wholly independent and externally-related to the other forms of Spirit. This independence and externality breaks down as we proceed through the argument of the text. Hegel sees consciousness not as something passive but, at every one of its stages, an *effort* on the part of the subject to fully grasp and to possess the object.

The first form of consciousness is what Hegel terms 'Sense Certainty', in which the subject naively believes it can adequately grasp an object through its bare sensory givenness alone (as a mere 'this'). Consciousness finds, however, that any attempt to understand or to say anything about the object involves transcending the level of the sensory given. In 'Perception', the second form of consciousness, the object is no longer merely a 'this' but is seen rather as a thing possessing properties (or universals). But we soon realize that the universals possessed by the object are also possessed by others. This calls into question the very individuality of

consciousness

the object. To resolve this problem, consciousness considers the 'subjectivist' suggestion that perhaps the universal properties of the object are ideas in our minds, and that the object is something quite apart from these ideas. This suggestion solves nothing, however. All we have done is to shift from the vague idea that the apparent conflict between the immediate individuality of the thing and the 'universality' of its properties is reconciled 'in the thing', to the equally vague idea that it is reconciled 'in us'.

In the next twist of the dialectic, we consider making a distinction between the essential properties of the thing, and those that are accidental, or only possessed through its relation to others. Perhaps, we reason, the essential properties will allow us finally to adequately grasp the thing itself. However, we soon realize that the thing must possess its 'inessential' properties precisely as a result of its essential ones (i.e., it can only possess inessential properties compatible with its essential ones). It follows that the inessential properties of the thing are very much a part of its nature, and thus there is no real basis here for distinguishing between the 'essence' of the thing and its accidental attributes.

It is but a short step from here to the next standpoint of consciousness reviewed by Hegel: why not adopt a kind of 'appearance' vs. 'reality' distinction? The multiplicity of changing properties, we might say, belongs to appearance, whereas beneath the appearances might be some deeper level of truth. If we could penetrate to this, then we could truly grasp the object. This approach, in fact, ushers in the first appearance of something that comes close to a scientific outlook (the standpoint Hegel here dubs 'Force and the Understanding'). Suppose we try to grasp the thing in its true form by explaining its appearances as the result of certain forces which do not themselves appear. Hegel shows, however, that even this move turns out to be fundamentally false. Force seems to be something separate and distinct from its manifestations. In fact, however, they are deeply connected. After all, what really is an unobservable force? Mustn't we understand it simply as something that manifests itself in certain observable ways? In sum, the appearance/reality and essence/accident distinctions come to naught.

Nevertheless, this 'scientific' standpoint of consciousness is one that, within a certain context, proves fruitful to human understanding. Hegel goes on to show how from the idea of force and its manifestations we develop the concept of 'laws of nature', according to which forces act to produce phenomena of various kinds. However, Hegel shows how such 'laws' ultimately explain nothing. Instead, they merely state general patterns or regularities. In fact, scientific 'laws' really just re-describe the very phenomena that we wanted to explain in the first place. From here, Hegel launches into one of the most notorious sections of *The Phenomenology of Spirit*, his strange description of the 'inverted world': a peculiar thought experiment apparently designed to show that it wouldn't matter what sort of explanatory forces or entities we posit, so long as we understand them as producing the appearances available to us.

The 'scientific approach' breaks down at this point, and Spirit thereby discovers something new about itself. It is clear that in each of the stages of consciousness described thus far, Spirit has not been a passive subject opening itself to reality: it has been actively involved, to the point where its own activity has shaped what it takes to be real. This is most obvious in the case of 'force and the understanding' – our attempts to explain the object involve our minds deliberately positing a reality beyond appearances, but, as Hegel's discussion of the 'Inverted World' shows, there is something fundamentally arbitrary and subjective about this procedure. The dialectic thus moves beyond 'Consciousness' to 'Self-Consciousness'. See also **force and the understanding**; **'inverted world'**; **perception**; ***Phenomenology of Spirit***; **self-consciousness**; **sense-certainty**.

consummate religion   See **Christianity**.

contradiction (*der Widerspruch*)   It is often claimed that Hegel denied the 'law of non-contradiction'. This law, one of the fundamental 'laws of logic', states that something, X, cannot possess characteristic Y and *not* possess that characteristic at the same time and in the same respect. Thus, while the apple could be both green and (at some other point on its surface) not green, or green at one time and red at another, it could not be both green and not green at the very same time or in the very same respect. More broadly, the law asserts that contradictory ideas or situations are nonsense. Thus, it cannot be both raining and not raining at the very same time in the very same place. Further, such things as 'square circles' are called contradictory: since by definition a square has four angles and a circle none, the 'square circle' is impossible. It is generally understood that any idea or assertion that is logically contradictory is also empirically impossible. (However, it is not the case that everything that is empirically

contradiction

impossible is also logically contradictory: e.g., a pig that has the power of flight is not physically possible, but there is no logical contradiction in the idea.) The importance of the law of non-contradiction is that it teaches us to recognize that because thought aims at truth, we must think again if we arrive at contradiction.

The sense in which Hegel is said to have 'denied' the law of non-contradiction essentially rests on an equivocation. The account given above understands contradiction in the strictest sense of the term, as the simultaneous assertion of two things that cannot be true simultaneously. However, in a looser sense we often dub contraries or opposites as 'contradictory'. Thus, it is often held that night 'contradicts' day, or the female is the 'contradiction' of the male, etc. It is this sense of 'contradiction' that provides us with a key to understanding what Hegel means when he speaks of contradiction as an inherent part of dialectic. Hegel, like Heraclitus, believes that contradiction – primarily in the sense of opposition or contrariety – is an inherent part of both thought and reality. One of the characteristics of what Hegel calls the understanding, a form of thought he regards as deficient, is that it has a tendency to hold opposites as fixed, and finds itself unable to think beyond them. Such thinking displays itself in ordinary 'commonsense' ('You're not conservative? Then you must be liberal'). But it also shows up in philosophy. For example, Kant's Antinomies of Pure Reason purport to demonstrate that certain questions have two equally good but completely opposed answers. Thought stops there, for Kant, concluding therefore that no 'real' (i.e., definitive) answer is possible to those questions.

By contrast, Hegel's dialectic uses contradiction – or, better put, *negation* – as a vehicle to find truth. For example, the Logic begins with the category of 'being'. When we think through this category and try to understand what it means 'to be' we find that this idea is quite empty and indefinite. It is difficult, therefore, to distinguish it from its opposite, nothing (which can be understood to be a literal contradiction, if nothing = 'non-being'). When the mind begins to consider what the substantive difference is between being and nothing, it finds itself at a loss. Thought shuttles back and forth between the two, one leading us to the other and back again, unable to actually define, in anything other than circular language, what the difference is. Here the understanding, or ordinary thought, stops. Hegel's dialectic goes further, however, recognizing in this shuttling back and forth between 'is' and 'is not' precisely what it means to 'become'. Thus, becoming stands as the third to being and nothing, and Hegel's dialectic moves on from there – making use of conflict, opposition and negation at every stage.

For Hegel, all finite concepts are inherently 'contradictory' because they are always partial and one-sided and usually derive their meaning from opposed ideas. As a result, when speculative philosophy thinks through one such finite concept, it is usually found to 'give way' and to transform into its opposite. This is very clearly illustrated in the example from the Logic given above, involving being and nothing. Another example of Hegelian 'contradiction' is to be found in *The Philosophy of Right*, where we find the idea of the family 'negated' by the idea of civil society (the family is characterized by love; civil society – essentially, the 'business world' – by divisive, competitive relations). Obviously, in the strict logical sense 'family' and 'civil society' do not 'contradict' each other – but they do oppose and negate.

Hegel also often speaks not just of thought as involving contradiction, but reality as well. Perhaps the most famous example of this occurs in *The Phenomenology of Spirit*, where Hegel tells us that 'The bud disappears in the bursting-forth of the blossom, and one might say that the former is refuted by the latter; similarly, when the fruit appears, the blossom is shown up in its turn as a false manifestation of the plant, and the fruit now emerges as the truth of it instead' (Miller, 2; PG, 4). (Again, if one were to gloss this passage it would be more straightforward to say that what is at work here is negation, rather than contradiction.) For Hegel, negation and opposition are an inherent part of all things, and all change and development – indeed, the realization of the Absolute itself – come about through their agency. In the *Encyclopedia Logic* he states that 'There is in fact nothing, either in heaven or on earth . . . that exhibits the abstract 'either-or' as it is maintained by the understanding' (Geraets, 187; EL § 119 A2).

The classical law of non-contradiction is often understood to rest upon the more fundamental 'law of identity': frequently stated as 'A is A'; a thing is what it is, it possesses a firm and fixed identity, and is not what it is not (A is not not A). In a certain sense, Hegel challenges this law as well through his conception of 'identity in difference'. For Hegel, something is what it is precisely by *not* being other things. Take anything – the aforementioned apple, for example. We could make a list of its positive characteristics (green, roundish, speckled with brown, bitter-sweet, etc.). But the apple's being any of these things involves simultaneously its not being a whole host

'cunning of reason'

of others. Thus, we can see that in a certain way the identity that things possess is always possessed in a kind of perpetual tension and opposition with others. Indeed, in the sense of the terms established above, we could speak of identity existing through contradiction and negation. See also **being, nothing, becoming**; **commonsense**; **dialectic**; **identity and difference**; **Kant, Immanuel**; **negation**; **understanding**.

corporations, the   See **civil society**.

correctness   See **truth**.

crime   See **wrong**.

'cunning of reason' (*die List der Vernunft*)   Hegel claims that we are compelled to ask whether 'beneath the superficial din and clamor of history, there is not perhaps a silent and mysterious inner process at work' (Nisbet, 33; VIG, 36). This 'silent and mysterious inner process' is the realization in time of the reason inherent in the world (Hegel also refers to this as 'the universal' and as 'the Idea'). For Hegel, history has a knowable pattern and moves toward an end result: the achievement by human beings of self-awareness, which is simultaneously the achievement of freedom. This process has always been at work in history, though human beings are usually unaware of it. The apparent difficulty with this view, however, is not only that so much that has happened in history seems irrational or accidental, but that the individual historical actors generally have had in view their own personal, selfish ends, not those of 'the Idea'. Hegel's answer to this problem is 'the cunning of reason' – one of his most famous theories, and a key idea in his Philosophy of History.

Hegel writes in the *Lectures on the Philosophy of World History* that 'the particular interests of passion cannot . . . be separated from the realization of the universal; for the universal arises out of the particular and determinate and its negation' (Nisbet, 89: VIG, 98). In other words, finite individuals act for their own finite ends, but in doing so they unwittingly bring about the realization of the universal. If there is an inherent order in existence, and in all things in existence, that order will tend to triumph regardless of the actions or wishes of finite beings. Indeed, Hegel sees all finite being as the expression or concretization of the universal. Thus, although we may think that we are acting purely for our own ends, we are nonetheless unwitting vehicles of the realization of the Idea in time.

To draw an analogy, suppose that we are observing the bees in a beehive, each of them playing their allotted role – workers, drones and queen. Suppose further we suddenly became able to read the minds of the bees and discovered, to our shock, that the bees believe they are acting for their own individual self-interest. We would conclude that though the bees may be motivated by self-interest, their inherent nature, and the nature of their society, causes them to pursue their self-interest in certain ways that bring about higher, collective ends. Finite individuals have all sorts of thoughts and wishes and plans – but in the end their actions serve to bring about ends of which they may be totally unaware, and in the end they perish, while the universal persists. Hegel writes: 'It is what we may call the cunning of reason that it sets the passions to work in its service, so that the agents by which it gives itself existence must pay the penalty and suffer the loss' (Nisbet, 89: VIG 98).

Hegel believes that retrospectively we can see that in some way all that human beings have done – including all war, cruelty and destruction – has served to lead us to the goal of reason actualized in the world. The cunning of reason is not unlike the Christian concept of divine providence (as well as Adam Smith's 'invisible hand'). However, it is important to note that neither reason nor Spirit is conceived by Hegel as an objectively-existing, sentient divinity (a frequent misunderstanding). See also **concrete universal**; **history and Philosophy of History**; **Idea**; **reason**; **'slaughter-bench of history'**; **world-historical individuals**; **World Spirit**.

death (*der Tod*)   Hegel discusses death in his Philosophy of Nature. In death and disease we find that the individual is, in a sense, 'inadequate' to express its universal nature. For example, the death of a man shows that his individuality cannot, in the end, fully or completely express the universal

desire

Humanity, or the human form. The individual is a 'specification' of the universal, but all such specifications are finite and limited. Each is thus 'overcome', in a manner analogous to how specific definitions of the Absolute are overcome dialectically in the Logic. In nature, the Idea expresses itself only as a series of imperfect and mortal organisms. In conscious thought, the Idea implicit in nature (Idea in-itself) has become explicit, or for-itself. Arguing very much at odds with commonsense (as does all true philosophy), Hegel asserts that this 'expression' of Idea is more adequate than the expression of Idea in finite, living things. See also **Absolute**; **dialectic**; **Idea**; **idealism**; **Logic**; **nature and Philosophy of Nature**; **organics**.

desire (*die Begierde*) Hegel introduces the term 'desire' in the 'Self-Consciousness' section of *The Phenomenology of Spirit*. In the preceding section, 'Consciousness', he shows how all of our attempts to know objects involve the covert activity of the subject and its concepts, assumptions and theoretical constructs. In 'Self-Consciousness' this 'self-centeredness' of Spirit is now revisited in a new form. Desire, according to Hegel, is our active will to *compel* objects to conform to our conceptions or wishes. Consciousness revealed itself to be subject-centred in a covert fashion. In 'Self-Consciousness' Hegel passes to an account of how our *actions* reveal themselves to be subject-centred as well: in one way or another, we are always trying to bend things to make them conform to the wishes of the subject.

Hegel writes that 'self-consciousness is desire in general' (Miller, 105; PG, 121). Spirit as self-consciousness has a dual object: the thing out there (given in perception), and itself, which is what it is in opposition to the thing. Self-consciousness, Hegel writes, 'presents itself as the movement in which this opposition is removed, and the identity of [the self] with itself is established' (Miller, 105; PG, 121). In short, Hegel shows that when the subject transforms objects according to its will it is really being moved by the desire to confront itself. The desire of the subject to annul the other and absolutize itself is just the same thing as the desire to be confronted by the self and *no other*. The nature of consciousness forces this state of affairs: consciousness is always a two-termed relationship requiring a subject and an object. Therefore, when the subject wishes to know itself, it must split itself into a subjective side, which knows, and an objective side, which is known. To know itself, consciousness must find a mirror. This means, however, that if the goal of consciousness is self-knowledge, it cannot achieve this by annihilating all objectivity, but only by making objectivity reflective, by transforming objects into a mirror of consciousness.

Just insofar as we desire to put our stamp on all that is, to create a world for ourselves, we desire total self-reflection. The transformed object becomes an extension of myself, and thus no longer truly 'other'. But although it becomes a 'part' of me it is not 'like' me; it is not a being like my self. The subject thus will not be satisfied until it has seen its own nature in another being, and that other being has *recognized* it. In short, this drive for self-consciousness can only be satisfied by a being like the subject. But the subject does not want simply to contemplate this other subject; it must be affirmed by it as well. The subject can only be assured that it confronts another being like itself if the other being in turn recognizes it as a being like itself. Thus, in one fell swoop the subject will satisfy the desire for self-reflection and individuation: the recognition of the other subject will affirm it in its identity; give it self-understanding as a being of a determinate sort. However, the first forms taken by self-consciousness, beginning with the famous 'master–servant dialectic', fail to achieve what Spirit desires.

Although Hegel discusses desire within the 'Self-Consciousness' section of the *Phenomenology*, it can be argued that he believed that something like desire is, in one way or another, at the root of all forms of Spirit. In the Philosophy of Spirit, Hegel writes: 'Every activity of Spirit is nothing but a distinct mode of reducing what is external to the inwardness which Spirit itself is, and it is only by this reduction, by this idealization or assimilation, of what is external that it becomes and is Spirit' (Wallace, 11; PS § 381 A). 'All the activities of Spirit' – all modes of human being – Hegel says, are forms in which we strive to overcome otherness. In the *Encyclopedia Logic*, Hegel states that 'In cognition what has to be done is all a matter of stripping away the alien character of the objective world that confronts us' (Geraets, 273; EL § 194 A-1).

Further, freedom for Hegel is only possible through overcoming otherness. 'Freedom,' Hegel states, 'is only present where there is no other for me that is not myself' (Geraets, 58; EL § 24 A-2). Elsewhere, he writes that 'freedom for which something is genuinely external and alien is no freedom; [freedom's] essence and its formal definition is just that nothing is absolutely external.'[8] Spirit's triumph over the other is only fully actualized

determinate being

in science (rational inquiry in general). Hegel states that 'the aim of all genuine science is just this, that Spirit shall recognize itself in everything in heaven and on earth' (Wallace, 1; PS § 377 A). At the very end of the Philosophy of Nature, Hegel remarks that Spirit 'wills to achieve its own liberation by fashioning nature out of itself; this action of Spirit is called philosophy . . . The aim of these lectures has been to give a picture of nature in order to subdue this Proteus: to find in this externality only a mirror of ourselves, to see in nature a free reflection of Spirit . . .' (Miller, 445; PN § 376 A). In short, Hegel shows that the highest achievements of human Spirit are at root transformations of desire – which seems at first glance to be wholly negative, destructive and self-centred.

Hegel believes that this will to overcome otherness is seen in all of non-human or pre-human nature as well. Faced with the opposition of an external world, the animal simply destroys or gobbles up the external. The difference between man and animal is that man can 'master' nature and 'absorb' the external without literally annihilating it. The dog can only eat its food, or chew up its master's slipper. It cannot make the world its own through thought. See also **consciousness**; **freedom**; **'master–servant dialectic'**; **organics**; *Phenomenology of Spirit*; **recognition**; **science**; **self-consciousness**.

determinate being (*das Dasein*)   In Hegel's Logic, in the subdivision of the Doctrine of Being designated 'Quality', 'Determinate Being' is the category which follows the famous triad being-nothing-becoming. (Translators differ on how to render *das Dasein* into English; 'being-there' and 'existence' are other possibilities.) Becoming reconciles being and nothing, but what is it that becomes? For Hegel, it is something whose being involves negation (or not-being). A 'determinate being' is one which is what it is by not being some other. In short, determinate being sublates the preceding three categories: its being is not static, but consists in *becoming* something which *is* in virtue of *not-being* something else. Further, the being in question here is *qualitied* being. Hegel is telling us, at this stage of the dialectic, that beings are only determinate through possessing qualities which mark them off from other sorts of things, with different qualities. See also **Being, Doctrine of**; **being, nothing, becoming**; **Logic**; **quality, quantity, measure**.

dialectic (*die Dialektik*) One of the most important concepts in Hegel is the dialectic, and it is crucial for understanding his philosophy. The idea of dialectic has ancient roots, and Aristotle credits Zeno the Eleatic with having invented it. Zeno's arguments in support of the monism of Parmenides involved displaying the contradictions generated by the belief that plurality exists. (For Hegel, as we shall see, negation or contradiction is the very essence of dialectic.) Plato discusses dialectic in a number of works. In *The Republic* it is portrayed as a progressive ascent to knowledge of the whole, via the overcoming of various *hypotheses* which are used as stepping stones on the path to truth. In *The Parmenides*, Parmenides practices dialectic with a young interlocutor named Aristotle, generating a series of paradoxes concerning 'the one'. Hegel regarded this dialogue as an extremely important demonstration of the dialectic. As Plato shows time and again, philosophical thought involves the recognition of the many contradictions inherent in commonsense (what Hegel would call 'the understanding').

The immediate source of inspiration for Hegel, however, is Kant's treatment of reason and the transcendental dialectic (as well as the ways in which these ideas were critiqued and developed by Fichte and Schelling). For Kant, reason is the faculty that strives to go beyond the understanding by attempting to effect higher-level syntheses of knowledge. For example, when psychology tries to understand not just this mental phenomenon or that, but to arrive at a total understanding of the 'complete subject' it is reason that is at work, pushing the mind to think beyond the given. Kant insists that we can never attain such total knowledge, but reason seeks it nevertheless, as a 'regulative ideal'. Reason functions negatively or falsely when it hypostatizes these ideals as transcendent objects (e.g. 'the soul') and tries to arrive at knowledge of them through 'pure reason' unaided by empirical evidence. Kant tries to demonstrate the fallacy inherent in this through the transcendental dialectic, which shows that there are equally good arguments for conflicting metaphysical claims (the so-called 'antinomies').

Hegel claims that Kant failed to see that the dialectic of reason can function as a means to achieve the total knowledge that he (Kant) believed impossible. Hegel distinguishes between negative and positive sides of reason (quite different from the Kantian understanding of reason's negative and positive aspects, mentioned above). Dialectic is the negative side,

dialectic

which (for Hegel, much as for Zeno) has the function of displaying the contradictions inherent in the concepts employed by the understanding. Kant's dialectic sets up antitheses, but he failed to see that these antitheses can be overcome through speculation, the positive aspect of reason. Speculative reason, as Hegel conceives it, is essentially the faculty that transcends the either-or thinking of the understanding. For Hegel, in sum, dialectic sets concepts in opposition to each other and reveals their problematic nature; speculation overcomes these dichotomies through a third term that reconciles or transcends their opposition.

Schelling's Absolute was an 'indifference' point which transcended the subject-object distinction, and all other distinctions. In *The Phenomenology of Spirit*, Hegel decisively rejects this way of conceiving the Absolute, arguing instead that it is the whole (of reality) itself conceived in 'the entire wealth of the developed form. Only then is it conceived and expressed as an actuality' (Miller, 11; PG, 15). Hegel identifies the whole with Idea, and dialectic is precisely what allows him to articulate the 'entire wealth' of its 'developed form'. The categories of the Logic are provisional definitions of the Absolute: each offers itself as a definition of the whole, yet each proves partial or incomplete and thus incapable of standing on its own. What moves the dialectic and makes possible the negation of one category and the transition to another is our pre-reflective 'intuition' of the Absolute, or the whole. Jean Hyppolite writes:

> In our opinion, if we are to understand Hegel's [dialectic] we must assume that the whole is always immanent in the development of consciousness. Negation is creative because the posited term had been isolated and thus was itself a kind of negation. From this it follows that the negation of that term allows the whole to be recaptured in each of its parts. *Were it not for the immanence of the whole in consciousness, we should be unable to understand how negation can truly engender a content.*[9]

In other words, we do not rest content with being, or with essence, or any of the other categories, precisely because we perceive a disparity between each category and what we somehow *already know* the whole to be. In the end, Idea proves the only adequate definition of the Absolute – but Idea 'contains' all the preceding categories as its conceptual self-differentiation; i.e., the earlier categories are not *simply* negated in the sense of being left behind.

Hegel uses the German verb *aufheben* to describe how the categories are overcome, but preserved at the same time. This word is notoriously difficult to render into English, but in recent years the seldom-used English term 'sublation' has become a popular translation. *Aufheben* has essentially three meanings: to cancel or abolish, to raise up, and to preserve or retain. Hegel's use of *aufheben* usually connotes *all* of these meanings simultaneously. Further, the dialectic is frequently described in terms of the formula 'thesis, antithesis, synthesis'. However, Hegel does not express things this way, and it is a problematic understanding of how the dialectic functions. Nor is it entirely correct to describe the dialectic as 'triadic'. A glance at how Hegel organizes his ideas, and at the many 'charts' of Hegel's system prepared by commentators, would certainly incline one to believe the claim that in Hegel everything comes in threes. Hegel himself makes it clear in the conclusion to the *Science of Logic*, however, that the triadic form is inessential. Though it is convenient to group Hegel's categories into threes, they could also be grouped in twos, fours, etc. What *is* essential to the dialectic is 'determinate negation', which is the 'mechanism' by which one category is supplanted by another. Negation in the Hegelian dialectic is always determinate – meaning that the negation of a category is a new, distinct category; e.g., the 'determinate negation' of nothing is not 'not-nothing', it is 'becoming'.

The real problem with all formulas such as 'triadicity' or 'thesis-antithesis-synthesis' is that Hegel makes it abundantly clear that the dialectic is not a *method* 'applied to' a given content or subject at all. In a literal sense, Hegel's philosophy does not tell us what the Absolute is; it gives form to the Absolute itself. The Absolute just is the Idea and its internal, dialectical self-differentiation. In short, Hegel maintains that in his philosophy there is in fact no distinction between form and content. This is the reason why all the attempts that have been made to 'formalize' dialectical logic are misguided.

Hegel's Logic offers us the paradigm of dialectic. In the Logic, the dialectic exhibits considerable rigor. In the other branches of Hegel's system (and especially in *The Phenomenology of Spirit*, the propaedeutic to the system itself) the transitions between ideas often seem considerably less rigorous and necessary. However, Hegel holds that dialectic is not just something to be found in philosophy; it is found in the natural world as well. (This should be unsurprising, for according to Hegelian philosophy the Logic essentially lays bare the formal structure of reality itself, and thus nature is a reflection or 'embodiment' of that dialectical structure.) In the *Encyclopedia Logic*, Hegel states that dialectic 'is in general the principle of all motion, of all life, and of all activation in the actual world' (Geraets, 128–29; EL § 81 A-1). Hegel sees the whole of reality as an internally related system of mutually dependent, and mutually negating or antagonistic elements. Dialectic is therefore involved in the being, and the coming-into-being, of anything. To adapt Hegel's metaphor from the Preface to *The Phenomenology of Spirit*, the bud is 'negated' by the blossom, which in turn is 'negated' by the fruit – but each is a necessary moment in an organic unity. See also **Absolute**; **Idea**; **Kant, Immanuel**; **negation**; **reason**; **relation**; **speculation**; **sublation**; **thesis, antithesis, synthesis**; **understanding**.

— E —

***Encyclopedia of the Philosophical Sciences in Outline** (Enzyklopädie der philosophischen Wissenschaften im Grundrisse)* Commonly referred to by scholars as the *Encyclopedia*, this work was published by Hegel originally in 1817, with further editions appearing in 1827 and 1830. It is one of only four books Hegel published under his own name (his first book having been published anonymously – see the Introduction to this volume). The *Encyclopedia* constitutes a summary of Hegel's entire philosophical system (with the exception of the *Phenomenology of Spirit*, which is a kind of introduction to the system itself) and was used as a basis for classroom lectures. The text consists of numbered paragraphs, many consisting of no more than a few lines. In class, Hegel would refer to these and then expound upon them. Because they are so terse, and intended merely as a basis for oral exposition, readers often find these paragraphs to be extraordinarily obscure. Today, they are almost always published along with the 'additions' (*Zusätze*) culled from the notebooks of Hegel's students, some of whom attempted to take down his words verbatim. The book is divided into three major sections: Logic, Philosophy of Nature and Philosophy of Spirit. The Logic portion is often referred to as the *Encyclopedia Logic* so as to distinguish it from *The Science of Logic* (or 'Larger Logic') a far more extensive presentation of the same ideas, published by Hegel in three volumes. Indeed, as the following chart reflects, Hegel expands upon the content of the *Encyclopedia* (and his lectures on it) in a number of places.[10]

Division of the Encyclopedia	Treated more fully in . . .
I. Logic	*The Science of Logic*
II. Philosophy of Nature	*not applicable* (our principal source here is indeed the *Encyclopedia* and Hegel's lecture remarks on it).
III. Philosophy of Spirit	
(A) Subjective Spirit	*not applicable* (see above)
(B) Objective Spirit	*The Philosophy of Right*; *Lectures on the Philosophy of History*
(C) Absolute Spirit	
1. Art	*Lectures on Aesthetics*
2. Religion	*Lectures on the Philosophy of Religion*
3. Philosophy	*Lectures on the History of Philosophy*

For an account of the content of the *Encyclopedia*, see the separate entries on Logic, Philosophy of Nature, and Philosophy of Spirit.

Enlightenment (*die Aufklärung*) 'The Enlightenment' refers to a Western intellectual movement, at its zenith in the late-eighteenth century, which emphasized reason as the only true authority in human life. It originated roughly at the same time in England, France, Germany and other Western European countries. The Enlightenment privileged science over religious faith, innovation over tradition, and advanced a political agenda championing (to one degree or another) equality, individual rights and democracy. Enlightenment principles were behind both the American and French revolutions. The English term 'Enlightenment' did not come into common usage until the mid-nineteenth century. However, the German term *Aufklärung* was current in the late-eighteenth century and was used by proponents of the movement itself (e.g., in Immanuel Kant's 1784 essay 'What is Enlightenment?').

Enlightenment

Hegel's relation to the Enlightenment is somewhat ambivalent. His early life shows signs of ardent support for Enlightenment principles. This was especially the case during the years in which he studied at the Tübingen theological seminary, where he and Schelling and Hölderlin were passionate supporters of the French Revolution, and passionate opponents of the traditionalism they found embodied in the seminary itself. Nevertheless, by the time he wrote *The Phenomenology of Spirit* Hegel seems to have developed a critical distance from the Enlightenment, a distance that increased over time. Thus, it is only in a heavily-qualified sense that one could describe him as an 'Enlightenment thinker'.

In the *Phenomenology* Hegel discusses Enlightenment in the section entitled 'Self-Estranged Spirit'. There, he describes a type of mentality, profoundly alienated from both nature and society, which feels itself called to remake these in order to 'perfect' them and to remove their opposition. This attitude is actually characteristic of modernity itself, and so Hegel's discussion of 'Self-Estranged Spirit' involves him in a sustained critique of the modern mindset.

As noted above, Enlightenment typically sets itself in opposition to religious faith, offering instead what Hegel calls the 'pure insight' of reason. In typical, dialectical fashion, however, Hegel sees an underlying identity between these two. Both seek an 'absolute unity' beyond appearances. Religious faith conceives this absolute unity as God, inaccessible to understanding. 'Pure insight' uses reason to seek some kind of source or principle behind all things – some ultimate condition, or ultimate explanation for why things are as they are. 'Pure insight', of course, derides and ridicules religion, but Hegel sees both as involved in metaphysical aims which, in the final analysis, are virtually indistinguishable. For example, materialism (one of the usual tenets of Enlightenment) attributes everything to an abstraction called 'matter' which is ultimately just as mysterious as the abstraction called 'God'. In fact, the materialism and (at least implicit) atheism of Enlightenment soon harden into dogma and Enlightenment becomes a substitute religion. Ultimately, Enlightenment issues in an utterly mundane view of the world, seeing everything in terms of utility. Having destroyed the idea that things have some value or significance in reference to a 'beyond', Enlightenment sets the value of things entirely in terms of their use. This must inevitably result in seeing human beings themselves in terms of utility – in other words, in an inhuman ideology. It is but a short step from here to 'the Terror' of the French Revolution. See also **absolute freedom and the Terror**; **abstract right**; **Phenomenology of Spirit**; **self-estranged Spirit**.

Essence, Doctrine of (*die Lehre vom Wesen*)   The Doctrine of Essence is the second major division of Hegel's Logic, succeeding the Doctrine of Being, and succeeded by the Doctrine of the Concept. The categories of being express the level of simple immediacy, or of the 'givenness' of things (quality, quantity, measure). The standpoint of being is essentially naïve, and Hegel's account of its categories shows how each fails as a provisional definition of the whole, and how each is therefore superseded. In the Doctrine of Essence we have achieved a critical distance from being. Nevertheless, essence does not simply leave being behind. Instead, in the Doctrine of Essence we turn back upon the categories of being and reflect upon them, trying to penetrate to some deeper level of truth. The transition from being to essence thus duplicates the traditional philosophical overcoming of commonsense: having discovered the contradictions inherent in the immediate world of experience, and in our conceptual understanding of it, we seek some truth that transcends that world. (This is the meaning – or one of the meanings – of Plato's 'allegory of the cave'.) The Doctrine of Essence, accordingly, is a sustained attempt to discover the inner truth that lies beneath appearances: essence is, as Hegel tells us, 'the truth of being' (Miller, 389; WL II, 3).

The foregoing represents, as it were, an 'epistemological' account of the difference between the two 'perspectives' given in the Doctrines of Being and Essence. In logical terms, the difference between the two is chiefly this: In the Doctrine of Being each category is simply supplanted or replaced by one which is wholly other. In the Doctrine of Essence, however, we continually encounter conceptual dyads, which are not so much 'opposites' as correlative terms. Hegel shows us that the relationship between these terms is one which is always far more peculiar and ambiguous than commonsense takes it to be. The categories, in fact, appear (*scheinen*; literally 'shine' or 'seem') in one another: for example, 'thing' is a part of the idea of 'properties' itself, and the same is true of 'matter and form', 'whole and parts', 'cause and effect,' etc. Each term is what it is only in relation to the other.

The categories of essence are those of what Hegel calls 'reflection', which is closely related to his concept of the understanding. Hegel explains that 'The term "reflection" is primarily used of light, when, propagated rectilinearly, it strikes a mirrored surface and is thrown back by it' (Geraets, 176; EL § 112 A). Something quite similar is happening when we say that we reflect on something or think it over. First, we consider it as it appears. Thought then, in a sense, 'bounces back' from the surface and tries to consider it in terms of deeper reasons or grounds which tell us why the thing appears as it does. It is for this reason that the dichotomy of appearance and (underlying) essence is basic to reflection.

Hegel regards reflection as an extremely important philosophical standpoint, which reaches its zenith in the thought of Immanuel Kant. However, from Hegel's standpoint reflection does not go far enough. It tends to think in terms of dichotomies, to which it adheres rigidly. It does not reach the standpoint of speculation (Hegel's own standpoint) in which appearances are grasped not as the deceptive covering of a hidden essence, but as the self-display of the whole (or Absolute). It is in this sense that the Doctrine of Essence and its categories of reflection describe a system of categories that is inherently 'false' in the sense of being partial or one-sided.

As noted earlier, the categories of the Doctrine of Essence tend to come in pairs. Again, dyadic, either-or thinking characterizes reflection. Typically, however, reflection takes one member of a dichotomy as primary. For example, it takes essence as primary, and appearance as somehow derivative. In Kant's philosophy, things-in-themselves are (implicitly) taken as primary, not phenomena, which are mere appearances somehow occasioned by things-in-themselves. Hegel deals with this Kantian distinction in the Doctrine of Essence. The advance from reflection to speculation involves, for one thing, seeing the members of such dyads as equally primary or mutually determining. To take one of Hegel's own examples, it is a mistake to regard essence as 'primary' and to subordinate appearance to it. After all, how are we to understand the relation of these two, except by understanding appearances as appearances *of essence*? Further, what sort of reality should we assign to essence considered apart from its appearances? Doesn't essence, in fact, realize itself precisely in its appearing (i.e., in its manifesting itself)? Essence considered apart from its appearances is an abstraction devoid of content. To take another example, Hegel provides a similarly speculative treatment of the dyad whole/parts. Reflection tends to take the whole as primary. But the whole is only a whole in virtue of the parts it unifies – and the parts are what they are only through being members of the whole. In every case, speculation involves thought pushing beyond dyadic terms and seeking some higher, wider, unifying conception that resolves oppositions.

It is within the Doctrine of Essence that we find Hegel's notorious discussion of the 'laws of thought': identity, non-contradiction and excluded middle. Contrary to what is often asserted, Hegel does not 'deny' these laws; he argues that they are valid within certain delimited contexts. Nevertheless, speculation involves reconciling oppositions between concepts which reflection takes as absolutely opposed, or even contradictory. A paradigm example of reflection's naivete is its insistence that the concepts of 'identity' and 'difference' are absolutely opposed. (The laws of thought are, in fact, founded upon this dichotomization of identity and difference.) In a famous discussion, however, Hegel argues that something only possesses identity in virtue of its differences from other things (the Hegelian doctrine of 'identity in difference').

The inadequacies of the Doctrine of Essence and its reflective standpoint eventually result in the transition to what Hegel calls the Concept. In the 'Objective Logic' of being and essence, categories are determined by, or related to other categories. In the 'Subjective Logic' of the Concept, however, categories are related *to themselves*. Hegel's dialectic shows how the pure thought-categories of being and essence pass over into the categories of the Concept; how the Concept constitutes the higher-level (or deeper-level) unity of being and essence. In the Concept, all the foregoing categories are understood to have their meaning and significance just in being 'comprehended' by a self-related, self-determining idea. The turn to the Concept is thus a kind of 'subjective turn' which issues first of all in a re-evaluation of the major concepts of traditional logic. See also **Being, Doctrine of; Concept, Doctrine of the; contradiction; identity and difference; Kant, Immanuel; Logic; reflection; understanding; whole and parts.**

estates, the   See **civil society**.

ethical life (*die Sittlichkeit*)   'Ethical Life' is the third major division of Hegel's *Philosophy of Right*, following 'Abstract Right' and 'Morality'. These sections depict the self-development of the idea of right and human

ethical life

will. Morality, a response to the moral bankruptcy of abstract right, looks to inner subjectivity (e.g., conscience) for ethical guidance. Hegel argues, however, that morality so understood is fundamentally empty, and cannot generate principles we experience as truly binding upon us. Ethical life represents Hegel's account of how ethics is in fact grounded not in abstract principles but in social institutions.

Hegel, like Aristotle, believes that ethics has an inescapably social dimension. There may be certain rules that can be expressed abstractly (e.g. 'hitting the mean'), but *how* we learn to apply these rules cannot be a matter of learning further, abstract rules (something which would obviously lead to an infinite regress: rules for applying rules for applying rules, etc.). Instead, we learn the 'knack' of applying rules to concrete situations through many years of having our moral sensibilities adjusted by the institutions of our society. There may be certain principles that all societies agree upon, for example that generosity is a good thing. But human beings never learn 'generosity' as such, they learn to practice generosity as their society does. For example, some societies practice a great deal more generosity toward guests than others do, and consider this obligatory.

To draw an analogy, ethical rules mean as little when separated from a social context as aesthetic rules mean when considered apart from the different art forms. We may say that the achievement of 'unity' is an important artistic goal: but it means very different things in music, painting, sculpture, drama and poetry. To understand what it means it is not enough to offer a definition in the abstract: we must discuss how the ideal is concretized in the different arts. Similarly, Hegel's discussion of ethical life is not devoted to a deduction of ethical principles. Instead, it is concerned with the primary social forms which make the ethical development of the individual possible. Essentially, Hegel argues that individuals develop ethically as a result of finding themselves situated within a social whole, and realizing their place in relation to others. It is within a social whole that I am led to rise above a narrow concern with the satisfaction of personal desires and to become aware of higher duties and obligations. Ethical life is concerned with the three most basic social wholes: family, civil society and the state.

Family is the most basic social institution of all, united by the bond of love. In marriage, husband and wife subordinate their individual, subjective wills to the good of the marriage and the family they create together. This is the reason why marriage is an *ethical* institution for Hegel. In this sphere, 'the good' is the good of the family. Civil society, which individuals enter into on reaching adulthood, is the antithesis of the family. It is a world characterized not by love but by competition. Nevertheless, it is through civil society that individuals acquire a determinate sphere in which they can realize who they are, and exercize freedom. People actualize their freedom in civil society principally through the choice of an occupation, and ethical development is made possible by membership in what Hegel calls 'corporations'. These are essentially guilds, unions and professional associations that unite those in a certain occupation. Each typically has its own 'code of ethics', and membership in a corporation encourages co-operation and fellow-feeling: it teaches us to see our fellow citizens as something more than competitors. Through participation in civil society, we come to see society itself and its economic arrangement as conditions for the possibility of our freedom.

Nevertheless, the public spiritedness engendered within civil society is largely motivated by self-interest. There must, Hegel argues, be something in society that binds people together and transcends purely individual concerns. This is the function of the state, which brings people together by embodying the spirit of the nation: its traditions, mores and customs. In the simplest possible terms, the state represents an ethical advance on civil society because it fosters a sense of common citizenship and obligation to the whole (whereas in civil society we may feel a bond merely with other members of our corporation). The state unifies the people and safeguards and supports the spheres of family and civil society. In fact, Hegel argues, the very existence of family and civil society presuppose the authority of the state. These 'private' spheres of relation and action are made possible by a public, legal order which overarches, protects and regulates them. However, Hegel sees the state as much more than just 'government'. The state is 'Objective Spirit', which provides a people with a reflection of itself: an embodiment of its culture and its ideals. Hegel's state is a constitutional monarchy, and the spirit of the people is, in fact, *literally* embodied in the sovereign.

Hegel argues in *The Philosophy of Right* that freedom is truly realized only through our coming to identify ourselves with the larger social whole. In other words, true freedom only comes about through membership in the state. (This does not mean, however, that our particularity is simply cancelled: Hegel's conception of society makes a place for freedom of choice, individual rights, and the authority of the individual conscience – in other words, in ethical life elements of abstract right and morality are sublated.) For Hegel, freedom must involve *willing our determination*: affirming the conditions that make true freedom possible, which are more or less the conditions that make possible the society in which we live. In one way, of course, these conditions limit us, but in another more meaningful way they open up for us a range of possibilities for action which would be denied us if the 'limitations' of society did not exist. See also **abstract right**; **civil society**; **family**; **freedom**; **morality**; *Philosophy of Right*; **state**.

evil (*das Böse*) In a remark appended to the text of the *Encyclopedia Logic* Hegel comments on the error of treating evil as something positive and says that in fact evil is 'the negative that does not subsist on its own account, but only wants to be on its own account, and is in fact only the absolute semblance of inward negativity' (Geraets, 73; EL § 35 A). Here, Hegel might be read as endorsing the medieval doctrine of evil as a *privation*: as nothing positive in itself, but rather a lack or absence of something else. In fact, Hegel's position is subtly different from this. He believes all finite particulars are subsumed within the Absolute: reality considered as a systematic whole. To be finite is to be limited, and the great majority of errors, defects and 'wrongs' come about simply as a result of the inherent limitations of finite things. Hegel argues that the Absolute is a dialectically self-differentiating whole, and that dialectic always involves opposition and negation. Thus, it is possible to argue on the terms of Hegel's philosophy that 'evil' – construed broadly to include defect, error, conflict and opposition – is inherent in the nature of reality. Indeed, the Absolute only has existence as a whole of mutually-antagonistic elements.

However, evil is often understood more narrowly as 'moral evil', which refers to certain consciously chosen human wrongs, as opposed to 'physical evils' like deformities and disasters, and unwitting evils like catastrophic errors committed without any ill intent. Still, Hegel understands moral evil on analogy with other sorts of evil: as involving the opposition of a finite part of existence to the whole. The criminal, for example, depends upon society but attacks it at the same time, making himself an exception to general laws. He is, in fact, part of the whole, but he sets himself and his desires up as absolute. In a certain way, it is as if he thinks he is the whole itself; he does not recognize his own finitude and dependence. Analogously, certain forms of bodily disease ('bodily evil', we might say) occur when an organ ceases to function in accord with the whole, thereby jeopardizing the whole itself.

Nevertheless, though finitude and the evil consequent upon it are inherent in the nature of reality, they are 'overcome' in the whole. Each finite and flawed being, each disaster and atrocity, is a moment in the self-development of the Absolute. This idea is most dramatically illustrated in Hegel's Philosophy of History. One can thus see that his position is, to a certain extent, similar to that of traditional theologians, who argue that from 'God's perspective' (which is that of the whole) what we call evil serves a greater, ultimate end. The difference is that Hegel thinks he knows what that ultimate end is, while for traditional theology it remains a mystery. See also **'cunning of reason'**; **history and Philosophy of History**; **law of the heart**; **morality**; **negation**; **punishment**; **right**; **'slaughter-bench of history'**; **wrong**.

evolution (*die Evolution*)   Hegel is notorious for having rejected the theory of evolution in his Philosophy of Nature. He writes that 'A thinking consideration must reject such nebulous, at bottom, sensuous representations, as in particular the so-called origination [*Hervorgehen*] . . . of the more highly-developed animal organisms from the lower' (Miller, 20; PN § 249. In the 'addition' to this passage Hegel uses the term *Evolution*). Charles Darwin's *On The Origin of Species* was not published until 1859, twenty-eight years after Hegel's death. However, the idea that species may have evolved over time predates Darwin. Something like a 'theory of evolution' has even been attributed to the Pre-Socratic philosopher Anaximander (sixth century BC). Prior to Darwin, however, evolution was considered a highly questionable idea by many scientists, partly because no one had yet identified *how* species might have evolved. Darwin's theory of natural selection changed that, by identifying an extremely plausible (and simple) mechanism by which species could, through many small changes over the course of long periods of time, emerge from others.

Within each population of organisms there is always genetic variation, and this entails that certain individuals, with certain inherited traits, will be

evolution

better able to survive and reproduce than others. Thus, Darwin reasoned, over time such individuals will proliferate, while others with less fortunate sets of inherited traits will die off. This is what Darwin meant by 'natural selection'. A classic example often used to illustrate natural selection is the British peppered moth. Some of the members of this species are light-coloured, others dark. During the industrial revolution many of the trees on which the moths rested were blackened by soot. This gave the dark-coloured moths an advantage, as the light-coloured ones could easily be spotted by predators against the background of the dark, sooty tree trunks. As a result, the number of light-coloured moths began to dwindle. After several generations, the majority of the moths were dark-coloured.

It is important to keep in mind that when Hegel rejected evolution, no one had yet arrived at a satisfactory theory of how evolution had happened. Therefore, *that* it had happened was by no means accepted by all scientists. Like Aristotle, Hegel recognizes a hierarchy in nature, with animals higher than plants, and plants higher than non-living, 'mineral' nature. At the top of the scale, for both Aristotle and Hegel, is man. Such a viewpoint naturally lends itself to an evolutionary perspective: i.e., to the claim that the higher and more complex has 'evolved out of' the lower and simpler. However, Hegel explicitly rejects this. He believes that nature is indeed a scale or hierarchy, but that the different species are present all at once, and have not emerged over time. For one thing, there are large 'gaps' in nature between the different forms, so it is hard to construct an account showing convincingly how complex forms evolved from earlier, simpler ones.

Hegel believes that all the different natural forms are ways in which nature is approximating to an adequate embodiment of Idea. However, he holds that there is no *serial* approximation to Idea. In other words, the different natural forms do not display themselves one after another *in time*, expressing Idea in increasingly adequate forms. Rather, the philosopher who knows the Logic is able to look at nature and see that each thing in its own way approximates to Idea.

During Hegel's time the primary piece of evidence for evolution was the fossil record. The different strata of soil contain fossilized remains of living organisms. The deeper the strata, the simpler these organisms appear to be; the more recent the strata, the more complex the organisms. This suggests, of course, an evolution of complex life forms from simple.

Strikingly, Hegel rejects the very idea that fossils are the remains of living organisms. Instead, he suggests that they are 'anticipations' of life forms produced spontaneously through inorganic processes. In a famous passage Hegel states that 'God does not remain petrified and dead; the very stones cry out and raise themselves to Spirit' (Miller, 15; PN § 247 A). Hegel's claim is that since the expression of Idea is the *telos*, the goal of all of existence, we should not be surprised to find dim anticipations of organic forms being produced in inorganic matter. Thus, the different 'fossils' that we find do resemble the remains of animals and plants familiar to us, only in distorted or even monstrous forms. These are, in Hegel's view, merely inorganic matter's abortive approximations to a higher form.

Hegelian philosophers writing after Darwin have often pointed out that despite what Hegel himself says, evolution fits the Hegelian philosophy beautifully. Some have even felt confident that Hegel would have embraced the Darwinian theory of evolution, had he lived to see it. However, the truth of the matter is almost certainly more complex. Contrary to what is often thought, in his Philosophy of Nature Hegel did not engage in armchair theorizing, or attempt to deduce empirical truths *a priori*. Instead, he embraced the best-confirmed scientific views of his day. Had Hegel lived to read Darwin, he might very well have conceded that here at long last was a convincing argument for evolution. However, Hegel would have utterly rejected the idea of evolution as without ultimate purpose – a tenet of evolutionary theory that has been emphasized greatly by recent followers of Darwin. Hegel might well accept the theory of natural selection, but he would insist that this is merely a mechanism which furthers the coming into being of species, each of which approaches in its own way the embodiment of Idea. This neo-Hegelian, evolutionary view (advocated by such contemporary interpreters of Hegel as Errol E. Harris) holds that nature is a progressive unfolding of Idea. Nature, in a very real sense, *presupposes* Idea – and all the natural forms exist so that Idea can come to embodiment, reaching its perfect expression in Spirit or mankind. See also **Absolute Idea**; **Aristotle**; **Idea**; **nature and Philosophy of Nature**.

existence   See **determinate being**.

— F —

faith and knowledge (*Glauben und Wissen*)   This was the title of one of Hegel's early essays (written in 1802), but it also refers to an issue with which he was concerned, in one way or another, throughout his career. Faith and knowledge, or faith and reason, seem utterly opposed, since religious faith demands that we believe certain things without evidence – things which scientific reason declares to be impossible. Nonetheless, Hegel argues that they can be reconciled. In fact, it is only the understanding which asserts that there is, or must be, a gulf between the two. The root of the problem is that the understanding sees reason as investigating a world of finite, contingent, externally-related particulars. Reason (so the understanding holds) cognizes these particulars by classifying them according to abstract universals – to which the particulars are also related externally. Any sense of wholeness, any sense that all of these particulars might be internally-related in some larger, meaning-conferring whole is banished from the realm of reason and consigned to faith. However, the understanding's perspective on reason is inadequate. According to Hegel, true reason is dialectical and involves the recognition of the internal relations of particulars. Once we adopt this standpoint, we can see that the particular things studied by empirical science are all contained as moments within a larger whole – which, in fact, corresponds to the God which is the object of religious faith. Therefore, reason (properly understood) and faith have the exact same content – the Absolute or God – and there is consequently no real conflict between them. See also **Absolute; dialectic; God; reason; relation; religion and Philosophy of Religion; science; theology; understanding.**

family (*die Familie*)   In *The Philosophy of Right*, Hegel discusses 'ethical life': his account of how ethics is founded upon social institutions and practices, not abstract rules. Ethical life has three dialectical moments: family, civil society and the state. Marriage is the most basic 'ethical' institution for Hegel because it involves two individuals coming together to create a larger whole to which they subordinate their personal, subjective wills. In marriage and family we have transcended the individualism of abstract right – which involves, at its most basic level, claims about what is 'mine' –

and also the pure interiority of morality, which sets up the personal, subjective sense of good as absolute. In ethical life the good, in fact, first becomes objectified as the family itself, to which, again, our individual feelings and desires must be subordinated. (Because Hegel regards marriage as the first and most basic concrete expression of ethical life, and thus a fundamental form in which freedom realizes itself, he holds that marriage is an ethical duty.)

Family is a miniature society and, like all societies, it is hierarchical: authority is exercized by the parents (pre-eminently by the father). However, its members are united by the bond of blood, and of love. Family is the first form in which individuals encounter authority, rules and obligations. However, in order for us to fully develop as autonomous individuals and realize our potential there must exist a sphere of freedom that transcends the family. This is what Hegel calls 'civil society', the second moment of ethical life. Civil society is the antithesis of the family, and is characterized not by love but chiefly by divisive relations of competition: adults striving against one another to make their way in the world. In time, the younger members of the family enter into civil society and establish themselves as autonomous individuals (who will, in turn, form their own families). Hegel argues, however, that though civil society is necessary, its divisiveness and concern with self-interest must be overcome in the state, which serves to bind people together irrespective of individual differences. See also **civil society**; **ethical life**; *Philosophy of Right*; **state**.

feeling soul (*die fühlende Seele*) Hegel's account of Subjective Spirit deals with the 'psychology' of the individual, including such matters as perception, will, imagination, memory and the passions, as well as all those aspects of ourselves which are unconscious or preconscious. It is divided into 'Anthropology', 'Psychology' and 'Phenomenology'. 'Anthropology' deals with what Hegel calls 'the soul' (*die Seele*), which is the part of ourselves that is really on the cusp between the animal and the human: all that which is not a function of self-conscious mind or intellect. Hegel subdivides his treatment of soul into 'Natural Soul', 'Feeling Soul' and 'Actual Soul'.

Hegel's discussion of feeling, and of the difference between sensation and feeling, is obscure to say the least. Whereas sensations are fleeting, feeling seems to involve the co-ordination of sensations. But we are not yet

feeling soul

at the conscious level, where sense-impressions have been transformed into a coherent experience of the world around us. The soul is, Hegel tells us, 'the sleep of Spirit'. The natural soul is nature within us; that which lives and works within us unconsciously. In feeling soul, on the other hand, we find the first glimmer of awareness. Feeling soul is the great depth of the psyche: a congeries of impressions, sensations, intuitions. At this level, however, no firm distinction has been made between the subjective and the objective. Human life begins at this level, and individual identity must be carved out of it (which is, in effect, what is involved in the transition to actual soul).

When the individual is at the level of feeling soul, it is possible for another subject to exercize control over it. Hegel calls this its *genius*. This can occur in at least two ways. First, early in life, when the child lives at the level of feeling soul, another individual (such as its mother) may play the role of genius. However, it is also possible for adult individuals to 'regress' to the level of feeling soul. In such a state, another individual may control them and become their genius. This occurs in parent–child relationships, and in the strange phenomenon of 'mesmerism' or 'animal magnetism'.

With respect to the parent–child relationship, Hegel discusses how the child can undergo psychic and even physical changes *in utero* as a result of the mother's thoughts or feelings. He refers to such relationships as involving 'a magic tie', and explains his use of the term 'magic' (*Magie*) as follows: 'this term connotes a relation of inner to outer or to something else generally, which dispenses with any mediation; a magical power is one whose action is not determined by the interconnection, the conditions and mediations of objective relations; but such a power which produces effects without any mediation is "the feeling soul in its immediacy"' (Wallace, 97; PS § 405 A). Hegel's definition comprises all those phenomena that we today term 'paranormal', and he lectured at length on such phenomena, especially animal magnetism. A magical relationship is one which operates without mediation and which seems to cancel the limitations of time and space. Given this, and as Hegel states explicitly, 'magic' is completely inexplicable to the understanding. It can only be comprehended by speculative philosophy.

Hegel also discusses insanity under 'Feeling Soul'. The madman is someone who has regressed into an identity with the primitive level of drives and instincts, which most adult individuals have managed to suppress or to control. Insanity often involves some aspect of the individual's psyche becoming 'dislodged' from the greater whole of his interior life and claiming for itself centrality, as well as immunity from rational evaluation or revision. This is what occurs, for example, in obsession and in the phenomenon of the *idée fixe*, which Hegel discusses extensively. See also **actual soul**; **animal magnetism**; **genius**; **insanity**; **natural soul**; **Philosophy of Spirit**; **Subjective Spirit**.

Fichte, J. G. (1762–1814) Johan Gottlieb Fichte was born at Rammenau in Saxony, to a poor family. As a boy, his intelligence aroused the attention of a local nobleman, who provided for his education. During his years as a student Fichte fell under the spell of Spinoza, and accepted the theory of determinism. While working as a private tutor in Zurich, however, he encountered the works of Immanuel Kant, who had argued that despite the appearance that our actions are determined, we nevertheless must *believe* that we are free. Fichte's encounter with Kant had a major impact on him, and he devoted the rest of his career to creating a philosophical system that would improve upon and 'complete' the Kantian philosophy.

In 1792 he published *Attempt at a Critique of All Revelation*. Because this work was issued anonymously, and because its basic premises were Kantian, many assumed that it had been written by Kant himself. Kant was quick to clear up this confusion, however – and to praise the work. When Fichte became known as the author he seemed destined for a stellar career in academia. However, he was not fully satisfied with Kant's philosophy, believing it to be insufficiently systematic. In particular, what bothered Fichte was Kant's claim that our minds are limited to awareness only of how things appear to us; what things are *in themselves* we can never know. Fichte believed that this concept of the 'thing-in-itself' was unacceptable. If we can never know the thing-in-itself, why should we believe that it exists? For Kant, the thing-in-itself guaranteed the objectivity of our experience: appearances must be appearances *of something*, something that exists and has a nature quite independent of us. To reject the thing-in-itself would seem to land us in subjectivism: the belief that reality as it appears to us is really a creation of the human mind. In fact, with some important qualifications, this was precisely the course taken by Fichte.

In 1794 Fichte published *Foundations of the Entire Doctrine of Science* (*Grundlage der Gesammten Wissenschaftslehre*; often referred to simply as

Fichte, J. G.

'the *Wissenschaftslehre*'). What he attempts to do in this work is to ground all human knowledge, and existence itself, in the activity of what he calls the Absolute Ego. This has nothing to do, however, with 'ego' in the sense of my conscious selfhood. Kant had spoken of a 'Transcendental Unity of Apperception', which was responsible for the co-ordination of the different impressions we receive into the unitary experience of a single subject. Fichte's Absolute Ego is essentially a development of Kant's Transcendental Unity of Apperception – with the difference that instead of merely co-ordinating our impressions of the world, the Ego is the *source* of these impressions. Fichte's rejection of the thing-in-itself forces him to take this position. If sensory impressions do not have their origin in an 'external world' of things-in-themselves but rather (somehow) in our minds, we must deal with the obvious fact that we do not *experience* ourselves as producing these impressions. Fichte's solution to this is to posit that the production of impressions happens at a level deeper than that of the personal ego; it is the work of the Absolute Ego.

To go into a bit more detail, Fichte states that Kant's account of human consciousness involves two poles: (1) the subject and its categories and modes of knowing; and (2) the object known by the subject. Fichte believes one can develop a consistent philosophy starting from either pole. If one starts with the object one will emphasize how the subject is affected by and acted upon by the object; how the object, in a way, 'creates' the subject. This leads to determinism – to believing that the subject is simply a plaything of external forces – and Fichte calls this position *dogmatism*. On the other hand, one can start with the subjective pole and show, as Kant only partially succeeds in doing, how the object is 'constructed' by the subject. This position leads to the affirmation of the freedom of the subject, since it is unconstrained by any external object, and Fichte calls it *transcendental idealism* (the name that, initially, Kant gave to his own philosophy). The trouble with Kant, Fichte claims, is that his philosophy is really a hybrid of the two. On the one hand, Kant explains how the object is (partly) a production of the subject (transcendental idealism) – but on the other hand he insists on things-in-themselves that transcend the subject's experience and constrain it (dogmatism).

Fichte aims to resolve this tension in Kant by developing a radicalized transcendental idealism, showing how the object is entirely a production of subjectivity (and, in the process, how the thing-in-itself is a pure fiction).

However, Fichte admits that *both* transcendental idealism and dogmatism are internally consistent and defensible positions, neither of which can be refuted by empirical evidence. Therefore, he says in the *Wissenschaftslehre*, 'What sort of philosophy one chooses depends on what sort of man one is.' Are we drawn to a philosophy that restricts our freedom (dogmatism) or to one that affirms it in the most radical way possible (transcendental idealism)? In the *Wissenschaftslehre* Fichte presents a complicated defense of transcendental idealism, purporting to show how all of our experience of the objective world can be accounted for in terms of the activity of the subject. If we ask *why* the Ego produces in us the impression of an objective world, Fichte's answer is that the world exists for us as a field for moral action. In other words, the object – that which stands opposed to the subject – exists in order to be conquered and re-made by us according to moral ideals. All of life, Fichte asserts, is an ongoing (and never-ending) attempt to collapse the distinction between subject and object, by remaking the objective world into an expression of the subject's ideals.

Fichte's contemporaries found his philosophy as difficult and strange as we do today, so in 1800 he published a short work entitled *The Vocation of Man* (*Die Bestimmung des Menschen*). This work succeeds admirably in putting his philosophy into clear language, although he modifies and simplifies his ideas in the process. Modelled on Descartes's *Meditations*, the text is written in the first person and details Fichte's (or the narrator's) quest for self understanding. In Book One ('Doubt') he begins by considering himself as a part of nature and winds up affirming a 'scientific worldview' which is completely deterministic and allows no room for freedom – the equivalent of what he earlier called dogmatism. At the end of Book One, however, Fichte proclaims that while his mind is convinced of this, his heart insists even more emphatically that he is free. Which should he be guided by?

In Book Two ('Knowledge'), which is a dialogue, Fichte is visited by a spirit who presents him with idealist arguments aimed at proving that he has no basis for believing that an objective world exists independently of his mind. In fact, this position (equivalent to transcendental idealism) is offered by the Spirit as a resolution of the problem of Book One: if nothing exists apart from the subject, by what can it be determined? Needless to say, however, our freedom is won here at the price of losing the entire objective world!

Since this outcome also seems unacceptable, Fichte argues in Book Three ('Faith') that the skeptical problems raised by the first two books are irrelevant in view of his drives and feelings, which are far more powerful than any facts or philosophical arguments. Philosophy or science may argue that I am determined, but I have a fundamental and ineradicable conviction that I am free. Philosophy may argue that the world is unreal, that it is the creation of an 'Absolute Ego,' but I shall never *truly* believe this, and shall always act as if I think otherwise (as when I swerve to avoid an oncoming car – despite having just left philosophy class, where I was told that objects are a creation of the subject). Our drives and our will compel us to believe in the world and have faith that there are objects existing independently of us.

Fichte says that we have a drive for action, for 'absolute independent self-activity'. We do not choose to have this drive, but we do insist that our actions be self-determined (i.e., free) and not determined for us by something external to ourselves. However, we also have the conviction that we can't act in just any way, for we have the voice of conscience in us. Our drive to act and awareness of obligations commits us to belief in the world and to 'taking an interest', even though reason cannot underwrite this belief. The world, Fichte says, amounts to the sphere in which I must act – and act ethically. But we cannot conceive that this world with all its problems is how things *must* be, and that the present situation of man is the final and permanent one. Therefore, Fichte proceeds to articulate the basic moral goals which he thinks must animate our action in the world. What he says near the end of *The Vocation of Man* constitutes one of the purest statements ever of the modern, Western project of Enlightenment and the mastery and control of nature. Fichte proclaims that we must work towards the achievement of total knowledge and mastery of nature through science; the spread of one, enlightened culture across the whole globe; the unification of all human beings; an end to war; and an end to inequality. Although we have no rational basis for believing that the world is anything more than a posit of an Absolute Ego, we must still act on our conviction that the real has to be brought into accord with the ideal. Fichte is careful to point out that this is a never-ending project: the real will always resist our attempts to perfect it.

Much of Fichte's influence on Hegel is by way of Schelling's appropriation and transformation of Fichte's ideas. Schelling allied himself early on with

Fichte, producing his own *System of Transcendental Idealism* in 1800. However, Fichte broke with Schelling when the latter insisted on supplementing transcendental idealism with a philosophy of nature. Schelling argued that nature is not merely raw material for our ethically-charged striving; rather it is something through which we can come to know ourselves: a great chain of being approximating to human subjectivity. For Schelling, the 'completion' of nature is nature's coming to consciousness of itself through human self-awareness. Hegel takes over this basic idea from Schelling. Further, he rejects Fichte's idea of an unending progression towards the unification of subject and object, or ideal and real. In response, he claims that the subject-object distinction is actually overcome in philosophy, which is thought thinking itself, or human self-awareness raised to its absolute form. (For Schelling, the overcoming of the subject-object distinction really occurs in art.) See also **idealism**; **Kant, Immanuel**; **Schelling, F. W. J.**; **Spinoza, Benedict**.

'foaming chalice'   Hegel ends *The Phenomenology of Spirit* with the famous image of the 'foaming chalice'. He tells us that Spirit as displayed in the *Phenomenology*'s 'way of despair' constitutes 'the recollection and the Golgotha [*die Schädelstätte*] of Absolute Spirit, the actuality, truth, and certainty of his throne, without which he would be lifeless and alone; only, "from the chalice of this realm of spirits, foams for him his own infinity"' (*Aus dem Kelche dieses Geisterreiches, schäumt ihm seine Unendlichkeit*; Miller, 493; PG, 531). Hegel has, in fact, deliberately misquoted Schiller's poem 'Friendship' ('Die Freundschaft', 1782), the last two lines of which read: 'From out of the chalice of the whole realm of the soul, Foams for him – infinity' (*Aus dem Kelch des ganzen Seelenreiches, schäumt ihm – die Unendlichkeit*).

To understand the meaning of Hegel's changes, one must look at the final stanza of Schiller's poem in its entirety:

Friendless was the great World Master
Felt a lack – thus He created spirits,
  Blessed mirrors of His bliss –
Still found the highest being no likeness,
From out of the chalice of the whole realm of the soul
  Foams for Him – infinity.[11]

force and the understanding

Hegel's claim in the *Phenomenology* is that any developmental account of the Absolute (or God) must understand Spirit (*Geist*) as its aim. Hegel thus chooses to identify Schiller's created *Geist* (literally, *Geister*, plural) with the soul of the World Master (God) itself: *Seelenreiches* ('realm of the soul') becomes *Geisterreiches* ('realm of spirits'). Hegel rejects Schiller's claim that 'Still found the highest being no likeness.' For Hegel, the 'world master' *does* find an adequate 'likeness': in mankind, or Absolute Spirit. Further, Schiller says that out of this 'realm of the soul foams for him – infinity', implying that infinity displays itself before God, as something external. Hegel revises the last line of the poem to read 'foams to him, *his* infinity [*seine Unendlichkeit*].' Spirit, for Hegel, must be identified with the infinite itself. This infinite, however, is not what Hegel calls a 'bad infinity,' one which stands in opposition to the finite. Such an opposition places a limitation on infinity, thus making infinity finite. True (or 'good') infinity must therefore contain the finite. The result of this is that, for Hegel, Spirit does not confront an infinity 'foaming' out away from it: *it is the infinite* (the embodiment of Absolute Idea).

At the end of the *Phenomenology* Hegel thus looks back upon the whole of the work and sees it as a *Geisterreich*, an exposition of the rich varieties of Spirit itself. Through this work, we have been brought to the recognition of our own identity with the true infinite. In more specific terms, Spirit at the end of the *Phenomenology* has transcended finite consciousness, which is always opposed to some specific object, and has readied itself to achieve Absolute Knowing. See also **Absolute; Absolute Knowing; infinity; Phenomenology of Spirit; Spirit.**

force and the understanding (*Kraft und Verstand*) In *The Phenomenology of Spirit*, Hegel treats 'Force and the Understanding' as the final form of 'Consciousness'. Perhaps, consciousness thinks, objects can be truly grasped through knowledge of the 'forces' underlying them, which make them what they are. Here we have the first glimmerings of scientific consciousness: we will understand things as bound by 'laws' to which they must adhere. If we can attain knowledge of these laws, we become master of things (if only in thought). Thus, for example, we explain the fact that objects fall by positing an occult force called 'gravity'. But this sort of approach really explains nothing about the object at all. It is reminiscent of the famous line in one of Molière's plays where a character explains the power of a drug to induce sleep in terms of its 'dormitive [i.e., sleep-inducing] virtue'. Once the emptiness of such 'scientific' explanation is realized, consciousness is embarrassed to find that it has succeeded only in revealing something *about itself*. See also **consciousness**; **'inverted world, the'**; ***Phenomenology of Spirit***; **science**; **self-consciousness**.

for itself   See **in itself, for itself, in-and-for itself**.

freedom (*die Freiheit*)   The idea of freedom is central to Hegel's philosophy. Indeed, the major point of Hegel's Philosophy of History is that history is the progressive achievement of human self-consciousness, which is simultaneously the realization of freedom. Hegel believes that unlike animals our nature is not fixed and 'determined'. Instead, human beings *determine themselves*, and our level or degree of self-determination depends upon the level of our self-understanding. If I am not aware that I have the capacity to determine myself and my destiny, if I imagine that I am constrained by factors which (in reality) could be overcome, then for all intents and purposes I am not free. I am potentially free, for I still have the ability in principle to come to realize that my capacities are greater than they are – but in actuality, lacking this realization, I am unfree. History is the story of how we, as a race, come to the realization that we choose to be what we are. This realization is, of course, liberating. Thus, for Hegel, the achievement of self-consciousness and the achievement of freedom go hand-in-hand.

However, it would be a gross error to think that Hegel believes that freedom simply means doing whatever we like. The 'classical liberal' concept of freedom (which Hegel critiques) rests upon the idea that the self has within it a kind of negativity, which allows it, in one fashion or another, to reject, deny, or otherwise separate itself from situations that confront it. Freedom, in this conception, rests upon the capacity to say 'No'. This negative aspect of freedom, however, goes together with a positive aspect: the capacity not just to say 'no' to certain options, but to say 'yes' to others. In making positive choices, however, we always retain our ability to change our minds and to negate them.

The classical liberal conception, in short, sees freedom as lack of constraint in making and rejecting options. However, Hegel regards this concept as fundamentally flawed. What is it, he asks, that determines the options we have to choose from in the first place? Freedom to choose from a number of *given* options – established by forces or circumstances external to us – is not true freedom at all. True freedom, for Hegel, consists in not having our options set for us by something (or someone) else. It will involve our freely choosing or identifying ourselves with the conditions which make freedom possible.

Hegel tells us that true freedom must will itself. This sounds like an odd claim, but it is in fact quite simple. Freedom, to be free, must not only choose this or that option, but must always choose in such a way as to safeguard or perpetuate freedom. However, Hegel argues at length in *The Philosophy of Right* that freedom is only possible under certain conditions. As discussed earlier, true freedom only comes about when human beings have achieved true self-consciousness. But this is not only an historical process, it is a socially-situated one: the realization of our nature as free and self-determining is something that occurs only in societies that have achieved self-understanding through the development of cultural forms such as art, religion and philosophy. True freedom, therefore, must always involve willing or choosing the social conditions that make our self-awareness, and thus our freedom, possible. In other words, paradoxically, true freedom involves *willing our determination* (choosing or affirming it).

Hegel's position really amounts to the dialectical overcoming of the traditional dichotomy of freedom vs. determination (or 'free will vs. determinism'). I said earlier that freedom to choose from a number of options established by forces external to us is not true freedom. Therefore, one might object to Hegel by asking how we can become truly free by 'willing our determination'. After all, true freedom, for Hegel, consists in not having our options determined for us by something (or someone) else. But in society, my options are *mostly* determined for me by others! Hegel's answer is that this situation is inevitable: society does constrain us, but those constraints simultaneously make our lives, our character, and our self-understanding possible. They also open up various determinate ways in which we can express ourselves and our capacity to choose. If we affirm this, then society and its constraints are suddenly no longer something alien and constraining. We have chosen, in essence, to identify ourselves with society, and thus what 'determines' us is no longer something external. Willing our determination becomes self-determination.

In short, Hegel is telling us that instead of seeing the social conditions of our freedom simply as *limiting* us, we must also see them as that which makes us who we are, and that which makes possible the options we freely choose from in life. The society I live in may limit me in various ways, but might some of those limitations be beneficial, and might some of them make it possible for me to realize my various potentials and even to attain happiness? In modern society we live with countless laws and regulations of all kinds, and sometimes we may yearn to 'return to the primitive'. But how could I even conceptualize the idea of 'returning to the primitive', or any other philosophical idea for that matter, except in a modern society that has removed from me the burden of securing my day-to-day survival and sustenance? Yes, we are determined – but our determination makes possible who we are and what we could become. So long as we see it as 'limiting' us in some negative sense we are unfree, because we live in a state of resistance to what must be. True freedom, again, can be achieved only in choosing to accept this determination: in identifying with this world around us and understanding it as making possible our very selves. Hegel's most penetrating and profound treatment of human freedom occurs in his last published work, *The Philosophy of Right*. See also **civil society**; **ethical life**; **history and Philosophy of History**; *Philosophy of Right*; **state**.

— G —

genius (*der Genius*)   In the Anthropology division of Hegel's account of Subjective Spirit he discusses the 'feeling soul': a welter of sensations, impressions and intuitions, without any firm distinction between the subjective and the objective. In this highly obscure section, Hegel claims that when the individual is at the level of feeling soul, it is possible for another subject to exercize a 'control function' over it. Hegel calls this its 'genius'. This can occur in at least two ways. First, early in life, when the child lives at the level of feeling soul, another individual (such as its mother) may play the role of genius. However, it is also possible for adult individuals to regress, for brief or extended periods, to the level of feeling soul. In such a state, another individual may control them and become their genius. This concept is crucial for comprehending Hegel's discussion of psychic abnormalities such as animal magnetism and insanity. See also **animal magnetism**; **anthropology**; **feeling soul**; **insanity**; **Philosophy of Spirit**; **Subjective Spirit**.

God (*der Gott*) Hegel frequently states that God is the true subject matter of philosophy. In his manuscript for the *Lectures on the Philosophy of Religion* (1824), Hegel writes that 'God is the one and only object of philosophy . . .' and that 'philosophy is theology' (LPR I, 84; VPR I, 3–4). In a famous passage of *The Science of Logic*, Hegel states that the Logic 'is to be understood as the system of pure reason, as the realm of pure thought. This realm is truth as it is without veil and in its own absolute nature. It can therefore be said that this content is the exposition of God as he is in his eternal essence before the creation of nature and a finite Spirit' (Miller, 50; WL I, 33–34). Finally, in the *Encyclopedia Logic*, Hegel states that both philosophy and religion hold that, 'God and God alone is the truth' (Geraets, 24; EL § 1).

Nevertheless, Hegel's idea of God is quite different from that of ordinary believers, and the place of God in his philosophy is both complex and controversial. To begin with, Hegel rejects the traditional idea that God transcends the world. Instead, he holds that nature is part of the being of God, and that God is truly actualized or realized in the world only through human consciousness. Furthermore, because Hegel holds that history is the story of the development of human consciousness, he also claims that in a sense God himself develops over the course of time. Hegel thus replaces the traditional conception of God as existing apart from creation, perfect and complete, with one which claims that God only truly becomes God *through* creation.

To fully understand what God is for Hegel, we must begin with the Logic, which is essentially an attempt to articulate the formal structure of reality itself. It is not, however, a mere catalogue of concepts (like Kant's Categories of the Understanding). The Logic is a systematic whole in which each element is what it is in relation to all the others, and all are necessary elements in the whole. It culminates in Absolute Idea, which is understood to 'contain' all the preceding categories as, in effect, its definition. Absolute

Idea is a purely self-related idea; in fact, it is idea of idea, in which all distinction between subject and object has been overcome.

Hegel speaks of Absolute Idea as 'the Idea that thinks itself' (Geraets, 303; EL § 236), and he explicitly likens it to Aristotle's concept of God: 'This is the *noésis noéseós* [thought thinking itself] which was already called the highest form of the Idea by Aristotle' (Geraets, 303; EL § 236 A). The argument of Hegel's Logic establishes that Idea is the Absolute, which contains all fundamental determinations within itself and is related to nothing else, only to itself. Furthermore, Hegel's philosophy attempts to demonstrate that everything is intelligible as an expression or concretization of this Idea. Therefore, Hegel believes that his Logic articulates the inner truth latent within the theology of Aristotle (and other philosophers), as well as the understanding of the ordinary man: God (or Idea) is a supreme being, everywhere yet nowhere (immanent and transcendent), from which all other things derive their being.

However, the Idea of the Logic is still *merely idea*: it is, in effect, 'God in himself', or God implicit. As Idea it is real or objective, but only in the sense that it is not a subjective creation of the human mind. Nonetheless, it lacks concretization in the world. Hegel believes, in fact, that nature must be understood precisely as Idea concretely expressing or 'externalizing' itself (and doing so eternally). Higher still than nature, however, is human Spirit and its achievement of self-consciousness, in which the subject reflects on itself as object or, to put it the other way round, the object becomes the subject. Either way, the subject-object distinction is overcome. Thus, Spirit – self-aware humanity – constitutes for Hegel the most adequate, concrete embodiment of the Idea that 'thinks itself'. In humanity, Idea truly comes to know itself through our philosophical reflection on the Logic. This is why he tells us that in the Logic we are merely given 'God as he is in his eternal essence *before the creation of nature and a finite Spirit.*' Hegel's language here must be understood as figurative: he does not believe that *first* comes Idea, *then* nature, *then* Spirit. Rather, he holds that Idea is eternally 'embodying itself' as nature and Spirit.

Another, less 'mystical' way to put the above is simply to say that the Logic constitutes a kind of formal ontology which can be used to understand the reason or rational order inherent within reality. Nevertheless, it is almost irresistible to employ a mystical way of speaking in trying to understand Hegel's conception of God. One reason for this is precisely that his conception has so much in common with how mystics have understood the divine, in both the Western and Eastern traditions. (Hegel himself defined mysticism simply as an older term for 'the speculative', Geraets, 133; EL § 82 A.) Like Meister Eckhart, for example, Hegel rejects any firm distinction between the infinite and the finite, or God and the world. Hegel's argument for this is one of his most brilliant: if the infinite stands opposed to (or distinguished from) the finite, then it is *limited* by the finite and cannot be genuinely infinite! Therefore, the 'true infinite' for Hegel can only *contain* the finite. To put this in theological terms, God cannot be understood as strictly separate from the world – or vice versa. Instead, we must understand God to contain the world, in the sense that it is a moment or aspect of God's being. Thus, Hegel's understanding of God has rightly been described as *panentheism*, which translates literally as all-in-God-ism: the belief that the world is within God. God is not reducible to nature, or to Spirit, for we have seen that God is also Idea, which transcends any finite being. However, nature and Spirit are, in addition to Idea, necessary moments in the being of God. The claim that God requires the world or requires creation goes against the orthodox theologies of all three of the major monotheist faiths (Judaism, Christianity and Islam), which hold that God is absolutely independent of creation and would have lost nothing if he had not created.

Furthermore, Hegel is notorious for having claimed that his philosophy reveals the inner truth of the Holy Trinity of Christianity – the religion which he claims to be 'absolute'. Briefly, the Trinity is Father, Son and Holy Spirit. For Hegel, the Father represents Idea-in-itself, 'prior to creation'. The Father/Idea must 'freely release' himself/itself as otherness. This occurs in nature, and so nature corresponds to the Son, the Idea 'made flesh'. The Holy Spirit, of course, represents Absolute Spirit, which is humankind come to consciousness of itself and of nature as an expression of Idea. Thus, in Absolute Spirit we 'return to the father'.

Because Spirit is one of the moments of God's being, and because it is truly in Spirit that Idea as self-thinking thought is 'actualized', students of Hegel often wonder if he has not really made man into God. This was what was claimed by the 'young Hegelian' Ludwig Feuerbach (1804–1872), who insisted that if Hegel had truly understood himself he would have realized that his philosophy leads to this conclusion. (Feuerbach heartily approved of this and is sometimes cited as one of the founding fathers of 'secular humanism', which holds that there is nothing in the universe that is higher than humanity.) This is not, however, an accurate understanding of Hegel's philosophy. As noted earlier, Hegel's heterodox theology rejects any firm distinction between God and the world. The world becomes a necessary moment in God's being, with God/Idea understood essentially as a 'process', rather than something static, final and complete. God/Idea continually 'expresses itself' as the world, and one moment in this process is its coming to consciousness of itself through self-aware Spirit. Like all beings, we are an embodiment of Idea, but because we are self-aware, Idea achieves consciousness of itself through us. Humanity, therefore, is a necessary, consummating moment in the being of God – but still only one moment. God as Absolute Idea – 'God in himself' – still exists quite independently of finite human beings. Without the consummating moment of Absolute Spirit, God/Idea would be 'incomplete', but Idea would still express itself in the form of nature.

Hegel understands all talk of God, and religious discourse in general, to be a figurative way of expressing philosophical truths, utilizing myths, images and metaphors (what he calls 'picture-thinking'). Nevertheless, Hegel continually slides back and forth between philosophical and theological language, as I have done above. See also **Absolute Spirit**; **Aristotle**; **Boehme, Jacob**; **Christianity**; **faith and knowledge**; **Idea**; **infinity**; **mysticism**; **picture-thinking**; **reason**; **religion and Philosophy of Religion**; **speculation**; **theology**.

ground (*der Grund*)   In Hegel's *Encyclopedia Logic*, the category of ground appears in the Doctrine of Essence, following the discussion of identity and difference. 'Ground is the unity of identity and difference', Hegel tells us. 'It is essence posited as totality' (Geraets, 188; EL § 121). Hegel argues that the concepts of identity and difference, rather than being polar opposites, actually involve one another. In fact, the identity of something is constituted through its differences from others, and the differences between things are just their identity. These opposing yet interdependent concepts seem, in a way, to cancel each other out, and so Hegel says that 'they fall to the ground' (*Sie gehen hiermit zu Grunde*; Geraets, 188; EL § 120). He is using a pun to make the transition to ground.

In philosophy, 'ground' typically means the basis or reason for something. When Hegel speaks of ground as unifying identity and

ground

difference he is in fact indicating that identity and difference only have meaning within some larger whole or system, in which concrete claims about identity and difference would become meaningful. The identity of each member of a system is determined through its place within the whole. This amounts to saying that each member is what it is through its differences from other members; but all are what they are through being contained within the same whole. The identity of the whole itself is constituted through its internal differentiation. As is the case with a number of other categories in the Logic, ground foreshadows Hegel's account of the Concept and, ultimately, of the Absolute Idea, which is precisely the sort of systematic whole just described. (In the 'addition' appended to paragraph 121 of the *Encyclopedia Logic*, Hegel tells us precisely this: see Geraets, 190.) The true 'ground' of everything will turn out to the whole itself. At this point in the Doctrine of Essence, the whole is only dimly prefigured as some sort of explanatory principle 'underlying' things, to which they must be referred.

In *The Science of Logic*, Hegel's treatment of ground is far more complex. First, the transition to ground is via Hegel's discussion of contradiction (which follows his discussion of identity and difference). Second, Hegel goes into much greater detail concerning the different forms of ground, subdividing his treatment into Absolute Ground, Determinate Ground and Condition. The complexities of his discussion are too involved to do justice to here. Suffice it to say that when we reach the idea of condition, we realize that the true 'explanatory ground' is the whole itself. The condition for all things being what they are and acting as they do is their relation to everything else; their place within the whole, the formal structure of which is set out in the Logic. See also **Essence, Doctrine of**; **identity and difference**; **Logic**; **whole, the**.

— H —

habit (*die Gewohnheit*)   In Hegel's account of Subjective Spirit, in the subdivision entitled 'Anthropology', he maintains that the concept of habit or habituation is involved in the transition from feeling soul to actual soul. This transition is, in essence, the move from being human in an undeveloped, quasi-infantile fashion, to becoming a true, self-possessed individual. In order for this to be possible, we have to achieve mastery over our bodily functions and feelings. In other words, that which is natural in us must be brought under the discipline of habit: 'first nature', if you will, must be constrained by 'second nature'. For Hegel, this is the first step on the way to the achievement of truly human personality, and all that has the potential to follow from it (such as, at the highest level, the development of the intellect and of self-knowledge). Hegel tells us that 'if I want to realize my aims', if I want to actualize my human potential and the higher levels of Spirit, I must tame the natural within me. 'My body is not by nature fitted to do this; on the contrary, it immediately performs only what conforms to its animal nature. The purely organic functions are not as yet functions performed at the behest of the mind. For this service my body must first be trained' (Wallace, 146; PS § 410 A). See also **actual soul**; **anthropology**; **feeling soul**; **natural soul**; **Spirit**; **Subjective Spirit**.

history and Philosophy of History (*die Geschichte; die Philosophie der Geschichte*)   Hegel's understanding of human history is one of the most important and influential parts of his philosophy. He sees history not as a series of random or contingent events, but as having a pattern and a goal towards which it is moving. For Hegel, history is the story of the progressive achievement of human self-consciousness, which is simultaneously the realization of freedom. Unlike all other creatures, whose natures are mostly fixed and unchanging, humans determine themselves, and our degree of self-determination depends upon the degree of our self-understanding. If we are unaware that we have the capacity to determine ourselves and our destiny, if we imagine we are constrained by factors which (in reality) could be overcome, then for all intents and purposes we are not free. Potentially we are free, because we still have the ability in principle to come to realize that our capacity for self-determination is greater than we think it is. Still, if we lack this realization, then in fact we are unfree; our potential for freedom has not been actualized, because we are still mired in an impoverished conception of ourselves and our abilities. History is the story of how humanity comes to the realization that in a sense we choose to be what we are. This realization frees us: it causes us to become what we always already have been; to make our potential freedom actual.

Thus, when Hegel claims that freedom and self-consciousness go hand-in-hand, he is really making the strong claim that if a people is not conscious of its fundamental nature as free and self-determining, *then in fact it is not free*. This gives Hegel a standard to evaluate different cultures and different historical periods. After all, cultures differ in the degree to which they recognize human beings as free and self-determining. In many cultures throughout history, only certain individuals were regarded as free. The most extreme example would be cultures with despotic regimes, in which essentially only the ruler is regarded as a free being, and all others are seen as his property. Still other cultures may recognize only a subset of humanity as free. For example, the Greeks practiced slavery. They regarded only citizens as free, whereas women and slaves were seen as unfree. Many peoples have recognized the freedom only of their own kind, and have regarded other peoples as less than fully human, and less than free.

Hegel's Philosophy of History surveys the different historical periods and different cultures, essentially showing that there is a progression of consciousness through time: as a race we began in a state of relative unconsciousness, but over time we have come to greater awareness of our true nature as self-determining. Hegel argues that Christianity is responsible for introducing the idea that *all* human beings are free – and possess thereby an innate and inviolable dignity. According to the Christian teaching, all men are 'equal in the sight of God'. Further, in the person of Christ, the human and the divine (the absolutely free and self-determining being) actually coalesce. Historically, it is Christianity, therefore, that is responsible for raising our consciousness of who and what we are, and thus for helping us to see that we are all (potentially) free. Nevertheless, this has only occurred in the West. One of Hegel's more controversial claims, in fact, is that other cultures still lag behind the West, in that they have not yet progressed to the realization that all human beings are free and self-determining. True freedom, for Hegel, is achieved through membership in the modern, Western state, in which all are equal before the law, individuals are free to choose their occupation, laws are codified and publicly accessible, and the voice of the people is heard in government.

Because Hegel sees the goal of history as our coming to consciousness of our freedom, an implication of his position is that history has a climax or, we could say, a consummation. Again, Hegel believes that Christianity introduced us to the idea that all humans are free, and that this realization has culminated in the modern, Western state. However, it took the *philosophical* understanding of Christianity really to make the nature of our freedom explicit. In fact, some have argued that for Hegel humanity *truly* achieves consciousness of its freedom through his philosophy. Hegel is, after all, the first philosopher to discover the rational order within history itself. He is the first philosopher to tell us that the story of mankind itself reveals to us our true nature: history is the tale of our gradual self-creation, and of our realization that it is our nature to be self-creating. If philosophy is really the human attempt at self-understanding, and if history is the story of our struggle to understand ourselves and actualize our freedom, then history is consummated, and freedom achieved (at least in principle) when a fully adequate philosophy comes on the scene.

As a result of this, in recent years it has been claimed that Hegel teaches a doctrine of 'the end of history', and that there is such a thing as a 'post-historical age'. This idea originates with the Russian philosopher Alexandre Kojève, who gave a series of lectures on Hegel in Paris in the 1930s. Many years later the American neo-conservative thinker Francis Fukuyama popularized this idea in a series of articles, and in a book entitled *The End of History and the Last Man* (1992). However, as many Hegel scholars have pointed out, there is little basis for the idea that there is an 'end of history' in Hegel's texts (and still less for Kojève's claim that Hegel believed history ended with Napoleon). However, as we have already seen, Hegel clearly believes that there comes a point where history's goal of human self-consciousness is achieved (at least in the West). Progressivist neo-Hegelians (like Fukuyama) maintain that now that the truth about humanity has been revealed, inevitably other cultures will come to realize this truth and affirm universal human freedom. But there is little reason to believe that Hegel thinks that this has to happen. Unlike Marx, Hegel maintains that it is impossible for philosophy to predict future historical events.

history and Philosophy of History

In setting forth his Philosophy of History, Hegel utilizes a great deal of complex terminology that is frequently misunderstood. Again, Hegel asserts that there is a rationally-intelligible pattern to history; history is governed by an inherent order which is gradually displaying itself in time. Hegel has various ways of referring to this order: he frequently calls it 'reason', but he also refers to it as 'the Idea', 'World Spirit' and 'the universal'. The sheer variety of terms he uses causes readers problems, but so does the fact that he seems to hypostatize some of them. In other words, he seems often to speak of reason, the Idea or World Spirit (especially the latter) as if it were a kind of divine being overseeing the course of history. However, his language is deliberately figurative.

'Idea', for Hegel, refers to the Idea of the Logic, which is a purely self-related concept (and the final, all-inclusive category of the Logic). Hegel sees nature as embodying this Idea, but not fully. Self-related Idea can be adequately embodied only in a self-related mind – in other words, in the self-consciousness of human Spirit. However, as we have seen, self-consciousness is achieved through the course of history. Therefore, history is the story of the progressive actualization of Idea through human consciousness. Hegel's term 'the universal' is roughly equivalent to Idea. When Hegel speaks of 'reason' in history what he is referring to is the dialectical unfolding of historical events, which, in a certain way, mirrors the dialectical unfolding of the Idea in the Logic. For Hegel, reason is always dialectical, and it is not just a feature of our minds but of reality itself. Hegel is famous for speaking about the 'cunning of reason' in his Philosophy of History. This is a figurative way of saying that in history finite individuals act for their own finite ends, but in doing so they unwittingly bring about the realization of the Idea or reason. Finally, Hegel's 'World Spirit' refers simply to Objective Spirit as it displays itself in history. For Hegel, Objective Spirit is Spirit expressing itself as societal forms and institutions. These are understood as more or less adequate depending on the degree to which they affirm and make possible the expression of freedom. Thus, we can see in history the march of the World Spirit, as progressively more and more adequate forms of social organization present themselves.

Finally, something must be said about the alleged 'historicism' that is often attributed to Hegel. In *The Philosophy of Right* Hegel tells us that 'philosophy . . . is its own time comprehended in thought', and that 'It is just as foolish to imagine that any philosophy can transcend its contemporary world as that an individual can overleap his own time or leap over [the statue of] Rhodes' (Nisbet, 21–22). Commentators have often charged that there is a tension in Hegel's thought between this 'historicist' claim about the limitations of philosophy, and Hegel's claim to have found 'absolute truth'. In reality, however, this tension is merely apparent. Hegel *does* claim that no philosophy may overleap its time, but he also claims that he is living in a unique time in which it is finally possible to know the objective truth about history and humanity itself. He can say this because, as we have discussed, in his own time the goal of human history has been consummated.

To employ an analogy, when climbing a mountain we only see part of the mountain and surrounding terrain at each stage of the climb; our perspective is determined by what part of the mountain we happen to be clinging to. But this is also true of the perspective of the man who makes it to the very top. His perspective is also determined by the part of the mountain he is on: but his perspective is superior to all others, because from the top he is able to perceive the entire mountain and surrounding terrain, *and* evaluate the progress of all others making the same climb. Thus, Hegel can truly say that all philosophy is 'its own time comprehended in thought,' *and* claim to have discovered absolute truth, for his own time is the time in which Absolute Knowing has become possible.

In his published writings, Hegel's theory of history is present in *The Phenomenology of Spirit*. Though that work does deal with certain historical events and the meaning behind them, it is not a philosophy of history *per se*, but rather a kind of philosophical anthropology. Hegel gave lectures on the Philosophy of History in Berlin in 1822, 1828 and 1830. An edition of these lectures was published six years after Hegel's death under the title *Lectures on the Philosophy of World History* (*Vorlesungen über die Philosophie der Weltgeschichte*), and this text is our primary source for Hegel's thoughts on history. (A second German edition was brought out by Hegel's son, Karl, in 1840, and a third edition appeared in 1917 under the editorship of Georg Lasson.) See also **Absolute Spirit; Christianity; 'cunning of reason'; freedom; Idea; Marx, Karl; Objective Spirit; reason; Spirit; 'slaughter-bench of history'; state; world-historical individuals; World Spirit.**

Hölderlin, Friedrich (1770–1843) Johann Christian Friedrich Hölderlin is considered today to be one of the greatest German poets. He

Hölderlin, Friedrich

was a student at the theological seminary in Tübingen, where he became close friends with Hegel and Schelling. Like his friends, Hölderlin's time at the seminary was marked by a strong interest in the philosophical idealism of Kant, and the political idealism of the French Revolution. The three friends felt that they were moving toward some great climax in Western history that would see the birth of a new, more enlightened society. Unlike many Enlightenment enthusiasts, however, they did not champion materialism and secularism. Instead, they felt that faith and reason needed to be reconciled through a new spiritual awakening in Europe.

It was during Hölderlin's time in the seminary that the so-called 'pantheism controversy' took place, centering on a work by Friedrich Jacobi in which he quoted Lessing as having praised Spinoza. Widely regarded as an atheist, Spinoza had in fact argued that nature and mind were different attributes of the same divine being. Thus, he came to be understood by more sympathetic readers as a pantheist (someone who finds God in all things, especially in nature). Hegel, Schelling and Hölderlin were all drawn to Spinoza and to pantheism. One of the attractions of his philosophy was that it seemed, perhaps, to provide some way to overcome Kant's rigid dichotomy between appearance and reality – as well as a way to overcome the mechanistic materialism popular at the time. The three friends were so enthused by Spinoza's philosophy that they adopted a Greek 'pantheist' motto, *hen kai pan* ('one and all' – i.e., the many is one), which Hölderlin inscribed in Hegel's yearbook of 1791. The poetry Hölderlin wrote while at Tübingen contains few allusions to Christian doctrine, and instead a kind of 'pantheistic paganism' predominates. In a letter to his mother dated February 1791, Hölderlin relates that he has immersed himself in works by and about Spinoza. Indeed, it may have been Hölderlin who encouraged Hegel and Schelling in their interest in Spinoza.

Like Hegel and Schelling, Hölderlin was a Swabian, born in the Duchy of Württemberg, and was influenced by the Pietist tradition of that region. Württemberg Pietism contained a strong element of millenarianism, the belief in a coming transformation or perfection of the world. It is this influence that may have contributed to the enthusiasm of the three friends for the French Revolution. It has also been argued that Hölderlin was influenced by the so-called 'speculative school' of Württemberg Pietism, as represented by figures like F. C. Oetinger and P. M. Hahn. Hölderlin wrote *Hyperion*, his only novel (and the major work published during his lifetime) in the years 1792 to 1799. Scholars have argued for the influence of Swabian speculative Pietism on this work, and on Hölderlin's poetic theory.[12] Like many of his contemporaries, Hölderlin was also a great admirer of classical Greek culture. In particular, he had a fascination for the Orphic and Dionysian mysteries. Alan Olson writes that Hölderlin, and also Hegel (at this stage of his development), were both 'convinced that the future of Germany, especially its political unification, depended upon the generation of a common spiritual bond among its people – a *Volksreligion* [i.e., a religion of a nation or people] wholly independent of the alien, imported orientalism of Christianity.'[13]

There are no references to Hölderlin in Hegel's writings (by contrast, there are numerous references to Schelling). Nevertheless, it is undoubtedly true that Hölderlin exercized an influence on him. After leaving the seminary, Hegel took up an unhappy post as tutor to a family in Berne, Switzerland. In 1796 he learned through Hölderlin that a more attractive post might be available for him in Frankfurt, where Hölderlin was then living. Hegel soon made arrangements to join his friend in Frankfurt. Hölderlin had also been making a go of it as a private tutor, but with disastrous consequences. He beat one of his charges, the ten-year-old son of Charlotte von Kalb, and was dismissed. Hölderlin's next post was in the household of the banker Jakob Friedrich Gontard, where he soon fell in love with his employer's young wife Susette, and she with him. Hegel – for whom Hölderlin felt great affection, and on whom he depended – was roped into acting as a go-between, relaying messages between the young lovers.

In addition to this intrigue, however, the two old friends had conversations which were to have a profound impact on Hegel's intellectual development. Since leaving the seminary, Hölderlin had attended Fichte's lectures in Jena, and he communicated his enthusiasm for post-Kantian philosophy to Hegel, along with his nascent ideas about its shortcomings. While in Berne, Hegel had written essays towards the development, essentially, of a new 'Kantianized' Christianity. His conversations with Hölderlin persuaded him to change direction. Hölderlin's conviction that it was his task as a poet to fashion a new language for the modern age also persuaded Hegel to write in a new way. The result is that by the end of his Frankfurt period Hegel was beginning to write in the unique (and, to be honest, sometimes infuriating) style for which he has become famous.[14]

Sadly (but predictably) Hölderlin's affair with Susette Gontard went badly, and the poet began showing signs of mental instability. This must have been very painful for Hegel, and may be one reason for his silence on Hölderlin. In 1806, Hölderlin was confined to a mental institution and released a year later, though he had been declared incurable. He lived out his remaining years in the home of an admirer, the carpenter Ernst Zimmer. Hölderlin died in 1843, forgotten by his family and by most of the world. It was really only in the following century that his work would receive the attention it deserved. Although Hegel never mentioned Hölderlin in his work, he remembered his friend with affection for the rest of his life. Years later in Berlin, invited to lunch by the Crown Prince, Hegel only came out of his shell when Princess Marianne asked him about Hölderlin. The Princess recorded in her diary that Hegel spoke of his old friend with great fondness. See also **faith and knowledge**; **Schelling, F. W. J.**

— I —

Idea (*die Idee*) The Idea is one of the most important concepts in Hegel, and one of the most frequently misunderstood. To clear up one misunderstanding immediately, there is nothing personal or 'subjective' about Idea; it is not, in other words, 'my idea', and it is not confined to the minds of individuals. Hegel is not a subjective idealist. Idea, for him, exists objectively.

Hegel's principal discussion of Idea is in the third and final major subdivision of the Logic, the Doctrine of the Concept. In *The Science of Logic*, Hegel designates the Doctrines of Being and Essence 'Objective Logic', and the Doctrine of the Concept 'Subjective Logic'. To put matters as simply as possible, though the categories of being and essence deal with 'the objective' they are also categories of thought, or concepts. In the Logic, the distinction between thought and being (or reality) is overcome, and its concepts are just as much categories of thought as they are of the real. In the Doctrine of the Concept, Hegel treats not this concept or that, but the nature of the Concept *as such*.

The Doctrine of the Concept deals with *ideas about ideas*, beginning, under the section 'Subjectivity', with a re-thinking of the traditional categories of logic. Under 'Objectivity' Hegel deals with concepts which represent basic ways of understanding objects, and objects in their interrelations. 'Idea' is the final subdivision of the Doctrine of the Concept. The dialectic of Idea reaches its climax with the category of Absolute Idea, in which the distinction between subjectivity and objectivity is finally overcome. Absolute Idea is literally idea of itself; idea of idea. Hegel, drawing on Aristotle's description of God, calls it 'thought thinking itself' (Geraets, 303; EL § 236 A). At this point the system comes to closure and perfect completeness: in a sense, it even contains an account of itself. The entirety of the Logic, in fact, is ideas about ideas. Thus, in the end the Logic becomes literally and explicitly what it has been all along: thought thinking thought, or idea conceiving of itself.

The whole of the Logic has served as the argument for Idea, and it is with Idea that Hegel's articulation of the whole or the Absolute is completed. In fact, Hegel tends to treat 'the Absolute' and 'the Idea' as interchangeable terms. If we think of the Idea merely as a category, or division, of the Logic this will seem confusing, as Hegel also refers to the Absolute as 'the whole'. This confusion vanishes, however, once we know that Hegel understands all the preceding categories of the Logic as immanent within Absolute Idea, since all the earlier categories are, again, the argument for it. Idea, properly understood, is the whole itself (at least it is the whole of the Logic, which identifies, in a sense, the 'formal structure' of all of reality).

Idea is not a static overcoming of subject and object, however. It is thus a mistake to think of it as if it were an 'idea' in the sense of a piece of information, fixed and complete. Hegel conceives of Idea as a dynamic overcoming of subject and object – closer to an *act*, than to an 'idea' in the ordinary, mundane sense. In truth, this dynamism is to be found in the whole of the Logic. Hegel sees the dialectic not as his creation, but as something that unfolds itself in the medium of pure thought, via the *conflict* of concepts. While we who work through the dialectic of the Logic may see Absolute Idea as its 'result', in fact Hegel understands the Logic as Absolute Idea's 'self-specification'. If, as stated earlier, the Logic is the argument for (or, we could also say, definition of) Absolute Idea, then all the 'preceding' categories are, in a sense, aspects or moments of Absolute Idea. For Hegel, the Logic is not a book: it is a self-generating system that is in fact the core of reality itself. Hegel's two versions of the Logic are attempts to express this system, which is continually creating itself in all its

Idea

internal, conceptual differentiations, both in the realm of pure thought or philosophy, and in the natural and human worlds, which are its 'embodiment'.

We can achieve a better understanding of Idea by looking a bit more closely at the beginning of the Logic. Just as we must understand all the categories of the Logic as immanent within its final category, it is also the case that the entirety of the Logic can be understood as immanent in its beginning. Hegel tells us that the Logic is a circle and that the end returns to the beginning. What the Logic actually begins with is an indeterminate immediacy which Hegel initially names 'pure being'. It is indeterminate because it is neither subject nor object. Hegel is quite clear that the Logic cannot begin with any determinate conception of a subject or object, because philosophy cannot simply presuppose the truth or reality of anything. Thus, the Logic requires a very special sort of thinking which is a kind of *pure thought*, devoid (at least at first) of any determinate content. (This is just precisely what Hegel calls 'Absolute Knowing' at the conclusion to *The Phenomenology of Spirit*, the text that prepares the way for the Logic.) This pure thought develops itself through the whole of the Logic, culminating, again, in Absolute Idea. We begin with a knowing that *cancels* the distinction between subject and object – and we end with Absolute Idea, which is the *unity* of subjectivity and objectivity. We begin with a knowing that effectively has no idea of what it is at all (no presuppositions about itself and what it is doing); and we end with a knowing that has become object to itself, it knows itself as idea of idea. The end returns to the beginning, though the movement from beginning to end involves the self-specification of Absolute Knowing into the myriad forms of the Logic. The goal of the whole system (and, Hegel thinks, of reality itself) is *implicit* in the beginning and, in a way, known immediately: the sublation of subject and object.

In the Logic, Hegel's treatment of Idea has three moments: life, cognition and willing, and Absolute Idea. The following very briefly summarizes Hegel's complex discussion of these ideas. The transition to life is via the concept of teleology, which is the final category of 'Objectivity'. (Hegel says that 'it is the realization of purpose that forms the passage to the Idea', Geraets 273; EL § 194 A2.) Teleology conceives objects as self-differentiating, self-sustaining systems. The paradigm for such systems is the Logic, or Idea itself. However, the examples most ready-to-hand would be living organisms. Hence, Hegel calls life 'the immediate idea'. In living things, sentience involves bringing external reality inward – as when an animal perceives another creature, via a perceptual 'representation'. Sense, in effect, duplicates the world in subjectivity, or we might say that in sense the objective becomes subjective, or inwardized. This is the first, most primitive indication of something like 'soul' opposing itself to nature. However, animals are not able to reflect on their own life and the nature of their consciousness. In higher-level cognition, however, this does become possible. To say that life is the 'immediate idea' means that it is the idea that is *there*, expressed or embodied concretely, but not aware of itself. In cognition, we are capable of turning inward and knowing the world in relation to ourselves. Willing, on the other hand, does not cognize the world, it is 'concerned to *make* the world finally into what it ought to be' (Gereats, 302; EL § 234 A; my emphasis). In short, both cognition and willing are processes of bringing the object into relation or conformity with the subject. But we are not consciously aware that this is what we are doing.

In Absolute Idea, however, we reach the standpoint where the subject recognizes itself in the object explicitly. Absolute Idea is literally idea of idea, or 'thought thinking itself'. Hegel states that:

> The defect of life consists in the fact that it is still only the Idea *in itself*; cognition, on the contrary, is the Idea only as it is *for itself*, in the same one-sided way. The unity and truth of these two is the Idea that is *in* and *for* itself, and hence *absolute*. Up to this point the Idea in its development through its various stages has been our ob-ject; but from now on, the Idea is its own ob-ject. This is the *noèsis noèseòs*, which was already called the highest form of the idea by Aristotle. (Geraets, 303; EL § 236 A; italics in original.)

In Absolute Idea subject has become object and vice versa; it is idea of itself.

But if we ask how, concretely, we come to recognize this identity, it is through seeing the 'filling' of Absolute Idea, the entire conceptual scheme of the Logic, reflected in nature. Or, more specifically, it is through seeing all of nature as intelligible only as a kind of concretized approximation to Absolute Idea itself, which in fact is only truly embodied in human thought. In the Philosophy of Nature, Hegel states that we come 'to find in this

idealism

externality only a mirror of ourselves, to see in nature a free reflection of Spirit . . .' (Miller, 445; PN § 376 A). In short, Absolute Idea is 'actualized' in our coming to see that self-thinking thought is the meaning and objective of reality itself. See also **Absolute; Absolute Idea; Absolute Knowing; being, nothing, becoming; Concept, Doctrine of the; idealism; Logic; subjectivity, objectivity, idea; sublation; whole, the.**

idealism (*der Idealismus*) The sense in which Hegel is an idealist is very often misunderstood, so let us begin with the sort of idealism Hegel does *not* espouse. 'Subjective idealism' is normally understood to be the theory that reality consists entirely in our perceptions and ideas; that there is, in short, no objective reality apart from our minds. This is the position often ascribed to Leibniz and to Berkeley. However, both Leibniz and Berkeley insist that our perceptions are 'objective' in the sense that they are somehow derived from or related to God's mind and God's perceptions. (In fact, no one in the history of philosophy has ever held the radically subjectivist position that 'reality just is *my* perceptions, or *my* creation'.) Kant, on the other hand, was a *transcendental* idealist: he believed that the way in which the objective world appears to us is partly a construction of the mind. What things *really* are apart from how we experience them is absolutely unknowable, Kant maintained.

Hegel's position is quite different from these, and is often termed 'Objective Idealism' (or sometimes, misleadingly, 'Absolute Idealism'). It traces its philosophical lineage back to Aristotle, who accepted the existence of Platonic forms but made them immanent in the world, by identifying them with the actualized function of an object or living thing. Hegel's Objective Idealism holds that Idea is ultimate reality, but that it expresses or 'externalizes' itself in the world of nature and finite Spirit. Hegel argues in the Logic that the Idea contains all determinations of being and is, in fact, the one true 'concrete' (thus turning on its head the standard understanding of ideas as 'abstract', and objects as 'concrete'). However, considered apart from its expression, it is *mere* idea.

Hegel sees all of nature as an imperfect 'embodiment' of Absolute Idea. Nature is a scale of forms understood as a progressive approximation to the self-related wholeness of Idea, with living organisms (self-maintaining, internally differentiated systems) at the apex. Thus, the *truth* of nature for Hegel is Idea. All finite beings are what they are only in terms of their place within the whole – in other words, only in terms of their relatedness to Idea. This is what Hegel means when he refers, in the *Encyclopedia Logic*, to 'the ideality of the finite', which he says is 'the most important proposition of philosophy, and for that reason every genuine philosophy is idealism' (Geraets, 152; EL § 95 A). However, Hegel is also very much a *realist* in that he believes that a world of material objects really does exist 'out there' (nature, he tells us, is an 'other' to Idea). He is also an idealist, however, because he holds that these objects have their being only in relation to Idea. (Much as Aristotle held that the things of the world derive their being from their relation to the self-knowing divinity – a theory which Hegel recognized as approximating his concept of the Absolute Idea's relation to nature.)

To repeat, Idea is only imperfectly expressed in nature. Self-related Idea only becomes concretely real when it is 'embodied' in a self-related thought. Thus, the ultimate expression of Idea is in human Spirit, specifically in self-consciousness or Absolute Spirit. Hegel understands Absolute Spirit – Absolute Idea concretized – as the *telos* or end of all of reality. Thus, all things have being and significance, for Hegel, only in their relationship to Idea. Human beings fully actualize Absolute Spirit as the result of a long, historical process – and so for Hegel the meaning of history is Idea as well. If we ask what Absolute Spirit knows that makes it absolute, essentially Hegel's answer is that it knows the Logic (at least insofar as Absolute Spirit is understood narrowly as philosophy). Hegel understands his Logic to be a delineation of categories that are simultaneously subjective and objective; i.e., the Logic is both a system of thoughts or concepts, and an account of the being of things. This means that for Hegel, there is an identity of thought and being; the structure of reality is identical with the structure of thought.

These are the primary reasons why Hegel is called an 'idealist': not because he denies the existence of an objective world, but because he insists that Idea is the *truth* of that world. The world is itself an expression of Idea. It exists so that it may know itself, and it does this, ultimately, through the philosopher who speaks the speech of Idea, the Logic. See also **Absolute Idea; Absolute Spirit; abstract and concrete; Aristotle; concrete universal; Idea; Kant, Immanuel; Logic; nature and Philosophy of Nature**.

identity and difference (*die Identität; der Unterschied*) One of the most famous and original claims in Hegel's philosophy is that the

identity and difference

identity of something is constituted through its differences from other things. Normally, we regard the concepts of identity and difference as utterly opposed. However, Hegel's speculative approach shows very convincingly that they are bound up with each other. For Hegel, to be something – to possess identity – really involves *not* being, or being different from other things.

Hegel claims that the identity of an object is not something that it possesses intrinsically, irrespective of its relations to other things. Quite the contrary: the identity of something is constituted in and through its relations to other things and their properties. The male is what he is in relation to females, through not being female. We may also say that a given male is what he is through not being other males; through possessing certain properties in different measure or degree, or simply through not possessing some of the properties of others. To be green is not to be any of the other colours on the spectrum. To be five-feet-wide is not to be greater or smaller than five feet. To be a rights-bearing citizen is an identity constituted through one's relationship to other individuals in one's society, one's powers or activities are limited or checked by other persons with differing aims.

Hegel's claim that identity involves difference is simply a consequence of his claim that identity consists in relations: x can be related to y only if y is different from x. Indeed, the act of identifying an object always involves at least implicitly differentiating it from others. In defining something we always locate the larger genus to which it belongs, then identify the *differentia* which marks it off from other members of that genus. Something akin to this takes place even on the level of simple visual perception, where taking an object *as* an object always involves differentiating it from its surroundings. To identify two things – as when we say that two objects are chairs – involves, at least at the subconscious level, first noticing their differences and then disregarding them, as when we say that one is wood and one is metal, but both are chairs.

Furthermore, individuals can be considered just in themselves to be identities in difference. A human being, for example, is a whole made up of numerous parts, many of which are composed of materials quite different from each other and which perform markedly different roles. The enamel of our teeth is quite different from the grey matter of the brain, stomach acid is quite different from bone, etc. Nevertheless, we understand these very different parts to co-operate in forming one identity, one whole which is composed of the parts yet is more than their sum.

Hegel's principal discussion of the concepts of identity and difference occurs in the Doctrine of Essence of the Logic. There, he not only discusses these ideas, but also offers a critique of the 'law of identity'. One of the classic 'laws of logic', the law of identity states that a thing is just what it is and is not what it is not. The law is often formulated as 'A is A', or as 'A is not not A'. Hegel does not 'deny' the law of identity, any more than he denies the law of non-contradiction (a frequent accusation levelled against him). In other words, he does not deny that things are what they are. However, he regards the traditional manner of understanding identity as defective – a product of the shallow, literal-minded thinking typical of the understanding. For Hegel, as we have seen, the identity of something reveals itself to consist of its differences from other things. Given this, we can say 'A is A' is at best a half truth. Rather than understand the identity of something as its relation to itself, Hegel understands it in its relation to others; in its not being others. See also **contradiction**; **Essence, Doctrine of**; **Logic**; **understanding**.

in-and-for itself   See **in itself, for itself, in-and-for itself**.

infinity (*die Unendlichkeit*)   Determinate being is finite being, and finite being naturally calls to mind the possibility of infinity. Hegel writes in *The Science of Logic* that 'finitude is only as a transcending of itself' (Miller, 145; WL I, 145). And he writes in the *Encyclopedia Logic* that 'the truth of the finite is rather its ideality' (Geraets, 152; EL § 95). In fact, Hegel's treatment of infinity is one of the most famous parts of his Logic, and justifiably so: his distinction between genuine infinity (*wahrhafte Unendlichkeit*) and spurious or bad infinity (*schlechte Unendlichkeit*) is one of his most profound insights.

In the Doctrine of Being of the Logic, Hegel argues that when we consider a finite something we are automatically led to think of its other, which limits it. This other, however, is what it is by not being an other – and so on, *ad infinitum*. This is what Hegel means by a 'bad infinity', and in fact it is what we normally think of as the infinite: that which simply goes on and on and on; an unending series of distinct, finite items which succeed one another without end. This is the infinity of the understanding, for it is generated simply by a negation: infinity is just the not finite, the unending. This infinity, Hegel argues, is fundamentally false. If the infinite is conceived simply as the not-finite, standing in opposition to the finite, then in fact it is *limited* by its opposition to the finite. But if the infinite is limited, it cannot truly be infinite! True or genuine infinity, therefore, cannot stand in opposition to the finite. This means that the only way that is left for the infinite to be genuinely infinite would be for it to *contain* the finite within itself. In other words, if the infinity of the infinite is negated by its standing in opposition to the finite, the only way for the infinite to be truly infinite would be for the opposition (or separation) between finite and infinite to be removed. The understanding finds this outrageous, and declares it impossible. But for Hegel there is a simple, speculative solution: the infinite can retain its infinity if, in effect, it absorbs the finite as its internal moments or internal differentiation. The shift here is from seeing the infinite and finite as externally related (which is how the understanding sees things), to conceiving them as internally related. The true infinite is infinite, then, not because it goes on and on, but because it contains finitude within itself and is thus not limited, restricted, or defined by anything outside itself.

The concept of the true infinite is extraordinarily important for Hegel's philosophy. In the Doctrine of Being of the Logic, it sets the stage for a major transition: to the concept of being-for-self, which Hegel describes as 'the infinite determinacy that contains distinction within itself as sublated' (Geraets, 153; EL § 96 A). Ultimately, Hegel will characterize the Absolute (the whole of the real) as precisely such an infinite which contains the finite within itself as its internal self-differentiation. The true infinite is also important for understanding Hegel's treatment of God (the equivalent of the Absolute). Traditional theology, Hegel holds, is fundamentally mistaken in claiming that the infinite God and finite creation must be absolutely distinct for, again, this distinction would actually cancel God's infinity. Therefore, God must 'contain' the world as a moment of his being; the infinite must contain the finite. See also **Absolute**; **being-for-self**; **Being, Doctrine of**; **concrete universal**; **determinate being**; **God**; **relation**; **speculation**; **Spinoza, Benedict**; **understanding**.

in itself, for itself, in-and-for itself (*an sich, für sich, an und für sich*) Kant is famous for having spoken of a 'thing-in-itself', which forever transcends our experience. We know only the appearances of things; what 'things-in-themselves' are (i.e., what they *really* are) remains, and must remain, a mystery for us. Most of the German philosophers who came after Kant considered this an intolerable (and untenable) restriction on our knowledge, and sought to overcome it. Hegel does so, in part, by showing that Kant's understanding of the 'in itself' is a product of reflective thinking, which absolutizes distinctions and fails to see their deeper connection. Hegel states that a thing considered 'in itself' is a thing considered in abstraction from its manifestations – purely in terms of its potentiality to become or to manifest itself in various ways. When these potentialities are actualized it becomes 'for itself'. What Kant failed to see is that the being of something consists precisely in all that the thing manifests itself as. In other words, the being of something is found in its appearances, not in the thing considered (artificially) in so far as it does not appear! For Hegel, we are not cut off from the reality of things – appearances give us that reality.

Essentially, what Hegel has done is to interpret the Kantian appearance/thing-in-itself distinction in terms of Aristotle's distinction between actuality and potentiality. For Aristotle when something is merely potential its true being is implicit ('in itself', as Hegel puts it). When that potentiality is actualized, the being of the thing is manifest (become 'for itself'). To use the classic example: the acorn is the oak tree merely *in-itself*. Though we might say that the acorn *is* the oak tree at an early stage of development, it is also legitimate to say that when it is merely an acorn the oak tree *is not*. When the implicitness or potentiality of the acorn is overcome and the oak tree comes into manifestation (and, thus, being), we may say that it has become *for itself*.

Hegel uses the terms 'in itself' and 'for itself' in a number of different ways, but usually to contrast the undeveloped, implicit being of something, with its developed, explicit and manifest being. In the *Encyclopedia Logic*, he gives the following illustration: '"man-in-himself" is the child, whose task is to not remain in this abstract and undeveloped [state of being] "in itself", but to become *for himself* what he is initially only *in himself*, namely a free and rational being' (Geraets, 194; EL § 124 A). Hegel also employs a third, rather puzzling expression, which expresses the unity of these two: 'in-and-for itself'. Essentially, something is in-and-for-itself when its potentialities have not just become manifest, but when they have become manifest *to it*. One might say that something is in-and-for itself when its being for-itself really is *for* itself: really is known to it. Thus, we can survey the course of human history and say that in the beginning our nature was 'in itself', unrealized. It gradually began to unfold itself – human beings began to realize or actualize their potential – and became 'for itself'. Hegel argues, however, that history reaches its consummation when we understand the whole process and see that it is precisely an unfolding of our nature as free, self-conscious beings. When that stage is reached, our nature is 'in-and-for itself': we are aware of what we are. Thus, in Hegel's Philosophy of Spirit, Subjective Spirit is Spirit in-itself; Objective Spirit is Spirit for-itself; and Absolute Spirit is Spirit in-and-for itself.

Hegel also uses 'in-and-for itself' to refer to the third division of the Logic, the Concept. He describes the Doctrine of Being (which deals merely with the simple externality of things) as 'the doctrine of the Concept *in-itself*'. The Doctrine of Essence gives us 'the *being-for-itself* and *shine* [*Schein*] of the Concept' (the inner truth of Being, which prefigures the Concept). And the Doctrine of the Concept gives us the Concept '*in-* and *for-itself*' (Geraets, 133; EL § 83). The Concept is the dialectical sublation of being and essence. When I work through the Logic I am, in fact, a being reflecting into myself, into my own essence. When I reach the stage of the Concept I become explicitly aware that I am doing this, for in the Doctrine of the Concept thought literally thinks itself. What it was in itself (potentially) has unfolded and become for itself (actual), and the system is completed when it comprehends this process *as* its own. See also **appearance**; **Aristotle**; **being-for-self**; **Kant, Immanuel**; **reflection**.

insanity (*die Verrücktheit*) In Hegel's discussion of Subjective Spirit, under the section entitled 'Anthropology', he offers his account of what he calls 'the soul' (*die Seele*), the part of ourselves that is largely unconscious, and not a function of self-conscious mind or intellect. We all begin our lives at this level, and in a certain sense it must be subdued in order for self-possessed, self-aware human personality to emerge. Within the subdivision 'Feeling Soul', Hegel discusses how, under certain circumstances, individuals can regress to identity with this atavistic part of the self. Hegel discusses animal magnetism and psychic phenomena such as clairvoyance as examples of this – but he also offers insanity as another instance in which such a regression takes place.

When an individual 'loses his mind', according to Hegel, he sinks down, wholly or partly, into an identity with the primitive level of drives and instincts, which most adult individuals have managed to suppress or to control. The result is that the individual not only loses self-control, but also any ability to see things objectively and rationally, since this is a function of the higher-level faculties of mind. Hegel's theory of insanity is similar to his theory of bodily disease in the Philosophy of Nature: he regards disease as a state in which one part of the organism 'separates' itself in some manner from the whole and works against the whole. Similarly, insanity often involves some idea or notion becoming 'dislodged' from the subject's experience and claiming for itself centrality, as well as immunity from rational evaluation or revision. Such is the nature of obsession.

Hegel's account of insanity is full of fascinating and often amusing case studies. His comments on the plight of the insane are eminently sensible and humane, and he praises Philippe Pinel (1745–1826) for his use of what has come to be called the 'moral treatment' of insanity. On Hegel's view, those who would help the insane must take advantage of whatever modicum of reason they still possess (only complete imbeciles, Hegel thinks, are beyond hope) and make them question their 'fixed ideas'. The insane must either reintegrate their ideas with the rest of the psyche in a positive way, or be gently led to reject them. Hegel's approach is highly eclectic, and opposes the rigid application of the same therapeutic approach to every case.

Hegel cites examples of patients whose derangement was entirely physical in origin. He also mentions approvingly certain cases in which patients have been cured through clever tricks played by their doctors. One man was cured of his delusion that he was the Holy Spirit by being placed in the same room with another madman, who proclaimed that it was impossible that he was the Holy Spirit, 'Because I am the Holy Spirit!' (Wallace, 139; PS § 408 A). See also **animal magnetism; anthropology; feeling soul; Subjective Spirit**.

'inverted world, the' (*die verkehrte Welt*) In *The Phenomenology of Spirit*, in the section on 'Consciousness', Hegel treats the 'scientific' approach of trying to grasp or understand particular things by positing the existence of forces or entities acting behind the scenes. What Hegel tries to demonstrate is that although this approach may be fruitful within a certain context, it ultimately fails to give us an account of why things are as they are, and is fundamentally vacuous. After discussing 'Force and the Understanding' Hegel introduces an apparent thought experiment involving what he calls 'the inverted world'. Here he suggests that we take the scientific approach of identifying laws of nature a step further. Suppose we reached a point, in fact, where we had posited that behind the appearances is a world (the 'real world') totally opposite to this one! Hegel writes: 'According, then, to the law of this inverted world, what is *like* in the first world is *unlike* to itself, and what is *unlike* in the first world is equally *unlike to itself*, or it becomes *like* itself' (Miller, 97; PG, 111–12; italics in original). What is sweet in this world is sour in the inverted world; what is black in this world is white in the other, and so on. Hegel's point seems to be that it really wouldn't matter what sort of explanatory forces or entities we posited as acting 'behind the scenes' to produce the appearances familiar to us, as long as the theory was internally consistent. In short, the whole approach of thinking we can grasp things through conceiving of invisible forces or 'laws' seems fundamentally empty and misguided. It is at this point that the 'scientific approach' breaks down, and Spirit realizes that it has not been a passive subject, but actively involved in shaping what it takes to be real. Hegel's discussion of the 'Inverted World' shows that there is something fundamentally subjective involved in our attempts (thus far in his discussion of 'Consciousness') to understand existence. At this point, the dialectic passes beyond 'Consciousness' to 'Self-Consciousness'. See also **consciousness; force and the understanding;** ***Phenomenology of Spirit***; **self-consciousness**.

judgement (*das Urteil*)   In the Doctrine of the Concept – the third and final division of the Logic – Hegel discusses the different forms of logical judgement under the section entitled 'Subjectivity'. In the Doctrine of the Concept, thought, in a sense, reflects on itself until, in the final category of Absolute Idea, perfect self-relation is achieved. In 'Subjectivity' this self-relation of thought first reveals itself through a concern with the different sorts of concepts, judgements and inferences that have been catalogued in the past by traditional logic.

Hegel's discussion of the universal, particular and individual leads him to a consideration of the classical judgement forms. These are essentially ways in which universal, particular and individual terms are related to one another through the medium of the *copula*: the verb 'to be' in such judgements as, for example, 'All S is P' or 'Some S are not P'. Traditionally, a judgement like 'This swan is white' is taken to refer to some existing thing or subject ('this swan') to which we have attached a predicate ('white'), which is a concept we have formed in our minds. Hegel argues, however, that this sort of interpretation of the judgement is typical of the understanding, which sees subject and predicate, thing and universal, as externally related. Furthermore, it implicitly claims that universals are 'subjective' ideas, mere mental categories. In fact, Hegel claims that what the judgement truly expresses is the self-differentiation of an objective universal. In the case of our example, 'this swan is white', what the judgement actually expresses is the self-differentiation of 'whiteness' into the many white things, including this swan. Hegel is treating the universal expressed in such judgements as a *concrete universal*, as a universal which 'contains' its particulars within itself, as its self-specification. What judgements like this really assert is that the meaning of the particular is to be found in the universal – its being is its relation to, or place within, the universal. Hegel tells us in the Encyclopedia Logic that '*every thing is a judgement*. That is, every thing is an *individual* which is inwardly a *universality* or inner nature, in other words, a *universal* that is made individual; universality and individuality distinguish themselves [from each other] within it, but at the same time they are identical' (Geraets, 246; EL § 167; italics in original).

Traditional logic also sees the different *forms* of the judgement as externally related. By contrast, Hegel sees the judgement forms as members of a self-specifying whole. He tells us that 'The various types of judgement must not be regarded as standing beside one another, each having the same value; instead, they must be seen as forming a sequence of stages, and the distinction between them rests on the logical significance of the predicate' (Geraets, 249; EL § 171 A). Hegel sees the judgement forms as existing on a continuum, each of them approaching, to one degree or another, a kind of ultimate judgement of strict identity in which the subject is identified with or absorbed into the predicate. The 'truest' judgement form for Hegel is really 'The Individual is the Universal'. This reflects the basic fact that for Hegel 'the true is the whole'. All judgements aim at truth, but ultimately the truth of anything can only be had in so far as we have been able to see in it the universal – i.e., to see it in terms of the whole. It is this 'absorption' of the individual into the universal that all judgement forms thus aim at, whether the judgers realize it or not. Obviously, in a judgement like 'This swan is white', this goal is only dimly realized.

Hegel's account of the judgement forms is typical of his desire to treat all topics in terms of the ideal of the concrete universal. Instead of simply *listing* judgement forms as traditional logicians have done (treating them as externally related particulars), Hegel treats them as members of a systematic, self-specifying whole – and as yet another instance in which human thought, even in its most mundane forms, aims at knowledge of the whole of reality. Hegel discusses at considerable length the judgement forms of traditional logic, which were classified under the four forms of Quality, Quantity, Relation and Modality (a classification scheme used by Kant in his 'Table of Judgements', but without anything approaching Hegel's speculative treatment). Hegel renders these as 'The Qualitative Judgement', 'the Judgement of Reflection', 'the Judgement of Necessity' and 'the Judgement of the Concept'. The details of his account of these judgement forms are far too involved to do justice to here. See also **Concept, Doctrine of the**; **concrete universal**; **Logic**; **subjectivity, objectivity, idea**; **syllogism**; **truth**; **universal, particular and individual**.

justice   See **right**.

Kant, Immanuel (1724–1804)   Born in the city of Königsberg, Immanuel Kant ranks as the pivotal figure in German philosophy, and one of the greatest philosophers in history. For many years Kant considered himself a follower of the school of metaphysics inaugurated by Gottfried Leibniz, and systematized by Christian Wolff. In 1781, however, Kant published his masterpiece, *The Critique of Pure Reason*, in which he argues that metaphysics simply cannot make good on its claim to reveal to us the ultimate nature of reality. When he was writing this work, Kant had the Leibniz-Wolff philosophy squarely in mind as a paradigm case of the sort of metaphysics he was attacking, but his conclusions are troubling for all metaphysicians.

The foundation of Kant's argument in *The Critique of Pure Reason* is his claim that our experience of the world is formed by certain structures in the mind. These structures are not derived from experience; our minds come equipped with them, and they make experience possible. The implication of this is that the world as we perceive it is largely a construction of our minds, and that we only know things as they appear to us (what Kant calls *phenomena*). We can never know *things as they are in themselves* – things as they are apart from how they appear to us. Nevertheless, Kant says, though we cannot know *what* things-in-themselves are, we must nevertheless grant *that* they are, because there cannot be appearances without something that appears. A further, fascinating implication of Kant's position is that there may be all sorts of things that exist beyond our senses which we can never know, or which we would judge 'impossible' based on the limitations of the way our minds structure experience. In *The Critique of Pure Reason*, Kant terms his position 'transcendental idealism'. This created some confusion among readers, who missed the fact that Kant had insisted on the reality of things-in-themselves, and took him to be offering up a version of subjective idealism. In truth, what Kant meant by 'transcendental idealism' is the position that, though objects are real in the sense of existing 'out there', the way that they appear to us is a product of mental or 'ideal' structures ('transcendental', means, for Kant, that which pertains to the conditions for the appearance of objects).

Kant divides knowledge into three main areas: sensibility, understanding and reason. Sensibility refers to what he calls the 'forms of intuition', which are space and time. These are 'transcendentally ideal', not real. Space and time are not 'things', they are that *in which* things appear to us. Nor are they concepts we have formed through experience, because they are the pre-conditions of any experience whatever. They are, in Kant's terminology,

Kant, Immanuel

a priori: structures which exist prior to and independent of any experience. Understanding, for Kant, involves structures of the mind which determine specifically how objects in space and time will appear to us. Again, these are structures the mind comes equipped with, and are not concepts formed from our experiences. Famously, Kant includes in his work a table of twelve categories of the understanding, divided into four main headings: Quantity, Quality, Relation and Modality. The mind 'processes' experience in terms of these categories automatically, and when we consciously think about things we employ these categories, even if we are not aware of it.

Because Kant asserts that the categories of the understanding exist in order to process our experience, they therefore have meaning only when applied to sensory experience. Science, Kant tells us, deals only with the phenomenal realm, or the realm of appearance. This is what it means to say that science is 'empirical'. The implication of this is that science cannot tell us how things *really* are – it can only talk about appearances in a manner more sophisticated than commonsense. However, some philosophers have tried to go beyond the limits of science and to know things that lie beyond the appearances. This sort of philosophy is called today 'rationalism', but Kant dubs it 'dogmatism'. Specifically, Kant charges that dogmatism illegitimately employs the categories of the understanding beyond experience to try and speculate about three main subjects: God, the soul and the cosmos. (These correspond to the traditional division of metaphysics into Theology, Rational Psychology and Cosmology – all of which Kant declares untenable.) For example, arguments about the existence of God play on concepts like existence and non-existence, necessity and contingency, and inherence and subsistence, which are all *a priori* categories of the understanding, according to Kant. But God, the soul and the cosmos (existence considered as a totality) cannot be *experienced* at all, so all such reasoning about them using the understanding is futile. Philosophers who use the categories of the understanding in this way, applying them to 'objects' which cannot be experienced, are simply building castles in the air. And that is why it is notoriously the case that philosophers can't agree, and why so much philosophy seems like empty armchair arguments about what Arthur Schopenhauer would later call 'cloud cuckoo land'. This sort of false philosophy employs the 'pure reason' Kant critiques.

Kant believes that his argument effectively eliminates all reasoning about matters theological, spiritual and cosmological. Nevertheless, Kant also believes that the mind is so structured that inevitably humans will be led into this kind of illusory thinking. Reason – a 'higher' faculty than understanding – tries to achieve a higher-level synthesis of knowledge by seeking ultimate answers. Therefore, it is simply one of the peculiarities of reason that it will tend inevitably to fall into speculation about 'transcendent' matters. Kant attempts to demonstrate the futility of pure reason through his 'antinomies', which purport to show how there are two equally well-supported and absolutely-opposed answers to fundamental questions of metaphysics.

Many people in Kant's time took him to be arguing that God and the soul do not exist. To make matters worse, Kant maintained that there is no empirical basis for believing in human freedom: everything in the realm of phenomena appears to be governed by the principle of cause and effect. However, Kant maintains that human beings have a fundamental, pre-philosophical conviction that God and the soul exist, and that freedom is a reality. Further, he says, we *must* believe in these or else our moral convictions would be nonsense. Individuals are only morally responsible for things they have chosen (or not chosen) to do. If freedom did not exist, the entire notion of morality would be baseless – yet we tend to believe in our moral convictions as strongly as we believe in the reality of an objective world. And Kant has no wish to undermine our moral consciousness, which he believes is the very essence of human dignity. Thus, he maintains that although we do not *appear* to be free, we must nevertheless *believe* that we are free, at least in the realm which exists beyond appearance.

A further necessary element in our moral consciousness is the conviction, however dimly held, that ultimately good will triumph and be rewarded, and evil will fail and be punished. Even atheists tend to think this way – but Kant points out that this presupposes a tacit belief in something like divine providence, or a 'cosmic justice'. Thus, God too is a 'necessary postulate' of the moral consciousness, even though we cannot *prove* rationally that God exists. For Kant, God is a *noumenon*: an object which we believe exists, yet which by definition can never appear to us. Kant's views on ethics were set out more fully in his *Foundations of the Metaphysics of Morals* (1785) and *Critique of Practical Reason* (1788; often referred to as the 'Second Critique'). Kant examined aesthetic and teleological judgement in his *Critique of Judgement* (1790; the 'Third Critique').

Kant, Immanuel

The impact of Kant's ideas on philosophy was truly revolutionary. Most influential of all were his claims regarding the limitations of knowledge: how we know only the appearances of things, never things-in-themselves, and how these appearances are structured by the mind. Further, his claim that metaphysics violates these limits and is therefore illegitimate also stunned the philosophic community (or, at least, those philosophers who could understand Kant, since his works were quite difficult). The German philosophers who came immediately after Kant had an ambivalent relationship with him, however. On the one hand they admired him and were tremendously influenced by his ideas. On the other, they found Kant's strictures on knowledge, his idea of the thing-in-itself, and his rejection of metaphysics to be intolerable, and sought some way to answer him while preserving the many positive insights his work contained. In particular, they did not want to abandon transcendental idealism, and the project of identifying the *a priori* conditions of human knowledge. J. G. Fichte radicalized transcendental idealism and declared the world to be entirely the creation of an Absolute Ego. F. W. J. Schelling (at least in his earlier phases) accepted Fichte's version of transcendental idealism, but supplemented it with a philosophy of nature, arguing that nature exists so as to give rise to human subjectivity. Both subject and object, for Schelling, are specifications not of the Ego, but of an Absolute that exists beyond all distinctions.

Kant is important for Hegel in large measure because Fichte and Schelling are important for Hegel; his objections to Kant are, to a great extent, their objections, or are developments of their objections. Like Fichte and Schelling, Hegel rejects the unknowable thing-in-itself. He argues that appearances do not shut us off from things: appearances, instead, are just things displaying their being to us. Hegel maintains that what things are 'in themselves' is the Absolute – i.e., what things *really are* is the Absolute. But unlike Schelling, who makes the Absolute a quasi-mystical beyond, Hegel insists that the Absolute is in fact the whole of reality itself, considered as an organic, dialectically-articulated unity. Thus, all finite beings are 'appearances' of the Absolute. Hegel also takes Kant's ethical views to task, principally in his *Philosophy of Right*, arguing that it is fundamentally wrongheaded to believe, as Kant does, that ethics can be founded upon decontextualized, abstract rules.

Nevertheless, the positive influence of Kant is clear in Hegel's writings as well. In the Logic, for example, one can find Kant's categories of the understanding re-conceived. On one level, the Logic can be seen as an elaborate articulation of the entire realm of the *a priori* – with the difference that Hegel sees his categories not just as categories of the mind, but as an articulation of the being of things. Putting it into the terminology of modern philosophy, for Kant the *a priori* categories are exclusively epistemological, whereas for Hegel they are both epistemological and ontological. Hegel's Logic, in fact, allows him to save metaphysics from Kant, since the categorial ontology of the Logic is simultaneously an articulation of the 'highest' or most fundamental of all beings, the Idea, which Hegel makes equivalent (on one level) to God. See also **appearance**; **Fichte, J. G.**; **in itself, for itself, in-and-for itself**; **metaphysics**; **morality**; **Schelling, F. W. J.**

— L —

law of the heart (*das Gesetz des Herzens*)   Hegel discusses the 'law of the heart' in *The Phenomenology of Spirit*, in the first subsection of Division C: (AA) Reason. The context is a discussion of life in human society. Hegel deals first with the sort of mindset of a person with a purely selfish focus on the satisfaction of desires. An entire society made up of such persons would mean a perpetual war of all against all. However, such a mindset may mature into one in which we reflect upon this conflict among persons and limit the pursuit of our desires according to the dictates of our heart. A person with such a mentality may spurn conventional customs and mores as oppressive and 'false', when set against the 'truth' of the heart's feeling. Nevertheless, this approach is just as capricious, subjective and individualistic as the first. After all, one man's heart may easily come into conflict with another's, and what then? Also, Hegel argues that the customs and conventions flouted by the man of the heart make possible the very life he enjoys in society. Reason, therefore, must transcend this form of individualism as well. This is a recurrent theme in Hegel's writings on society and the individual: true freedom must always involve

Logic

acquiescing, in a fundamental sense, to the conditions that make society possible, for it is only in society with others that true human freedom emerges. This argument is developed most fully by Hegel in *The Philosophy of Right*. See also **ethical life**; **morality**; **Phenomenology of Spirit**; **Philosophy of Right**.

life, cognition and willing, idea   See **Idea**; **subjectivity, objectivity, idea**.

light (*das Licht*)   In the Philosophy of Nature, within the section 'Physics of Universal Individuality', Hegel discusses the nature of light, which he describes as the 'universal self' of matter (Miller, 87; PN § 275). Light is, as it were, a kind of infinite filling or propagation in space. Later, in the Philosophy of Spirit, Hegel will refer to light as 'physicalized space' (Wallace, 78; PS § 401 A). In the case of material bodies (and Hegel does not believe light to be composed of material bodies) space is only actualized in terms of a number of finite points. The 'filling' of space by light, however, is infinite and thus light infinitely actualizes spatial extension. Light is the 'universal self' of matter because in light everything reveals itself.

Light connects everything, and thus functions as a kind of overcoming of the force of repulsion – without, of course, actually affecting the position of bodies. Hegel's treatment of light is similar to his understanding of time: it is a kind of existent ideality; it is in the world, yet not a material thing. Hegel writes that 'Light is incorporeal, it is in fact immaterial matter; although this appears to be a contradiction, it is an appearance which cannot depend upon us' (Miller, 93; PN § 276 A). Because light, as pure manifestation, unifies all things without physically affecting them, it is an imperfect, spatialized reflection of the Idea. Light is also a prefiguration of philosophical thought which, grasping the Idea, sees everything as parts in a whole, but without physically affecting anything. See also **Idea**; **matter**; **nature and Philosophy of Nature**; **physics**; **space and time**.

Logic (*die Logik*)   Hegel published two versions of his 'Logic': the *Science of Logic* (*Wissenschaft der Logik*, 1812–16), as well as the so-called *Encyclopedia Logic*, the first book of his *Encyclopedia of the Philosophical Sciences in Outline* (1817). The former is verbose and obscure, the latter terse and obscure. In the account which follows (and in all entries in this volume dealing with the Logic), Hegel's remarks in both versions will be amalgamated, for the simple reason that 'the Logic' is not two books, but rather a single, conceptual content which its discoverer, Hegel, elaborated in two versions. The differences between these two versions have to do mainly with presentation: e.g., certain transitions or categorial structures are elaborated more fully in the *Science of Logic*, whereas in the *Encyclopedia* they are simplified. Except where indicated otherwise, in this entry – and in this entire volume – the term Logic is used to refer to the content of both texts in general, and neither in particular.

Lecturing on one of the early paragraphs of the *Encyclopedia Logic*, Hegel remarked that the subject matter of the Logic is truth (Geraets, 46; EL § 19 A-1). If we ask Hegel what 'truth' is, we find his most famous statement in *The Phenomenology of Spirit*: 'the true is the whole' (Miller, 11; PG, 15). In brief, for Hegel the truth of something is its place within the total system of reality. And what the Logic gives us, quite simply, is Hegel's account of the whole, of the formal structure of reality itself, its inner truth. The Logic is an account of pure categories or ideas which are timelessly true (Hegel tells us that what thought thinks in the Logic is 'what is eternal', Geraets, 47; EL § 19 A-2). But these categories are considered in complete separation from how they might be 'applied' to the sensible world. The categories of the Logic form an organic whole which is 'contained' in the final category, Absolute Idea (because, as we shall see, all the categories that precede Absolute Idea constitute the argument for it). Further, Hegel argues that Idea is God 'in himself'.

The Logic can be understood as a radically new form of metaphysics or ontology. Ontology is the study of what it means to be *as such*, whereas metaphysics studies the highest or truest of the things that *have* being. Hegel's Logic is, in fact, both a metaphysics and an ontology. The Logic is an account of being (or reality) as such, but it is simultaneously an account of the highest or most complete *individual being*, which Hegel refers to variously as the Concept, or the Idea, or the Absolute. So why did Hegel call this new metaphysics 'Logic'? A clue is to be found in the derivation of the term 'logic' from the Greek *logos*. In the Preface to the second edition of the *Science of Logic*, Hegel discusses the Concept as follows: 'This Concept is not sensuously intuited or represented; it is solely an object, a product and content of thinking, and is the absolute, self-subsistent thing, the *logos*, the reason of that which is, the truth of what we call things; it is least

Logic

of all the *logos* which should be left outside the science of logic' (Miller, 39; WL I, 19). Hegel's Logic is an account of this *logos*.

True to the spirit of Greek philosophy, Hegel's *logos* is *objective idea*: there is nothing subjective about Hegel's idealism, and it is worth repeating that the Logic must be understood as setting forth the ultimate categories of the real; it is not a discussion of subjective 'ideas' invented by human beings. In the *Encyclopedia Logic*, Hegel states that, 'ideas are not just to be found in our heads, and the Idea is not at all something so impotent that whether it is realized or not depends upon our own sweet will; on the contrary, it is at once what is quite simply effective and actual as well' (Geraets, 214; EL § 142 A). Hegel's Logic, in fact, promises to deliver knowledge of the objects of traditional, classical metaphysics (though Hegel radically re-conceives these objects). The Logic is simultaneously an account of the *formal structure* of God (the self-knowing Idea), the soul or mind (the living embodiment of Idea), and the Cosmos (the whole whose every part is an approximation to the being of Idea). It is thus at one and the same time a theology, rational psychology and cosmology. Hegel can accomplish this, however, because he has gone beyond classical metaphysics. He stands on the shoulders of the earlier German idealists, Kant, Fichte and Schelling.

The foregoing gives us a general idea of the aims of Hegel's Logic. The rest of this entry is devoted to a very brief, highly compressed sketch of its argument. The reader is encouraged to consult the entries dealing with the major divisions of the Logic for more details.

Hegel's Logic is divided into three major divisions: the Doctrine of Being, the Doctrine of Essence and the Doctrine of the Concept. To begin with the Logic, however, is to begin with Absolute Knowing, with which *The Phenomenology of Spirit* concludes. This work shows how, in Absolute Knowing, Spirit's goal of self-confrontation is achieved by developing an account of substance (or being) which is simultaneously subject. This is not actually set forth in the 'Absolute Knowing' section of the *Phenomenology*, however, but only in the Logic. As is well known, Hegel's Logic opens with the category 'pure being' (the first category of the Doctrine of Being). But this is not the first object or category 'known' by Absolute Knowing. Having cancelled the subject-object distinction, Absolute Knowing is, paradoxically, not really a type of knowing, or a property or activity of a subject at all. In reaching and realizing Absolute Knowing we do not 'know' anything.

Instead, we give rise to a pure indeterminate 'immediacy' which is *neither* subjective nor objective, but which will – through the self-development of the dialectic – mediate itself and reveal itself to be *both* subjective and objective. 'Pure being' is simply the initial name Hegel gives to this immediacy. This pure being, which is also pure or absolute 'knowing', appears again at the end of the Logic, in a transformed state, as the Absolute Idea, which is a self-related, self-determining idea. (Thus, the 'Absolute Knowing' of the end of the *Phenomenology* and the beginning of the Logic may be said to be a psychological depiction of the transcendence of the subject-object distinction, whereas the Absolute Idea at the end of the Logic is a purely logical, non-psychological expression of the unity of subject-object.)

The Doctrine of Being covers the most basic concepts involved when we deal with objects in their immediacy: i.e., how they present themselves to simple, unreflective consciousness. Hegel begins with the pure, empty immediacy of being and shows, dialectically, how it goes over into its opposite, nothing, and how this is reconciled by a further concept, and so on. In this way, Hegel derives all the categories of the first division of the Logic.

The categories of being, however, only partially and inadequately describe the whole. The surface givenness of things is not the entire truth. Therefore, Hegel's attempt to articulate the whole must of necessity go beyond (or beneath) the surface. This is exactly what is realized in the transition from being to essence. The Doctrine of Essence, accordingly, is an attempt to discover the inner truth that lies beneath appearances: essence is, as Hegel tells us, 'the truth of being' (Miller, 389; WL II, 3). The movement of the dialectic also undergoes a transformation in the transition from being to essence. In the Doctrine of Being categories are simply supplanted or replaced by others. In the Doctrine of Essence, however, we continually encounter categories which are paired with others. Hegel demonstrates that the relationship between these paired concepts is always far more ambiguous than ordinary commonsense takes it to be. The categories of essence appear or 'shine' (*scheinen*) in one another; each term is what it is only in relation to its complement.

The standpoint of essence is what Hegel calls 'reflection', which is closely related to his concept of the understanding. Hegel regards reflection as a very important philosophical standpoint. After all, in a sense the transition

Logic

from being to essence replicates the traditional philosophical transcendence of commonsense, and the search for a deeper truth. However, Hegel holds that reflection does not go far enough. It tends to set up conceptual dichotomies, and to adhere to them rigidly. It fails to reach the standpoint of speculation, in which appearances are seen not merely as something that veils a hidden truth, but as the self-display of the truth (or Absolute) itself.

The inherent problems with the Doctrine of Essence and with reflection necessitate the transition to the Doctrine of the Concept. Though Hegel calls the categories of being and essence 'Objective Logic', they are also categories of thought; they are concepts. (In the Logic, in fact, the distinction between thought and being, or thought and reality, is overcome, and its categories are both categories of thought *and* of the real.) In the Doctrine of the Concept – 'in Subjective Logic' – Hegel treats not this concept or that, but the nature of the Concept *as such*. In the Concept, we find that all the foregoing categories of being and essence have their true significance in being 'comprehended' by a self-related, self-determining idea.

In the Objective Logic of being and essence, categories are related to and determined by other categories. In the Subjective Logic of the Concept, however, categories are related *to themselves*. The Doctrine of the Concept deals with ideas about ideas, and reaches its dialectical climax with 'Absolute Idea', in effect the idea of idea itself. In the first division of the Concept, 'Subjectivity', Hegel completely re-thinks the traditional categories of logic. He begins with a consideration of the most basic concepts about concepts: universal, particular and individual. Hegel next turns to the different forms of judgement and the syllogism, treating their different forms as attempts, ultimately, to express the whole (recall that for Hegel 'the true is the whole'). In the succeeding subdivision, 'Objectivity', Hegel deals with concepts which represent our most basic ways of understanding the objective world: mechanism, chemism and teleology. Teleology describes a self-differentiating, self-sustaining whole which is, in effect, the objectified Concept. In the idea of teleology thought confronts itself in still another way, and reveals that the true end of objectivity is thought finding itself objectified within the world. In 'Idea', the third division of the Concept, the distinction between Subjectivity and Objectivity is overcome. Idea is object aware of itself, or, subjectivity that has itself as object.

Throughout the Logic, Hegel has been articulating the idea of wholeness or system. The transitions in the dialectic are made possible by the fact that each category is offered as a 'provisional definition' of the whole (or Absolute), but each turns out to be an inadequate, merely partial representation of it. We are able to transcend these partial standpoints because we have an implicit awareness of the whole at each stage. Still, every category may be understood as an amplification or supplementation of what has come before. Thus, everything after 'pure being' in some sense expands upon what it means 'to be' (this is the sense in which the Logic is ontology). Hegel is careful to tell us that his Logic is a circle; that the end returns to the beginning.

But exactly how does Absolute Idea (the end) 'return to' pure being (the beginning)? And how is Absolute Idea an account of the whole? Hegel tells us that the entirety of the Logic is an argument for Absolute Idea — the categories of the Logic form an organic whole which is 'contained' in Absolute Idea. Pure being is empty and indeterminate because it has no content. Absolute Idea, on the other hand, contains all determinations within itself: there is nothing outside it to determine it, so in a sense one can say that it is also undetermined. Yet, at the same time, it is *fully determinate* precisely *because* it contains all determinations within itself; it is self-determining. Absolute Idea is the true infinite.

Considered in itself, however, Absolute Idea is still 'merely idea'. Absolute Idea 'contains' within itself a complete system of ideas: it requires no other category or concept to complete it. However, on its own, Logic is formal and one-dimensional. To be fully realized, the Idea must 'express itself' in the world of space and time. In other words, for Absolute Idea to become truly absolute, it cannot abide simply in the realm of ideas: it must become 'embodied'. This occurs when Absolute Idea becomes actual in the world through an embodied thought which reflects on itself. Speaking figuratively, Absolute Idea 'strives' for realization in the world, and finds it only in Absolute Spirit — pre-eminently in the self-thinking thought of the philosopher.

Hegel tells us that the object of philosophy is God, and he identifies God with the Absolute Idea, just as Aristotle identified God with self-thinking thought. However, if this is the case, if God = Absolute Idea, it follows that Hegel must hold that God is merely formal and irreal. God 'in his eternal essence' (which the Logic unveils) is deficient. Spirit is a necessary moment in God's becoming fully realized in the world – in Absolute Idea's becoming true Absolute. To express Hegel's theory of the Absolute Idea achieving realization in the world, it might seem that he need only have written the Logic, and the Philosophy of Spirit. Hegel, however, also insists on including the Philosophy of Nature as a distinct branch of his system. The Philosophy of Nature covers the fundamental categories pertaining to the entire natural world, excluding mankind or Spirit, showing how they are intelligible when Spirit is taken as their *telos*, or ultimate goal. Hegel's aim is to work out a developmental account of reality as a whole, in terms of which everything is significant or intelligible. The *telos* of the universe is the Absolute Idea's realization in the world through the speculative activity of the philosopher, which is achieved through a long historical process. The non-human cannot, however, drop out of this picture as unintelligible. Thus, in Hegel's philosophy, the Logic leads to the Philosophy of Nature. See also **Absolute**; **Absolute Idea**; **Absolute Knowing**; **Absolute Spirit**; **Being, Doctrine of**; **Concept, Doctrine of the**; **dialectic**; *Encyclopedia of the Philosophical Sciences in Outline*; **Essence, Doctrine of**; **God**; **Idea**; **metaphysics**; *Phenomenology of Spirit*; **sublation**.

madness   See **insanity**.

Marx, Karl (1818–1883)   Karl Heinrich Marx was a German-Jewish philosopher and political economist. It is his ideas that form the foundation of the economic and political ideology known as communism (or 'scientific socialism'). Marx began his university studies at Bonn, and later transferred to the University of Berlin, where he was influenced by the 'Young Hegelians' (or 'Left Hegelians'). These men tended to be highly critical of the theological or metaphysical element in Hegel's thought. One of them, Ludwig Feuerbach, argued that God is simply a projection of human nature or human qualities. The Young Hegelians also opposed what they saw as the conservative tendency in Hegel, and often adopted radical agendas for social reform – or revolution.

The philosophy Marx subsequently developed involves a radical critique of capitalism, the social and economic system in which property is privately owned and products and services are traded in a market. Marx is also famous for his theory of history, which predicts that capitalism must of necessity be displaced by a more advanced, socially just system (communism) in which private property and the market will have been eliminated.

The early Marx offered 'humanistic' criticisms of capitalism. In the so-called 'Manuscripts of 1844' (or 'Paris Manuscripts') Marx argued that private ownership of the means of production and the division of labour lead to a condition he called 'alienation'. Under capitalism, the majority of people must sell their labour to a boss, who takes the product of their labour from them and sells it himself. Thus, under capitalism, our labour no longer belongs to us, nor is the product of our labour under our control. This is problematic, Marx maintains, because it is labour that principally characterizes our nature: we are the beings who take what is found in nature and transform it. Capitalism therefore alienates us from our very being as a species. According to Marx, it turns people into soulless, dehumanized automata who have little respect for themselves, or others.

Furthermore, since in a capitalist system the means of production is controlled by the few, this inevitably means that the many have no choice but to sell their labour to others (i.e., they do not work for themselves). Employers take the products of our labour from us, and pay us, as a wage, only a fraction of the profit they make from selling them. In short, under capitalism, workers are exploited, and the concept of exploitation is one of the central ideas in the Marxian theory. If we decide to quit our jobs and go to work for someone else, we will encounter much the same situation. Thus, capitalism produces a condition Marx called 'wage slavery'. We become not literal slaves, but *de facto* slaves nonetheless: forced to sell our labour to bosses who exploit us, labouring most of our lives at jobs that are deadening and often degrading.

Marx's solution to these problems is not to reform capitalism but to destroy it. One destroys it by eliminating the distinction between bosses and workers, and creating a classless society. This is only possible, however, if we shift from a system where the means of production is privately owned,

Marx, Karl

to one where it is owned publicly by the people themselves. In such a system, the profit motive would be largely eliminated. We would no longer work solely for our personal profit, but for the good of the whole. People would no longer have to compete for resources, and there would be no distinction between the 'haves' and the 'have nots'. Instead, Marx tells us that communist society would be ruled by the principle 'from each according to his abilities, to each according to his needs.' In other words, we would all labor to produce goods for society, and would receive in exchange all that we need not only to survive, but also to flourish. It was Marx's contention that under modern capitalism (and earlier forms of social stratification and exploitation) human potential has been stifled. He believed that once alienation and exploitation are eliminated, people would be free to realize more aspects of their nature.

Marx sees all history as the history of class struggle. In modern, industrialized, capitalist society there are essentially two classes: the *bourgeoisie*, the middle class who own the means of production, and the *proletariat* (or proletarians), the working class who live in thrall to the bourgeoisie. However, things have not always been this way. Under medieval feudalism, for example, the Church and the landed aristocracy ruled society, not the merchant class. Classes have always existed (though they have changed forms) and all history is the history of their struggle. Marx holds, further, that in all historical periods the nature of society has been determined by economic relations (or 'relations of production'). This theory is referred to by followers of Marx as 'historical materialism'. Culture, mores, and even religion, are merely a 'superstructure' reflecting underlying economic conditions. Marx is famous for having declared religion 'the opium of the people'. In other words, Marx believes that religion has functioned to distract people from the injustice under which they live, by promising them justice in the afterlife. It is for this reason that Marx's philosophy is atheistic.

Marx adapted Hegel's dialectic into a theory of history which claims that different, succeeding phases in history come about through the negation of earlier phases. Although something like this view is to be found in Hegel, Marx departs from Hegel radically in claiming that he can predict the next phase of history. He argues, in fact, that capitalism will of necessity be displaced by the social system he advocates. (This claim leads to a major problem for Marxists: how one can reconcile the call to revolution with the claim that change is destined to happen anyway.) Marx's support for his position depends upon economic arguments showing that the capitalist system is inherently unstable (Marx makes these arguments in his magnum opus, *Das Kapital*, the first volume of which was published in 1867). For example, he claims that capitalism inevitably leads to endless cycles of booms and busts; of plenty succeeded by poverty.

Marx believes that when the 'workers' revolution' comes it will appear in two stages. The first stage is that of the 'dictatorship of the proletariat', in which the working class will wrest control of the means of production, and of the entire society, from the bourgeoisie. It will be necessary for the workers (or those who represent them) to establish absolute power and to destroy all remnants of the capitalist system, including private property. Marxian theory predicts that the dictatorship of the proletariat will eventually give way to a stage of 'ultimate communism', in which the political state will simply 'wither away'. With exploitation and alienation eliminated, there will no longer be crimes motivated by material envy or despair, and thus, for example, no need for police. Of course, the state cannot simply wither away if it is surrounded by hostile, non-communist states. Thus, followers of Marx typically hold that true communism cannot be achieved in one place unless it is achieved everywhere else as well. Critics of Marxism therefore claim, clearly with some justification, that it is an ideology of world domination. Critics further point to the death and destruction wrought by communist regimes worldwide in the twentieth century (some estimates of the dead approach 100 million). Marxists point out, however, that these 'communist' regimes never advanced beyond the stage of the dictatorship of the proletariat; true communism, they say, has never been tried.

The question of Marx's relation to Hegel is a complex one. Hegelian terms like 'dialectic' were co-opted by Marx and his followers, with the result that the ideas of Hegel and Marx are frequently confused with each another. To compare and contrast the two in terms of essentials, both Hegel and Marx believe that human beings are social animals, who achieve true freedom only in society. Also, both men hold that a society dominated by self-interest and the pursuit of profit will result in the alienation and disenfranchisement of many people. However, Hegel believes that private enterprise is a basic freedom, and that self-interest can be tempered by social controls and institutions which foster civic-mindedness. Hegel would therefore reject Marx's contention that private ownership of the means of production must be abolished.

Hegel would also reject Marx's belief that dialectic can predict the course of history. For Hegel, philosophy is like the 'owl of Minerva' that takes flight only at dusk, commenting upon that which has already happened, and unable to predict the future. Further, Hegel would see Marx's understanding of religion and culture as reductive. For Hegel, religion is an expression of Absolute Spirit, a way in which we come to understand our own nature. The customs, mores and institutions of society also have this function (as Objective Spirit) and cannot be understood solely in terms of economic factors. For his part, Marx's criticisms of Hegel often rely upon a misunderstanding of Hegel's idealism as something that is decidedly 'otherworldly'. Marx fails, in short, to appreciate that Hegel is very much a 'this-worldly' philosopher, who tries to discern the inherent reason in nature, history and human society. See also **dialectic**; **history and Philosophy of History**; **'owl of Minerva'**; *Philosophy of Right*.

'master–servant dialectic' The so-called 'master–servant dialectic' is one of the most famous episodes in *The Phenomenology of Spirit*, and occurs in the section on 'Self-Consciousness'. Under 'Consciousness', the preceding section, Hegel covers certain fundamental ways in which the subject seeks to know objects. However, simple awareness of objects (in whatever form) cannot produce consciousness of self. This comes about, Hegel argues, not through *knowing* objects but through *acting* on them – acting to change or to overcome them. Human beings possess a basic will to alter objects in order to bring them into accord with the subject's wishes, and Hegel calls this will *desire*.

However, Hegel argues that true self-consciousness is only achieved when our desire is directed on other desires: on other beings like ourselves. We only attain self-consciousness in interaction with other human beings who reveal us to ourselves, and recognize and affirm us as human. This desire is so important to human beings that they are willing to risk death in order to win recognition from others. In the *Phenomenology* Hegel imagines a kind of primal, historical scene in which two individuals fight to *compel* recognition from each other. Inevitably, there will be winners and losers in such a contest: one will typically yield to the other. The winner becomes what Hegel calls 'master' (*Herr*) and the loser becomes 'servant'

(*Knecht*). The servant is essentially an individual who has chosen life over honour, or life over recognition. But a man who values biological survival more than recognition is, Hegel claims, in a real sense not truly human. The master is one who has triumphed over his 'instinct for self-preservation' and achieved a truly human ideal: he has won recognition from another individual. The servant has not won recognition from the master, as the master regards him as an inferior. However, the recognition the master has won from the servant is flawed for this very reason: the recognition of inferiors can hardly be very satisfying.

Though the servant serves the master, Hegel argues that all is not how it appears on the surface. In a real sense it is the master who is enslaved and the servant who becomes truly free. The servant labours for the master, and the master is free to enjoy himself. But the consequence of this is that the master *loses* himself in enjoyment, in his passions and desires. Thus, he seems to revert to a subhuman level. Meanwhile, through his labour, the servant works to transform nature. Given Hegel's position that the transformation of the objective world is one of the primary means to the achievement of self-consciousness, this means that in his service to the master the servant actually begins to advance in self-consciousness. The master, on the other hand, does not advance. Further, because the servant's work is not done in the service of his own desire, his forced servitude actually becomes a means to suppress his own natural passions and inclinations for the sake of something else. Ironically, the inhumanity of servitude becomes the path to the coming-into-being of the truly human. In working for the master, the servant creates science, technology and the arts.

Nevertheless, though the servant creates much, he is fundamentally unfulfilled: his desire for recognition remains unsatisfied. Hegel turns from the 'master–servant dialectic' to a discussion of the stages of development of what we can call the 'servant consciousness'. Specifically, Hegel deals with 'stoicism', 'scepticism' and 'the unhappy consciousness' as further manifestations of the servant's standpoint. These are all forms in which the servant seeks freedom and recognition, but always *in thought*, never in reality.

The 'master–servant dialectic' is probably the single most influential section of *The Phenomenology of Spirit*. It has been widely discussed by Marxian interpreters of Hegel, notably Alexandre Kojève. See also

matter

freedom; *Phenomenology of Spirit*; recognition; **self-consciousness; stoicism, scepticism, unhappy consciousness**.

matter (*die Materie*) In the Philosophy of Nature, in the division entitled 'Mechanics', Hegel's discussion of matter follows his discussion of space, time and motion. In truth, these concepts presuppose the concept of matter. Without material objects there is no space (no 'externality'), and no motion through space in time.

In *The Phenomenology of Spirit* Hegel writes that 'Matter . . . is not an existent thing, but is being in the form of a universal, or in the form of the Concept' (Miller, 292; PG, 144). Matter is not a thing – a distinct entity or a substance out of which things are made. Instead it is 'universal being' in the sphere of nature, because in that sphere what is real is 'material'. 'Matter' is just another way of talking about extension and spatial separation. Hegel states this outright: 'Matter is spatial separation' (Miller, 46; PN 262, A). The substantiality of matter consists specifically in its weight: 'matter itself is essentially *heavy*; this is not an external property, nor can it be separated from matter. Gravity constitutes the substantiality of matter; this itself is the *nisus*, the striving to reach the *center*; but – and this is the other essential determination of matter – this center falls *outside it*' (Miller, 45; PN § 262). What Hegel is alluding to in the last sentence is the material object's reference beyond itself, to another, more powerful body. This is a dim, mechanical reflection of the relationship of the Concept to its moments, and a prefiguration of the organism and the relation of its parts to the whole.

Gravity negates the mutual externality of material objects. Hegel speaks of matter's tendency to collect together to form primitive systems. He also refers to gravity as attraction and opposes it to repulsion (here we have the material expression of the categories of attraction and repulsion in the Logic). Repulsion is the force which works against matter's tendency toward homogeneity, and maintains a universe of separate material beings. Without this frustration of attraction, matter would fuse together and nothing else would ever come into being. Once again, negativity plays a role in the actualization of the Idea's higher purposes. See also **mechanics; nature and Philosophy of Nature; repulsion and attraction; space and time**.

measure   See **quality, quantity, measure**.

measureless, the (*das Maßlose*)   In the Doctrine of Being of the Logic, Hegel argues that the categories of quality and quantity must be supplemented by measure. Beings are what they are through possessing qualities in some quantity, but qualities may not exist in just any quantity. Some standard must establish a quantitative range in which the qualities of something can exist. The idea of a limit to quantity leads us to measure.

In a subsection of 'Measure' entitled 'Nodal Line of Measure Relationships', Hegel discusses the interdependence of quality and quantity in more detail, and how qualities are dependent upon measures. If quantity is altered beyond a certain measure or degree, qualitative change will occur. To put things in the abstract, quality A exists within a range of quantitative variations, but once we pass a certain 'node' A changes to B. If the variation continues, further on B changes to C, and so forth. Hegel uses a number of examples to illustrate this principle, drawn from a variety of fields. For example, in chemistry, alteration of the quantity of elements in chemical compounds will eventually lead to the coming-into-being of a different compound. The quantity of the elements of that compound can then be varied to produce still another compound, etc.

Here we have the 'bad infinite' (which first occurred under the discussion of quality) rearing its ugly head again. We can see that this process of overcoming quality-determining measure could be drawn out to infinity, at least in principle. As a result, Hegel argues that the dialectic has arrived at a new category: a continual passing of one quality into another without end. Taken as a whole, this process has no measure, no limit, and is hence the measureless. This measureless, however, emerges in Hegel's discussion as a new kind of whole: a substrate out of which determinate qualities and qualitied things seem to 'emerge' (not unlike the 'infinite' of the pre-Socratic philosopher Anaximander). The significance of the measureless is that with it we have arrived at the idea of a 'ground' of being which subsists beneath the surface appearance of things. As a result, it is at this point that the dialectic shifts to a consideration of essence. See also **Being, Doctrine of**; **Essence, Doctrine of**; **infinity**; **Logic**; **quality, quantity, measure**.

mechanism, chemism, teleology

mechanics (*die Mechanik*)   The Philosophy of Nature consists of three main divisions: 'Mechanics', 'Physics' and 'Organics'. Mechanics treats inert matter which is acted on and caused to move by external forces. The first category of mechanics is space, which Hegel tells us is the idea of externality as such. What chiefly characterizes nature, and makes it different from the Idea of the Logic, is the irreducible fact of one thing being external to, or physically opposed to another. Hegel explains that time is not a container in which things exist, rather it is the *idea* of their negation or overcoming in space. Time is 'the Concept itself that is there' (Miller, 487; PG, 524): time is, in a sense, an existent ideality, not a 'thing'.

Hegel moves from here to a discussion of place and motion. What all of these concepts presuppose, however, is the concept of matter: without material objects there is no 'externality' (of one thing to another), and no motion through space in time. Essentially, matter for Hegel is just another way of talking about extension and spatial separation. The primary characteristic of matter is gravity, which negates the mutual externality of material objects through attraction. This means that matter is characterized by a tendency to come together to form larger wholes – a prefiguration, at this primitive, mechanical level of the organism. However, if there were not a negative, repulsive force opposed to the attractive force of gravity, matter would simply fuse together and organic being would never arise.

With what Hegel calls physics we leave behind the 'externality' of mechanics and penetrate into matter itself, to discover that the individual material body must be understood as containing *within* itself a complex order and structure. See also **matter; nature and Philosophy of Nature; organics; physics; space and time**.

mechanism, chemism, teleology (*der Mechanismus, der Chemismus, die Teleologie*)   In the Doctrine of the Concept – the third and final major section of the Logic – thought reflects for the first time consciously and explicitly on thought itself, and all the earlier categories are understood to have their significance just in being comprehended by a self-aware thought. The first subdivision of the Concept, 'Subjectivity', concerns itself with the most basic forms of judgement and inference (thought, literally, about the forms of thought). In the following subdivision, 'Objectivity', Hegel turns to an account of the 'Objective Concept', which specifies itself into three forms: mechanism, chemism, and teleology. In the simplest possible terms, what Hegel canvasses in this section is certain fundamental ways in which we understand the 'objective world'. In fact, as we shall see, these consist ultimately in a projection of the fundamental nature of Idea itself. Hegel is leading up to the third and final division of the Concept – Idea – which is the unity or sublation of subject and object.

Mechanism, chemism and teleology are homologous with the major divisions of the Logic (Being, Essence and Concept), and they look forward to the major divisions of the Philosophy of Nature: Mechanics, Physics and Organics. Mechanism sees the world as a set of externally related particulars, in which each makes no intrinsic difference to the others. Their arrangement may change, and some may come and go, but it makes no difference to the nature or makeup of the individuals. What Hegel is describing here sounds straightforwardly like the image of the 'clockwork universe' which was dominant in the science of the Enlightenment period, and still constitutes what many people think of as a 'scientific' way of looking at things. It also sounds quite a lot like what he calls mechanics in the Philosophy of Nature – but in this section of the Logic Hegel is describing certain general 'styles of thinking' applicable to more than just observable, physical nature. In other words, it is possible to apply this 'mechanical' way of thinking to many things, even to ideas. (The political philosophy of Thomas Hobbes, for example, essentially views society and human relations on the mechanical model.) It can become the basis of an entire worldview – and, it is important to note, within certain delimited contexts it is an entirely legitimate way of looking at things. (However, only teleology, as we shall see, is adequate to conceiving the whole.)

Chemism consists of the recognition that objects cannot be entirely understood as related externally: objects have affinities or antipathies for others, and these relations and interactions may cause them to change in fundamental ways. In short, in chemism we recognize that objects are internally as well as externally related: objects are what they are, in their intrinsic nature, through their relations to other things, and interactions between objects can result in changes to that intrinsic nature. Hegel calls this chemism because he has in mind the sorts of chemical changes which can be produced when one substance is brought into contact with another. The substances do not remain pristine, ever the same: their intrinsic nature may be broken down or changed through the chemical process. (It is this turn towards concern with an 'inner' dimension of things that makes

metaphysics

chemism homologous with essence in the Logic.) Still, chemism is intended to have a wide application, beyond the 'chemical'. For example, we find chemism present in the complexities of human relationships, where persons express affinities or antipathies for others, and may undergo radical, internal changes (e.g., to their tastes, attitudes and temperament) as a result of forming relationships of various kinds.

In teleology, the object is seen as a whole of distinct but internally-related parts. Thus, teleology seems to 'synthesize' or sublate elements of mechanism and chemism. The object is 'once more a self-enclosed totality', as in mechanics, 'but it is enriched by the principle of difference which came forth in chemism' (Geraets, 273; EL § 194 A). In the object seen 'teleologically', each part is internally related to, and dependent upon every other. Each can be seen as the 'end' of the others: that for the sake of which they perform their function. For example, in the human body it is possible to understand all the different organs and processes as intersecting so as to keep the heart functioning, or the brain functioning. But it is equally the case that each is the 'means' to the others. Thus, the heart and the brain can also legitimately be seen as functioning for the sake of the other parts. In truth, all the organs exist for the sake of the whole – and the whole only has being through the parts. The term 'teleology' connotes purpose, but the only purpose Hegel has in mind here is the self-maintenance of the whole, which has no purpose beyond itself. The ideal of the whole expressed in teleology is self-sustaining, and self-differentiating. Hegel tells us that mechanism and chemism are the Concept *in itself*, whereas with the emergence of purpose in teleology we have 'the Concept as it exists *for itself*' (Geraets, 277; EL § 200 A). Thus, in the idea of teleology, thought confronts itself in yet another way, and reveals the true point of 'Objectivity': thought discovering itself objectified within the world. From teleology, Hegel passes to the final category of the Concept and the climax of the Logic: Idea, which is the Concept *in-and-for itself*. Idea is object aware of itself, or, subjectivity that has itself as object. See also **Concept, Doctrine of the; Idea; in itself, for itself, in-and-for itself; Logic; mechanics, physics, organics**.

metaphysics (*die Metaphysik*)   Recently, it has become controversial to claim that Hegel was a metaphysician. Metaphysics is often defined as the study of the fundamental nature of reality. However, when scholars challenge the idea that Hegel has a metaphysics they generally have in mind something more specific – something closer to what Kant called 'special metaphysics', which involves the study of certain fundamental entities which do not appear to the senses, such as God and the soul. 'Non-metaphysical' readers of Hegel specifically reject the idea that his philosophy contains such a metaphysics.

In the Introduction to the *Encyclopedia Logic*, Hegel writes that, 'Speculative Logic contains the older logic and metaphysics; it preserves the same forms of thought, laws, objects, but it develops and transforms them with further categories' (Geraets, 33; EL § 9). The Logic is, quite simply, a transformation of the older form of metaphysics, one which unites 'special metaphysics' with ontology (or 'general metaphysics'). Ontology is the study of what it means to be *as such*, whereas metaphysics, again, is the study of the highest, truest, or most fundamental of the things which *have* being. More succinctly, ontology studies *Being* (as such), and metaphysics studies certain rather special *beings*. Hegel's Logic is both a metaphysics and an ontology simultaneously. The Logic is an account of what it means to be, but it is simultaneously an account of the highest or most complete individual being.

The first category of the Logic is Being ('Pure Being', or Being-as-such). However, this category is quickly left behind as the dialectic passes on to myriad others. This may give the impression that the Logic drops the subject of Being. Another way to look at the matter, however, is that the succession of categories that follow are in fact attempts to more adequately articulate the nature of Being, which appears initially in a thoroughly indeterminate form. The Logic culminates in the Absolute Idea, which is unique in that it is not an idea *of* something, nor is it somehow defined by contrast to, or relation with, other ideas. Absolute Idea is purely self-related (it is idea of idea), and 'contains' all the preceding categories which have led up to it (and which constitute, in fact, the 'definition' or articulation of Absolute Idea). In truth, Absolute Idea is an eidetic (idea-like), individual being; i.e., *it is* – and Hegel explicitly compares it to Aristotle's God. Thus, on one level we may understand the Logic straightforwardly as metaphysics: as the articulation of the 'highest' (or most paradigmatic) of all beings. The Logic, in fact, accomplishes all the aims of special metaphysics at one and the same time: it is theology, rational psychology and cosmology. The Absolute Idea gives us a formal, eidetic account of the nature of God (the self-knowing

metaphysics

individual Idea), the Soul (or Spirit: the living embodiment of the Idea), and the Cosmos (or nature: the whole whose every part is an approximation to the being of the Idea).

At the same time, however, the Logic may be understood as a formal ontology: an articulation not just of the nature of *a* being, but of Being, or what it means to be *as such*. For Hegel, things are what they are through their relation to the whole. All of reality is an organic, internally-differentiated system. The parts of this whole are the individual things we encounter all around us, including ourselves, and the Being of these things is their place within the whole. For Hegel, further, the systematic whole that is the universe just is an embodiment of the systematic whole that is Absolute Idea. Thus, another way to put this is to say that *things have their Being in their relation to Absolute Idea*. Absolute Idea is therefore not just *a* being, but the *idea* of Being as such.

In truth, the debate over whether Hegel's philosophy is metaphysical or non-metaphysical, metaphysical or ontological, or however one wishes to put it, is not only misguided, it rests on an underestimation of Hegel. In true dialectical fashion, Hegel's Logic overcomes and transcends these dichotomies.

Hegel's sublation of special metaphysics and ontology in the Logic is structurally analogous to Aristotle's solution to the problem of Being in the *Metaphysics*. In that text, Aristotle begins by asking about the nature of Being-as-such. However, the climax of his argument involves his discussion of God, the highest of the things that *have* Being, and his assertion that everything else that exists is 'imitating' God. Aristotle thus seems to change the subject from ontology to (special) metaphysics or theology. In fact he does indeed seem to be saying that the Being of things consists in their relation to one particular, necessarily existing being. In the twentieth century, Martin Heidegger famously objected to this shift from ontology to metaphysics, as an instance of a philosopher 'forgetting Being' and constructing an *onto-theology* (a theology masquerading as an account of Being-as-such).

In Hegel, we find an argument similar to Aristotle's: to be is to be a reflection of Absolute Idea, which is the most fundamental being there is. Nevertheless, Hegel does not fall into the same error Heidegger found in Aristotle. Hegel's Logic shows that the definition of Being-as-such *necessarily* leads to Pure Being's supplementation by other categories and, in fact, the articulation of an entire system. Taken as a totality, this system of categories – this 'definition of Being' – is a being. Hegel can thus be seen as not only overcoming the traditional distinction between special metaphysics and ontology, but also Heidegger's distinction between Being and beings, or the ontological and the ontic (a fact which Heidegger himself did not seem to appreciate). See also **Absolute Idea**; **Aristotle**; **being, nothing, becoming**; **God**; **Idea**; **Kant, Immanuel**; **Logic**.

mind   In older English translations of Hegel, *Geist* is often rendered as 'mind'. Two notable examples of this include J. B. Baillie's 1910 translation of *Die Phänomenologie des Geistes* as *The Phenomenology of Mind*, and William Wallace's 1894 translation of *die Philosophie des Geistes* (a subdivision of *The Encyclopedia of the Philosophical Sciences*) as *Hegel's Philosophy of Mind*. Today 'Spirit' is almost universally preferred as a translation of *Geist*. The reason is that the term 'mind' tends to be rather narrowly associated with the intellect (the thinking, conceptualizing, reasoning part of us), whereas Hegel's use of *Geist* has a much broader connotation than this. *Geist*, in fact, covers all aspects of human nature, including the lower, primitive parts of our consciousness (covered in Hegel's account of Subjective Spirit), the concrete expressions of our nature found in social institutions (Objective Spirit), and in art, religion and philosophy (Absolute Spirit). His treatment of what would be called today 'philosophy of mind' is to be found under 'Subjective Spirit', where he covers such topics as the senses, reasoning, imagination, memory and madness. See also **Absolute Spirit**; **Objective Spirit**; **Philosophy of Spirit**; **Spirit**; **Subjective Spirit**.

moment (*das Moment*)   Hegel sometimes uses the term 'moment' to refer to an 'aspect' of something, or, more technically, a part which is separable from the whole only in thought. The term is often used by English-speaking Hegel scholars. It appears again in the phenomenology of Edmund Husserl, who makes a useful distinction (helpful for understanding Hegel) between 'pieces' and 'moments'. A piece is a part which is literally separable, such as the carburetor in a car engine. A moment, on the other hand, is a part or aspect of something not literally separable. For example, hue, saturation and brightness are 'parts' of colour – but one could not literally separate these from each other. In Hegel's Logic, each category is a

morality

moment in the whole. Each is a part, but not a literal, physical part – and each derives its meaning from its place in the whole, and is thus not fully intelligible considered in separation from it. The Logic is an articulation of the whole, via a demonstration of the dialectical relationship between its moments. See also **dialectic**; **Logic**; **whole, the**.

morality (*die Moralität*) In *The Philosophy of Right*, Hegel's discussion of morality (a term he uses in a special, technical sense) follows his discussion of abstract right, which is essentially the 'classical liberal' view of society as founded upon a contract, existing for the narrowly-conceived self-interest of individuals. Hegel argues that the world of abstract right cannot maintain itself unless individuals are able to adopt a standpoint of impartiality (in fact, a *moral* standpoint) in which they set aside personal interests and apply universal principles – as in deciding a criminal case, and determining how a wrong-doer is to be punished. However, abstract right does not foster such impartiality, for it encourages individuals to think exclusively in terms of their personal interests.

In short, the system of abstract right is morally empty. The dialectic therefore passes beyond abstract right – right in its external or objective form – to morality, which deals with right as it develops itself in the subjective, inner life of the individual. (These two moments, the objective and subjective sides of right, will be reconciled in 'Ethical Life'.) In what Hegel calls morality, individuals look *within* for guidance. They look for it in the form of sentiments or conscience. Or they look for it in abstract, philosophical theories of morality which may have no relation to actual morality, as it is practiced in a concrete social setting. Hegel identifies Kant's ethics as one such theory, and he attacks it vigorously.

Freedom expresses itself in morality through the exercize of autonomous moral judgement: the subject insists that it will follow only its own feelings, or only those moral principles on which it has put its imprimatur; i.e., principles somehow derived from, or legitimated by its own nature. Essentially, Hegel's objection to morality is to point out that it is empty of content. How exactly is the subject supposed to derive ethical principles out of its own subjectivity? Hegel argues that Kant's principle of universalization does not generate concrete moral rules: 'the proposition "Consider whether your maxim can be asserted as a universal principle" would be all very well if we already had determinate principles concerning how to act' (Nisbet,

163; PR § 135 A). Furthermore, a clever enough person can universalize anything he'd like to get away with. This means that the moral standpoint can quite easily become the standpoint of pure evil – of the individual setting himself up as absolute. Hegel writes that 'Where all previously valid determinations have vanished and the will is in a state of pure inwardness, the self-consciousness is capable of making into its principle either *the universal in-and-for itself*, or the *arbitrariness* of its *own particularity*, giving the latter precedence over the universal and realizing it through its actions – i.e., it is capable of being *evil*' (Nisbet, 167; PR § 139; italics in original).

At a basic level we understand that ethical principles must be binding upon us: they must express what we *ought* to do, not what we *might* do if we felt like it. But it is seldom the case that some rule we have devised ourselves, or some 'feeling' can have this sort of binding force. In fact, ethics must consist in something more than subjects simply 'giving a law to themselves'. Ethics really requires a social setting and social institutions which concretize moral rules in terms of evolved customs and practices. The dialectic of the *Philosophy of Right* thus passes beyond morality to ethical life. See also **abstract right**; **ethical life**; **evil**; **Kant, Immanuel**; **law of the heart**; *Philosophy of Right*.

mysticism (*der Mystizismus*) Hegel's philosophy is often described as being in some way 'mystical'. Hegel himself says little about mysticism. Perhaps the most significant text is a remark appended to a passage in the *Encyclopedia Logic*, where Hegel says that 'the meaning of the speculative is to be understood as being the same as what used in earlier times to be called "the mystical" [*das Mystische*], especially with regard to the religious consciousness and its content' (Geraets, 133; EL § 82 A). Hegel makes similar claims, likening the speculative to the mystical in the *Lectures on the Philosophy of Religion* of 1824 and 1827. These statements are significant because 'speculative' is Hegel's term for his own philosophy; therefore he seems to be saying that his philosophy is mystical. In fact, he is saying this but only in a qualified sense. In the *Encyclopedia Logic* Hegel goes on to explain that the mystical is what transcends the understanding, which holds commonsense dichotomies to be absolute. Speculation is a higher level of thinking, for it goes beyond the oppositional thinking of the understanding through dialectic. Speculation, therefore, is mysticism simply because speculation, like mysticism, goes beyond the understanding.

Natural Religion

However, when mystics themselves assert that their knowledge goes 'beyond the understanding', they often mean that it is ineffable, or beyond the ability of human language to express. Hegel completely rejects the idea that the truth cannot be put into words. Furthermore, mystics sometimes claim that their knowledge is inexpressible because it involves a non-rational, non-verbal *experience* of the Absolute. Hegel rejects this as well. The speculative is the mystical for Hegel – but he believes he has eliminated the mystery in mysticism, and unveiled the truth in the language of philosophy. Nevertheless, Hegel's treatment of the mystics elsewhere also shows that he regards the content of their thought as identical in important respects to his own. His comments on Jacob Boehme and on Meister Eckhart, for example, show that he regarded himself as revealing the inner meaning of mystical claims. See also **Absolute**; **Boehme, Jacob**; **Christianity**; **reason**; **speculation**; **Trinity**; **understanding**.

— N —

Natural Religion (*die natürliche Religion*) Hegel discusses 'natural religion' in The Phenomenology of Spirit, in Subdivision 'CC. Religion,' which falls within the larger section he designates as Division C. All religion, for Hegel, is an attempt to express the Absolute Idea in sensuous terms, using images, myths and metaphors. What religion does not realize is that it is Absolute Spirit itself – the highest manifestation of human nature – that is the true expression or embodiment of Absolute Idea. Thus, all religious forms will somehow involve the *unconscious projection* of human consciousness into something exalted beyond the human. In natural religion, natural objects or nature itself is so exalted.

Hegel's treatment of natural religion involves him in discussing certain actual, historical religions. His discussion is frequently inaccurate and surprisingly superficial, owing mainly to the rudimentary state of scholarship on religion in his time. (Hegel read voraciously in all areas, but of necessity he had to rely on texts which have long since been superseded by subsequent research.) First, Hegel discusses Zoroastrianism as the 'religion of light'. Here we find religion flowing from the standpoint of something like the primitive sense certainty with which the *Phenomenology* began. It seeks the divine in something to be found in immediate sense awareness – and finds it in light, which is perceptible, but suitably intangible. The very indefiniteness of this symbol for divinity is its undoing, however, and Spirit seeks to 'specify' God in terms of tangible, natural forms. Thus are born the animal and vegetable gods of certain polytheistic religions. Hegel has Hinduism in mind (here and elsewhere, Hegel displays a disappointingly inadequate understanding of Indian thought). Next, God is conceived on the model of a craftsman, and religion expresses itself in the sort of monumental structures produced by the ancient Egyptians. Here Spirit becomes especially opaque to itself, as in the mysterious Sphinx. In fact, all of these religious forms are inadequate, and so Hegel turns from them to the religion of art, and to ancient Greece. Many of the ideas Hegel covers under natural religion in the *Phenomenology* are developed more fully in *The Lectures on the Philosophy of Religion* and *Lectures on Aesthetics*. See also **Absolute Spirit**; **art and Philosophy of Art**; ***Phenomenology of Spirit***; **religion and Philosophy of Religion**; **religion of art**; **symbolic art**.

natural soul (*die natürliche Seele*) In the Philosophy of Subjective Spirit, Hegel initially treats what he calls 'Anthropology', which deals with 'the Soul' – all that within us which is unconscious. Hegel subdivides his treatment of soul into 'natural soul', 'feeling soul' and 'actual soul'. Hegel describes the natural soul as an *anima mundi*, a world-soul, and as a 'single subject'. He speaks as if this single subject divides into the many individual subjects, but his language is figurative: 'Just as light bursts asunder into an infinite host of stars, so too does the universal natural soul sunder itself into an infinite host of individual souls; only with this difference, that whereas light appears to have an existence independently of the stars, the universal natural soul attains actuality solely in individual souls' (Wallace 35; PS § 390 A). What Hegel is saying is that in the most primordial levels of our psyche, we are in a sense identical. And through this natural soul we are in sympathy with the natural world.

Hegel tells us, furthermore, that the natural soul, in its individual determination, is influenced by such things as climate and geography, and thus it subdivides itself into what we might call 'regional souls'. There follows his notorious discussion of racial and national characters. The specification of the soul into what we think of as truly individual character is, Hegel believes, logically posterior to its specification into racial and ethnic types. When he turns to the development of individual character, Hegel makes some of his most penetrating and profound observations on human life, as he takes us through the life course of the individual from childhood to old age. There follows a discussion of the nature of sensation, and then we pass to the section on 'Feeling Soul', the second major division of 'Anthropology'. See also **actual soul**; **anthropology**; **feeling soul**; **Subjective Spirit**.

nature and Philosophy of Nature (*die Natur; die Naturphilosophie*) As early as 1801 Hegel began making notes towards developing his Philosophy of Nature. He continually revised these notes – many of which still survive – during his time in Jena. Hegel lectured on the subject eight times: in Jena in 1805–06, in Heidelberg in Summer 1818, and in Berlin in 1819–20, 1821–22, 1823–24, 1825–26, 1828 and 1830. His only published account of the Philosophy of Nature, however, was the second division of the *Encyclopedia*. This material was published in two other revised editions (1827 and 1830, the latter edition containing some 3,600 alterations). In 1847, Karl Ludwig Michelet published an edition of the Philosophy of Nature with additions (*Zusätze*) compiled from Hegel's manuscripts and lecture notes, chiefly from the periods 1805–06 and 1819–30. (Michelet did not have access to the manuscripts from the period 1801–04.)

No part of Hegel's philosophy has drawn more criticism than his Philosophy of Nature. However, the criticism often comes from the ill-informed, who assert that it is merely a product of 'armchair theorizing'. Thanks to the research of J. M. Petry, Errol E. Harris, H. S. Harris and others, scholars are being forced to reconsider this judgement. In the *Encyclopedia Logic*, Hegel writes that, 'the relationship of speculative science to the other sciences is simply the following: speculative science does not leave the empirical content of the other sciences aside, but recognizes and uses it, and in the same way recognizes and employs what is universal in these sciences, [i.e.,] the laws, classifications, etc., for its own content; but it also introduces other categories into these universals and gives them currency' (Geraets, 33; EL § 9). Hegel makes things even clearer in the *Encyclopedia*

Philosophy of Nature: 'Not only must philosophy be in agreement with our empirical knowledge of nature, but the *origin* and *formation* of the Philosophy of Nature presupposes and is conditioned by empirical physics' (Miller, 6; PN § 246; italics in original).

This does not mean that Hegel's Philosophy of Nature is merely a compilation of data taken from the science of his day. In a sense what he does is to take that data and, guided by the categories of the Logic, give it rational, systematic order. Hegel is aware that science is not 'finished' and that it will continue to make new discoveries. However, Hegel believes that the *basic structure* of his Philosophy of Nature is final and complete, because it is a reflection of the Idea. On one level, Hegel is simply claiming that there is an inherent rationality, a definite order in nature – but this is the tacit assumption of all scientists, whose work consists always in seeking to identify laws, regularities and interconnections. In the Logic, Hegel believes he has discovered the objective order of existence – the 'pattern', if you will, of reality itself. In the Philosophy of Nature he attempts to demonstrate, with striking imagination and insight, how nature conforms to this pattern. This allows us to define the basic difference between *philosophy* of nature and the natural sciences. The natural sciences do not ask the question 'what is nature?' The Philosophy of Nature does ask this question, however. It attempts to understand nature as a whole, and to understand its place within the larger whole of existence itself.[15]

On another level, Hegel's Philosophy of Nature can also be seen as a revival of an older, pre-Modern way of understanding the natural world. Hegel understands each of the forms of nature in very Aristotelian terms: as constituting an approach to – one might even say (to speak purely metaphorically) an imitation of – Absolute Idea's actualization as Spirit. To continue to speak in Aristotelian language, for Hegel each level of nature 'strives' to be an independent, self-sufficient system, like the Idea itself. On Hegel's account, nature is seen to 'give way' to Spirit, which 'is the truth and the final goal of nature and the genuine actuality of Idea' (Miller, 24; PN § 251).

In developing his Philosophy of Nature, Hegel is following in the footsteps of Schelling, though Hegel's work is far more systematic than Schelling's and reflects a more solid grasp of contemporary science. Still, there are many significant similarities between their theories, including their highly critical attitude toward Newtonian science. Both men regarded the

Newtonian conception of the universe as that of a dead, mechanical system of externally-related entities. Instead, Schelling and Hegel saw the world as a *cosmos*: an internally-related, organic whole. In his later Philosophy of Nature Hegel seems to anticipate modern theories of the ecosystem and of the holism of nature (or perhaps we should say he paved the way for these). He speaks of the 'whole organism of the Earth' and writes that 'The total state of the atmosphere . . . including the trade-winds forms a vast living whole' (Miller, 122; PN § 288 A). The Newtonian model represents, for both Schelling and Hegel, the physics of the understanding, which holds that even living things should be understood as mere mechanisms.

Turning now to the notorious transition from Logic to nature, Hegel says that at the end of the Logic the Idea 'freely releases' itself as nature. In the Philosophy of Nature he states that, 'Nature has yielded itself as the Idea in the form of otherness' (Miller, 13; PN § 247). The realm of the Idea is purely ideal or irreal (Hegel refers to his Logic as a 'realm of shadows'). Nature, as the 'real world', is completely different from Idea, but Hegel claims that it is nonetheless a physical reflection of Idea. At the very end of the *Encyclopedia Logic* Hegel remarks that 'What we began with was being, abstract being, while now we have the *Idea* as *being*; and this idea that is [*diese seiende Idee*], is *Nature*' (Geraets, 307; EL § 244 A; italics in original). In other words, nature is the Idea concretized; the Idea existing in the world. Hegel does not think that nature can be *deduced* from Idea. Instead, to pass from the ideal realm of the Logic to nature is simply to pass to a discussion of another realm entirely, but one which, in essence, 'embodies' the categories of the Logic.

Hegel's claim that nature must be understood as an expression of Idea is often dismissed as arbitrary and fanciful. It is neither of these, however. What Hegel means is simply that in order to truly understand nature we require knowledge of the Idea. In his Introduction to the Philosophy of Nature, Hegel alludes to the blurry distinctions between classes and species in nature, and the proliferation of monstrosities or deformities in all species. Nature is seldom neat and tidy. Hegel points out, however, that 'In order to be able to consider such forms as defective, imperfect, and deformed, one must presuppose a fixed, invariable type. This type, however, cannot be furnished by experience, for it is experience which also presents these so-called monstrosities, deformities, intermediate products, etc. The fixed type rather presupposes the self-subsistence and dignity of the determination stemming from the Concept' (Miller, 24; PN § 250). Here Hegel sounds rather Kantian, claiming, it seems, that the determinations of the Idea are what we always 'bring to' our understanding of nature. The difference, however, is that for Hegel the Idea and its moments are not 'subjective'. Hegel's Logic is an account of *objective* Idea, not a psychology or phenomenology. Whatever one may think of Hegel's claims about the ontological status of the Idea, his claims about the relationship of Idea to nature are quite sound: only our presupposition of the logical or ontological categories of universal, particular, individual and the rest, can explain our experience of nature's products as imperfect, partial, fuzzy or monstrous.

This relationship between nature and Idea is recapitulated throughout the Philosophy of Nature. Things in nature 'endeavour' to stand apart from others as independent; everything is an approximation to or imperfect 'imitation' of the one truly independent existent object: Idea realized in Spirit. Hegel has collapsed Aristotle's two-tiered scale of being into one tier. Whereas Aristotle held that man is the highest terrestrial being, but that man and his world are only a part of what 'strives' to imitate the Unmoved Mover, Hegel has actualized the Unmoved Mover (Absolute Idea) in man himself. For Hegel, all beings 'strive' not to imitate a transcendent Unmoved Mover, but to be *understood* by that 'Active Intellect' which is Spirit, their 'natural end'.

Despite his use of creation imagery and neo-platonic emanation language, Hegel says that he does not believe that the universe was created in time. He writes that 'The world is created, is now being created, and has always been created; this becomes apparent in the conservation of the world' (Miller, 15; PN § 247 A). In other words, the world and all its states and processes – the coming into being of new individuals, the maintenance of individuals over time, etc. – is a perpetual expression of Idea. Hegel's Philosophy of Nature presents us with a system of categories in increasing order of complexity, but they should not be conceived as temporal stages. Hegel writes, 'Nature is to be regarded as a *system of stages*, one arising necessarily from the other and being the proximate truth of the stage from which it results: but it is not generated *naturally* out of the other but only in the inner Idea which constitutes the ground of nature' (Miller, 20; PN § 249). Notoriously, Hegel rejects evolution.

The Philosophy of Nature consists of three main divisions or moments. 'Mechanics' treats inert matter which is acted on and caused to move by

negation

external forces. (Here Hegel finds a place for Newtonian science, as a correct, though limited, description of one aspect of the natural.) 'Physics' deals with the intrinsic nature of corporeality as such, its elements, powers, etc. In 'Organics' we find matter forming itself into systems which aim at being self-sustaining and complete. It is easy to see how this final division corresponds to the Doctrine of the Concept in the Logic: organic systems are, in fact, dim corporeal reflections of the Idea, a whole of parts internally (i.e., 'organically') related to one another. (Physics corresponds to the Doctrine of Essence in so far as in physics we 'look within' matter to see its inner qualities, and Mechanics corresponds to the Doctrine of Being insofar as it deals with immediate, superficial externalities.) See also **Aristotle; evolution; Idea; Logic; matter; mechanics; organics; physics; relation; Schelling, F. W. J.; space and time**.

negation (*die Negation*)   Hegel's dialectic operates through negation – in fact it would be accurate to describe negation as the 'mechanism' of dialectic itself. The passage from one category to another in the Hegelian dialectic always involves negation. The paradigm for such dialectical transitions is to be found in the Logic, where the transitions between categories are thought by Hegel to exhibit strong necessity and rigor. Each category in the Logic is understood to be a provisional definition of the Absolute (of the whole), but each proves inadequate given that it is always found in some manner to presuppose, depend upon, or simply be related to another category, often what seems at first glance to be its opposite. Thus in the dialectic each category is negated by the category that follows it. This continual negation of one category by another allows Hegel to progressively articulate the Idea, which is the system of these mutually dependent, yet mutually negating concepts.

As noted above, the Logic provides the Hegelian paradigm for dialectical negation – but within the Logic the paradigm of dialectic is the sequence of concepts at the very beginning: being-nothing-becoming. Furthermore, dialectic is not simply something characteristic of concepts: Hegel sees the entire world as an internally related system of interdependent yet antagonistic elements. As Heraclitus famously said, 'the finest harmony is composed of things at variance, and everything comes to be in accordance with strife.'[16] Negation is involved in the coming into being of anything. To borrow (and adapt) Hegel's metaphor from the Preface to *The Phenomenology of Spirit*, the bud is negated by the blossom, which in turn is negated by the fruit. Yet each is a moment in an organic unity. They negate each other, but are absolutely necessary for each other. See also **being, nothing, becoming; dialectic; Logic; moment; sublation; thesis, antithesis, synthesis; triads.**

'night in which all cows are black' Hegel's first philosophical work was a defense of Schelling's thought: *The Difference between Fichte's and Schelling's Systems of Philosophy*, published in 1801. Soon, however, Hegel became more critical of Schelling's philosophy. He effectively announced his break with Schelling in the Preface to *The Phenomenology of Spirit* (1807), via an attack on Schelling's way of conceiving the Absolute:

> Dealing with something from the perspective of the Absolute consists merely in declaring that, although one has been speaking of it just now as something definite, yet in the Absolute, the $A = A$, there is nothing of the kind, for therein all is one. To pit this single insight, that in the Absolute everything is the same, against the full body of articulated cognition, which at least seeks and demands such fulfillment, to palm off its Absolute as the night in which, as the saying goes, all cows are black – this is cognition naively reduced to vacuity. (Miller, 9; PG, 13)

Hegel takes over the idea of an Absolute from Schelling, including the idea that the Absolute transcends the distinction between subject and object. He contends, however, that 'the Absolute' is an empty surd unless we can give a developmental account of how it becomes actual. A couple of paragraphs later in the *Phenomenology* Hegel speaks of the Absolute as, 'the process of its own becoming, the circle that presupposes its end as its goal, having its end also as its beginning; and only by being worked out to its end, is it actual' (Miller, 10; PG, 14). And he tells us that the Absolute must be conceived in 'the whole wealth of the developed form. Only then is it conceived and expressed as an actuality' (Miller, 11; PG, 15). The true, Hegel proclaims, is 'the whole'. He uses the dialectic to show how the Absolute is, in fact, reality understood as a system; as the whole come to consciousness of itself in human thought. (It is debatable how fair Hegel has been to Schelling, and whether he has faithfully represented Schelling's

Objective Spirit

conception of the Absolute.) See also **Absolute**; *Phenomenology of Spirit*; **Schelling, F. W. J.**; **system**; **truth**; **whole, the**.

non-contradiction, law of   See **contradiction**.

notion, the   See **Concept, Doctrine of the**.

number (*die Zahl*)   In the Logic, number results from the derivation of quanta, a subject Hegel treats under 'Quantity' in the Doctrine of Being. Quanta result simply when a given quantity is segmented or broken up into separate units through the application of some kind of limit. Quanta are qualitatively indistinguishable from one another, and are externally related. When such quanta are collected together into 'sums' we have the basis for enumeration, for numbers are simply unities of bare quanta, without qualities. For example, the number 'Five' is a unity of bare, indistinguishable units or quanta: . See also **Being, Doctrine of**; **quality, quantity, measure**; **quantum**.

— O —

Objective Spirit (*der objektive Geist*)   Objective Spirit is the second division of Hegel's Philosophy of Spirit. The principal texts that treat it are *The Encyclopedia of the Philosophical Sciences in Outline*, *The Philosophy of Right* and the *Lectures on the Philosophy of History*. In the *Lectures on the Philosophy of History*, Hegel states that 'After the creation of the natural universe, man appears on the scene as the antithesis of nature; he is the being who raises himself up into a second world' (Nisbet, 44; VIG, 50). This 'second world' is the world of Objective Spirit (and also Absolute Spirit, though we are not concerned with Absolute Spirit in the present context). In Hegel's system every aspect of Spirit above Subjective Spirit constitutes a world created by man, standing in opposition to the merely natural.

In his discussion of Subjective Spirit, Hegel shows how reason and autonomy arise through the subjection of natural impulses. However, his description of this process is, on one level, merely formal because individuals do not tame their natural impulses and learn to think rationally all by themselves. They do so with the help of others, living in a human community. It is only through our interactions with others that we learn to control the baser parts of ourselves, and to develop the higher parts; only through society, in other words, that our humanity emerges. Hegel subsumes under the rubric of 'Objective Spirit' a great number of subjects: the nature of the family and the basic forms of social organization, morality, contracts, government, law and world history. All of these constitute an *objective expression* of our human nature.

Subjective Spirit is Spirit *in itself* or merely implicit, whereas Objective Spirit is Spirit *for itself*. Through the phenomena of Objective Spirit we are, in fact, confronting ourselves – but we do not do so with full consciousness. It is often the case, for instance, that individuals living in different societies do not appreciate the fact that their customs and laws are their own creation, and may regard them as 'natural', or as expressions of divine law. It is only in Absolute Spirit (Spirit *in-and-for itself*), the standpoint pre-eminently of philosophy, that we come to appreciate that Objective Spirit is one form in which humanity objectifies its nature. In fact, Hegel sees all of world history as an account of our subduing nature and creating the human world, and, in the process, coming ever closer to the achievement of full self-awareness. (In the sphere of world history, Hegel refers to Objective Spirit as the 'World Spirit'.) See also **Absolute Spirit; history and Philosophy of History; in itself, for itself, in-and-for itself;** *Philosophy of Right*; **Subjective Spirit; World Spirit.**

objectivity   See **subjectivity, objectivity, idea**.

one and many   See **repulsion and attraction**.

organics (*die organische Physik*)   Hegel's Philosophy of Nature is divided into three main topics: mechanics, physics and organics. Mechanics deals with the 'external' aspect of material reality: things acting on one another. With physics we leave behind the 'externality' of mechanics and penetrate into matter itself, to discover that the individual material body must be understood as containing *within* itself a complex order and structure. In short, physics deals with the interiority of natural bodies, treated as internally-differentiated wholes. At the end of Hegel's treatment of physics, we find an anticipation of an individual which is a complex system of parts, and which can effect its own chemical and other processes *without* the continual intervention of external forces. Such an individual is, of course, a living, organic being. For Hegel, this is the highest form of nature. He states that 'The organic being is totality as found in nature, an individuality which is for itself and which internally develops into its differences' (Miller, 27; PN § 252 A). As a genuine whole, the parts of which can have no separate existence, organic being resembles the internally-differentiated and self-determining Idea of the Logic.

Hegel discusses in turn the terrestrial, plant and animal organisms. The terrestrial organism is simply the earth, which Hegel treats as a vast, living whole. The plant or vegetal organism is the halfway house between terrestrial and animal life. It is with plants that life first truly individuates itself – yet individual plants themselves (unlike animals) exhibit a lack of differentiation in terms of inner organs. Further, they are largely insentient and incapable of locomotion. The animal represents an ideal of wholeness and self-sustaining individuality. Every animal is an internally differentiated whole of parts or organs which are what they are in terms of their function within the whole. Further, animals are sentient and capable of 'internalizing' their environment in sense experience. Unlike plants, they are not rooted to a specific spot, and are capable of movement from place to place. The animal's sentience and ability to move means that it has a far greater capacity for independence and self-maintenance.

Hegel states that 'The animal organism is the microcosm, the center of nature which has achieved an existence for itself in which the whole of inorganic nature is recapitulated and idealized' (Miller, 356; PN § 352 A). The animal organism is a 'recapitulation' of all that has gone before in that it has sublated all the preceding moments or levels of nature. Animal organism is thus the highest form of organic being. Hegel states that, 'The animal is the existent Idea in so far as its members are purely and simply moments of the form, perpetually negating their independence and bringing themselves back into their unity, which is the reality of the Concept and is for the Concept' (Miller, 352; PN § 350 A). In short, the animal organism is a material embodiment of the internally differentiated, dialectical whole that is the Idea of the Logic. Hegel states earlier that 'Animal life is . . . the Concept displaying itself in space and time' (Miller, 277; PN § 337 A).

'Desire', the dark egoistic will to cancel the other which appears in *The Phenomenology of Spirit*, is prefigured in animal nature. The difference between man and nature is that man can 'master' nature and 'absorb' it without literally annihilating it through the use of his mind. It is in animal sex and nutrition that Hegel sees human science prefigured. He sees eating as the most primitive form in which conscious beings seek to make the object their own, or to collapse the distinction between subject and object. However, the 'otherness' of things can only be truly overcome in thought. In the Philosophy of Nature, Hegel treats excretion as an acknowledgement of this 'error' on the part of the animal. Thus the organism's conflict with the other cannot be resolved through nutrition. In reproduction, on the other hand, the animal confronts an other which is like itself (notice the analogy to Self-Consciousness and its treatment of 'recognition' in the *Phenomenology*). The animal recognizes itself in its mate, and in the sex act the individuality of both is momentarily annihilated and they are submerged into the unity of their genus. Because the animal is neither thoughtful nor thoughtfully self-aware, it cannot make the genus its object; it can only momentarily become one with it in an unconscious manner.

Nevertheless, in reproduction the animal comes the closest it can to what in man becomes speculative science. The animal cannot truly rise above its individuality and grasp its concept, or genus, let alone the Concept itself. Thus, it is simply an expendable, replaceable expression of its genus, one destined to no greater achievement than to produce another of its own kind. We can thus see why Hegel considers human being or Spirit separately from nature: human nature is fundamentally 'supernatural' in that it breaks this cycle and rises above the merely natural. And so, following Hegel's treatment of organics, the dialectic passes from Philosophy of Nature, to Philosophy of Spirit. See also **Concept, Doctrine of the; death; desire; evolution; Idea; mechanics; nature and Philosophy of Nature; physics; recognition; self-consciousness; sublation.**

organism   See **organics**.

'owl of Minerva, the'

'owl of Minerva, the' (*die Eule der Minerva*)   In the Preface to *The Philosophy of Right*, Hegel writes: 'When philosophy paints its grey in grey, a shape of life has grown old, and it cannot be rejuvenated, but only recognized, by the grey in grey of philosophy; the owl of Minerva begins its flight only with the onset of dusk' (Nisbet, 23). Minerva was the Roman equivalent of the Greek goddess Athena. Her owl symbolized wisdom, and has become a symbol for philosophy, the 'love of wisdom' itself. The 'owl of Minerva' is probably the best-known image in Hegel's writing. So closely is it associated with him that the Hegel Society of America chose to name its journal *The Owl of Minerva* (printed, since 1969, on light grey paper, using dark grey ink).

In this passage Hegel is, of course, discussing the nature of philosophy itself. Philosophy cannot predict the future. In a real sense, in fact, it can only understand something once it is finished. The meaning of historical events is never clear until well after they are over and done with, and so the philosopher of history cannot pronounce judgements until events have played themselves out. Hegel believes that he stands at a privileged point in history – able to look back at the course of human events and see that they were aiming at a goal which, to all intents and purposes, has been reached in his own time: self-knowledge. As a philosopher, Hegel believes that he is able to see how all older philosophies have played themselves out and made possible his own, as the consummation of the history of philosophy itself and simultaneously the consummation of the human quest for self-knowledge. He applies the same approach to art, attempting to show how art also aims (inadequately) at human self-understanding, and how it can now be fully understood by the philosopher because all of its basic possibilities have already displayed themselves. Thus, philosophy only takes flight when certain forms of Spirit are, in essence, completed. It is worth noting that one of the most important ways in which Marx departs from Hegel is in insisting that dialectic can be used as a tool to predict the next phase of history. See also **art and Philosophy of Art**; **history and Philosophy of History**; **Marx, Karl**; **philosophy and the history of philosophy**; **Philosophy of Right**.

— P —

perception (*die Wahrnehmung*)   The first major section of *The Phenomenology of Spirit* is devoted to a discussion of the forms of what Hegel calls 'consciousness'. The first and most primitive form of consciousness is 'sense certainty', in which we naively believe that we can grasp an object through its bare, sensory immediacy alone. The object is taken as a 'this here'. Consciousness discovers, however, that all attempts to understand or to say anything about the object – even calling it a 'this' – involve us in employing concepts, and thus actually transcending the level of pure sensory immediacy. Thus, in 'perception', the second form of consciousness, the object is conceived of as a thing possessing universal properties or qualities. This standpoint also purports to give us the thing just as it is. However, perception cannot succeed here either, for we soon realize that the universals possessed by one object are also possessed by others. Once we realize this, the very individuality of the thing is called into question.

To resolve this problem, consciousness considers the possibility that the universal properties of the thing are merely our ideas, and that the thing is something quite apart from our perception of it. Or, perhaps, the thing *just is* the conjunction of these universal properties, but that this conjunction happens in us. However, these suggestions don't resolve our basic problem, which was how to reconcile the apparent individuality of *this here thing* with our awareness of its multiple, universal properties. All we have done is to suggest, vaguely, that these differing aspects are reconciled 'in the mind' rather than in the object (i.e., we have simply shifted from the vague idea that they are reconciled 'in the thing' to the vague idea that they are reconciled 'in us'). But the relation between the concrete, immediate individuality of the thing and the 'universality' of its properties remains mysterious.

The dialectic of consciousness then moves on to a position that distinguishes between the essential and inessential properties of something. Perhaps, consciousness thinks, we can distinguish between the surface appearance of the object – its multiple, apparent properties – and what it *really* is. However, we soon realize that the thing has to possess its 'inessential' properties as a direct result of its essential ones (i.e., its essential

phenomenology

properties will determine which inessential properties it may possess). Thus, the inessential properties of the thing are very much a part of its nature, and the basis for distinguishing between the 'essence' of the thing and its accidental attributes becomes murky at best.

The next move of the dialectic involves the introduction of a distinction between 'appearance' and 'reality'. The many changing properties of the thing belong to appearance, whereas beneath the appearances might be some deeper level of truth. If we could know this, then we could truly grasp the object. This move gives rise, in fact, to the first appearance of something approaching a scientific outlook, the standpoint Hegel here dubs 'Force and the Understanding'. See also **consciousness**; **force and the understanding**; *Phenomenology of Spirit*; **sense-certainty**.

phenomenology (*die Phänomenologie*)   Hegel employs the term 'phenomenology' in two major contexts: in *The Phenomenology of Spirit* and in his Philosophy of Subjective Spirit. The term appears to have first been used by the Swabian mystical theologian Friedrich Christoph Oetinger (and not, as is often claimed, Johann Heinrich Lambert). Oetinger used the term as early as 1736 to refer to the procedure of displaying the moments of the 'divine system of relations'. In the twentieth century, 'phenomenology' became the name of a philosophical movement inaugurated by Edmund Husserl. The term literally means 'science of phenomena', where 'phenomena' simply means 'appearances'. This is what 'phenomenology' means for both Hegel and Husserl. *The Phenomenology of Spirit* is therefore the science of the appearances of Spirit. The text is a 'recollection' of the different forms in which Spirit has displayed itself and continues to display itself. *The Phenomenology of Spirit* was intended by Hegel as a kind of introduction to his tripartite system of Logic-Philosophy of Nature-Philosophy of Spirit. What has always puzzled commentators, however, is that in Hegel's Philosophy of Spirit, in the section on Subjective Spirit, a subsection appears entitled 'Phenomenology', the content of which seems to repeat much of *The Phenomenology of Spirit* in a highly compressed form. However, this confusion is easily overcome.

Hegel divides Subjective Spirit into 'Anthropology', 'Phenomenology' and 'Psychology'. Anthropology deals with what Hegel calls 'the soul', which is, as it were, the 'natural' or animal part of our selves. Phenomenology, on the other hand, deals with 'consciousness'. In consciousness, ego or selfhood appears, whereas in the soul it is absent. The level of the soul in effect becomes an 'other' for consciousness, and one reflects on one's natural predispositions as if they were alien, especially when those predispositions are difficult to control. The ego must, of course, sublate this other, and take control of it, just as it would any opposing object.

In the 'Phenomenology' section, Hegel follows the pattern of Consciousness-Self-Consciousness-Reason laid down in *The Phenomenology of Spirit*. What he says about 'Phenomenology' in the Philosophy of Subjective Spirit can help clarify the 1807 *Phenomenology*. The latter work presupposes the ego and excludes from consideration subconscious or unconscious processes (the soul), even though Hegel was well aware of them and of their relevance to a science of Spirit. In the 1807 *Phenomenology* Hegel is consciously narrowing his scope and presenting only the material on Spirit which is needed for his purposes.

In the material covered by 'Phenomenology' in Subjective Spirit, the ego has distinguished itself from the natural world. In 'Consciousness' we find ourselves aware of a world of objects as an other. The dialectic then turns (just as it does in the 1807 work) to 'Self-Consciousness', in which ego gropes for awareness of itself. In 'Reason', the final division of 'Phenomenology' (at least so far as Subjective Spirit is concerned) a form of conscious thought is attained which is intersubjective, and hence 'objective' rather than being merely personal. (Reason and all that it makes possible – such as scientific thought – must be publicly verifiable, according to standards held in common.) The dialectic of Subjective Spirit then moves beyond 'Phenomenology' to 'Psychology'. See also **anthropology**; **Phenomenology of Spirit**; **Philosophy of Spirit**; **psychology**; **recollection, imagination, memory**; **Subjective Spirit**.

Phenomenology of Spirit (Phänomenologie des Geistes)
Famously, Hegel is supposed to have completed writing *The Phenomenology of Spirit* on the eve of the Battle of Jena in October 1806. When published, its full title was *System of Science: First Part, The Phenomenology of Spirit*. Hegel's 'system' is ordinarily understood to consist of three branches: the Logic, Philosophy of Nature and Philosophy of Spirit. What is the relationship of the *Phenomenology* to this tripartite system? Commentators often refer to it as an 'introduction' to the system (and Hegel himself spoke this way). Indeed, there is material in the *Phenomenology* that is

Phenomenology of Spirit

developed more fully in Hegel's other writings. Further, the famous 'Preface' to the *Phenomenology* can certainly be read not just as an introduction to the text itself, but to the Hegelian system as such.

Nevertheless, the term 'introduction' is too weak. The *Phenomenology* is actually a propaedeutic to the system: in other words, it consists of material that must be gone through before one turns to the system. The reason for this is that the *Phenomenology* culminates in the identification of a standpoint of thought which makes possible the development of the Logic. This standpoint is called 'Absolute Knowing'. Furthermore, to put the point more strongly, Hegel believes that the reader who has followed his argument in the *Phenomenology* will actually stand at the threshold of Absolute Knowing.

Phenomenology literally means 'science of phenomena', where phenomena means appearances. Thus, The *Phenomenology of Spirit* means the science of (or study of) the appearances of Spirit. The simplest possible explanation of Hegel's use of Spirit is that it refers to human nature: Spirit is us. *The Phenomenology of Spirit* is basically an account of the different forms in which Spirit displays itself. Hegel wrote the following advertisement 'blurb' for the publishers of the *Phenomenology*:

> It includes the various shapes of Spirit within itself as stages in the progress through which Spirit becomes pure knowledge or Absolute Spirit. Thus, the main divisions of this science, which fall into further subdivisions, include a consideration of consciousness, self-consciousness, observational and active reason, as well as Spirit itself, – in its ethical, cultural and moral, and finally in its religious forms. The apparent chaos of the wealth of appearances in which Spirit presents itself when first considered, is brought into a scientific order, which is exhibited in its necessity, in which the imperfect appearances resolve themselves and pass over into the higher ones constituting their proximate truth. They find their final truth first in religion and then in Science, as the result of the whole.[17]

This is possibly Hegel's clearest statement about the content and purpose of the *Phenomenology* – but (as is always the case with Hegel) it is far from straightforward. What follows is a brief, highly compressed account of what Hegel is up to in this extraordinarily complex, rich and difficult work.

The reader is encouraged to consult the other entries in this volume dealing with the *Phenomenology.*

Following the Preface and Introduction, the actual body of the *Phenomenology* has a curious structure. It is not only divided into numbered chapters (eight of them), but into major divisions, designated by letters. These begin normally: 'A' is 'Consciousness'; 'B' is 'Self-consciousness.' But C is followed on the same line by 'AA' and the term 'Reason', as follows: 'C. (AA) Reason.' No 'D' follows. Instead, on the following lines, we have '(BB) Spirit', '(CC) Religion' and '(DD) Absolute Knowing'. Commentators have suggested various explanations for this. J. N. Findlay suggests that 'The numbering of the sections seems to mean that Hegel regarded all the parts of the work after the part entitled "Self-Consciousness" . . . as constituting the single third member of the main triad of his work.'[18] This is a reasonable hypothesis. A, B and C do form a dialectical triad, for C and all of its moments are a return to A, 'Consciousness', in which all the later phases of the dialectic are prefigured.

In 'Consciousness', division A, the first standpoint we encounter on the way to Absolute Knowing is 'sense-certainty'. At the root of sense-certainty – as well as all the forms of Spirit – is a primal drive for complete possession or mastery of the object, for, in effect, the overcoming of otherness. By implication, this drive is simultaneously a will to remove the divide between subject and object, for by cancelling 'otherness' it seeks to exalt the self (this implication will become crucial for understanding the section on 'Self-Consciousness'). Sense-certainty is the most basic, primitive form in which the urge to cancel or master the other manifests itself in consciousness. Spirit in sense-certainty believes, tacitly, that the object in its real, concrete particularity can be adequately 'grasped' through bare sensory experience alone. It is easy for Hegel to demonstrate the fundamental flaw in this position: Sense-Certainty fails in what it aims for because intuition cannot fully grasp or absorb its object. (See the separate entry on 'Sense-Certainty' for his full argument). Hegel's *fundamental* critique of this form of Spirit, and of all others that fall short of Absolute Spirit, is that the true unity of subject and object, ideal and real, can only be achieved through the total, thoughtful grasp of the whole of reality in the System of Science. The *Phenomenology* shows how this urge to cancel or 'master' otherness makes possible the actualization of Absolute Knowing and, through it, the realization of Idea and of Idea's expression as nature and as human Spirit.

Phenomenology of Spirit

The dialectic continues with 'Perception', in which we consider the object as a congeries of universals. But the universals which describe the thing's nature are shared by others. We have thus, again, failed to grasp the object in its individuality. In the final form of consciousness, which Hegel treats in the section 'Force and the Understanding', consciousness thinks the individual can be grasped through a knowledge of the 'forces' underlying it, which make it what it is. But this form of explanation is tautological, and merely involves us in making empty claims about occult forces. All that we have accomplished here is to discover something about *ourselves*.

We can now glimpse the end of the Hegelian philosophy already in its beginning. In Absolute Knowing the drive to totally grasp the object, and to annul the subject-object distinction will be realized. Absolute Knowing will be the total grasp of the only true, unique individual there is: the Absolute. In Aristotelian terms, it is the grasp of true being or substance. But in Hegel's thought substance has become subject: 'what seems to happen outside of [the self], to be an activity directed against it, is really its own doing, and substance shows itself to be essentially subject' (Miller, 21; PG, 28). This is because the Absolute is Idea, which sublates the distinction between subject and object. Knowledge of this individual is thus simultaneously self-knowledge. Otherness still exists, but it is now understood in terms of its place within the whole. Substantive otherness, however, has passed away, because the other is shown to be an expression of Idea, just as the self is. In short, Absolute Knowing achieves exactly what is desired, covertly, by sense-certainty (and the other forms of Spirit).

Absolute Knowing is 'Consciousness' transformed. Absolute Knowing will be a move beyond sense (as in force and the understanding), but it will not be concerned with the universal (contra perception) but rather with the individual (just as in primitive sense-certainty). Nevertheless, Absolute Knowing will preserve the moment of concern with the universal, for the individual it ultimately grasps is the 'concrete universal' – the universal which contains the particulars within itself. Finally, just as in force and the understanding, we will find in the end that we have only succeeded in discovering something about ourselves, for, again, Substance = Subject.

In introducing 'Self-Consciousness', Hegel uses the term 'desire' to describe this primal urge for the cancellation of otherness and the absolutization of the subject. But Spirit is not just this desire to absolutize itself, for when the subject transforms objects according to its will it is really being moved by the desire to confront itself. To know itself, consciousness must find a mirror. But we cannot fully or truly confront ourselves through malleable objects. This drive for self-consciousness can only be satisfied by a being like the subject, who recognizes it as another subject. The first attempt to achieve this occurs when subjects relate to one another through force, seeking to compel recognition. This is Hegel's famous 'master–servant dialectic', in which both fail to achieve the recognition they desire. The servant, however, fares better. Put to work by the master, he creates culture.

The next phases of the dialectic follow the development of the servant's consciousness. Hegel first discusses 'stoicism', in which the servant aims at freedom through detaching itself from the world. But this is a false freedom: freedom only in thought, not in reality. Stoicism gives way in Hegel's dialectic, therefore, to 'scepticism', an outright denial of the world, and to the 'unhappy consciousness', a yearning for recognition by a transcendent God (a cosmic 'master'), and for freedom in the afterlife. Of course, the relation of man to God simply recapitulates the master–servant antithesis, on a new level. In fact, Hegel maintains that true freedom and recognition are won only through membership in the modern state. In the dialectic of servant consciousness, we see only the first historical, and philosophical, glimmerings of what will ultimately make the achievement of the modern state, and the consummation of history, possible. Though the unhappy consciousness may seem a thorough failure, it is nevertheless an attempt by human beings to put themselves into accord with the universal. This sets the stage for the next phase of the dialectic, 'Reason.'

Hegel designates the division of the *Phenomenology* which follows 'Self-Consciousness' simply as 'C'. 'Reason' is its first subdivision, 'AA'. In AA through to CC, all the preceding ground is covered again. The doubling of the letters suggests a kind of reflexivity, a doubling back. This is indeed what happens, for these sections represent humanity's developing self-awareness. Consciousness and self-consciousness, as discussed by Hegel, were largely naive and reactive. In 'C', the standpoints of Spirit become more and more self-directed and self-aware. For example, reason can easily be seen to be a return, on a higher level, to the standpoint of consciousness. In consciousness we could clearly see the first glimmerings of the

Phenomenology of Spirit

scientific mentality: the concern with empirical 'verification', and the understanding of the object as a collection of universals or forces which transcend experience.

Reason is, in fact, the dialectical sublation of consciousness and self-consciousness. Hegel's treatment of reason involves humanity groping towards self-consciousness by (1) trying to find ourselves through the study of nature, and (2) through the re-shaping of the objective world to bring it into accord with our wishes. However, these activities are carried on without awareness that this is in fact what we are doing. In 'Observation of Nature' we search for reason in nature in the form of laws. This search eventually leads us to turn inwards and to attempt to understand the human subject using the same scientific approach. However, this project is ultimately a failure, since Spirit simply cannot be 'reduced': it cannot be understood adequately in the same terms we use to describe material objects. Hegel illustrates this with his famous critique of phrenology, the 'science' of determining a person's character from the bumps on his head. Spirit, Hegel tells us, is not a bone.

At this point, Hegel's account of reason turns abruptly from the realm of empirical science to that of the social world, in which the individual is still groping to find himself. In a sense, he is striving to give his individual existence some connection to the universal. This expresses itself in several different manifestations of what can be called 'individualism'. The individual becomes a sensualist, then a romantic idealist championing the 'law of the heart'. He immerses himself in work, in the humbug of narrow, blinkered specialization ('the spiritual animal kingdom'). Finally, individualism expresses itself in something like the ethics of Kant, which attempts to derive moral principles from individual subjectivity. What emerges from all of this is a rejection of individualism and of the fetishizing of individual autonomy. We know what we are, and become what we truly are, only in society – not through withdrawing from it or standing opposed to it.

'Spirit' (subsection BB) is Hegel's treatment of man seen as a social being. Hegel's allusions to actual history and culture remain largely indirect, but an historical, cultural context always makes itself felt. We should not be confused by Hegel's use of the term 'Spirit' at this point. Here he means it more or less in the sense of what is called in the *Encyclopedia* 'Objective Spirit', Spirit expressing itself in the institutions of society. Hegel's account of the forms of Objective Spirit draws upon history: the Greek polis, Roman civil society, the enthusiasm of Enlightenment, the French Revolution and the 'Terror', etc. Spirit begins in unreflective commitment to the ethical order of family and community. This is broken down through the imposition of a political system in which individuals are externally related and vie with one another over 'rights'. The consequence is alienation from the 'natural' ethical order. Spirit – now estranged from itself, as Hegel says – sets itself up as judge and 'reformer' of society. This ultimately results in the Terror of the French Revolution, the ultimate consequence of Enlightenment's ruthless criticism of the existing order. Spirit then attempts to recreate the ethical order it feels it has lost, but it knows that this is a mere contrivance. It moves from a Kantian concern with disinterested duty-following, to a commitment to 'individual conscience'. Hegel's account culminates in his memorable treatment of 'the beautiful soul', the man who is so terrified of sullying his moral purity that he simply cannot act.

What is obvious from all of this is that while the original phase of ethical life may be unreflective, no adequate replacement for it can be found through relying entirely upon the rational, critical faculties of the individual. However, if Hegel opposes 'unreflectiveness' in general, then he cannot advocate a return to the initial phase of ethical life – our uncritical immersion in the social order and in traditional folkways. On the other hand, as we have seen, separation from this initial phase appears disastrous. Hegel's resolution of this problem involves his claim that the rationality of Spirit, its ability to know itself and its world, is a communal affair; it is realizable only through civilized society, and as a result of a long, historical process. Thus, freedom, if it is to avoid the 'fury of destruction', must involve willing or affirming the concrete social conditions that make freedom possible. In fact, Hegel argues that it is only through being members of the modern state that we are truly free at all. Hegel develops these ideas much more fully and clearly in the later *Philosophy of Right*.

When Hegel turns from 'Spirit' to 'Religion' (subsection CC) he is in fact making a transition from Objective Spirit to Absolute Spirit (these distinctions become clearer in the later *Encyclopedia*). In 'Spirit' Hegel sketched how human beings must realize themselves in the social order. But Spirit's expression of itself in the institutions of society still does not provide us with full or absolute self-consciousness (which, we must always keep in mind, is the true end or goal of Spirit itself). Religion is one of the forms of Absolute Spirit, and it typically involves an unconscious projection of Spirit into

Phenomenology of Spirit

something exalted beyond the human. In other words, Spirit is knowing itself through religion, but it does not know that it is doing this.

In all of the forms of religion the divide between finite and infinite, human and divine, remains intact – yet religion seeks to overcome this divide. Christianity, in Hegel's account, is 'revealed religion' or the 'Absolute Religion'. In Christianity, man becomes conscious of God as Spirit itself, for Christianity teaches that God became a man, Jesus Christ. But the inner truth of Christianity, Hegel holds, lies not in the historical Jesus but in the idea of the realization of God *through man*. This truth is not revealed explicitly by Christianity. It is revealed by speculative philosophy, which Hegel sketches in the final sub-section of the *Phenomenology*, 'Absolute Knowing' (DD). In this short and difficult chapter, Hegel runs through the forms Spirit has taken thus far in the *Phenomenology*. Hegel now explicitly speaks of 'Absolute Knowing' as the true reconciliation of consciousness and self-consciousness. We have seen all along how this must be the case: Hegelian Science will be the total grasp of the one, true 'individual', the Absolute or 'the whole'. But this Absolute is 'substance become subject': the consummation of the whole consists in its coming to consciousness of itself in humanity. Human self-consciousness is thus the completion or perfection of existence itself.

In 'Absolute Knowing' Hegel also sketches out the direction in which the remainder of the System of Science will go. In sense-certainty consciousness began its attempt to grasp the object at the level of simple immediacy. Immediacy, however, was taken for granted as a 'category' or 'structure'. In the Logic, we return to the level of immediacy in the 'Doctrine of Being'. The Hegelian Logic is an expression – a recollection, in fact – of the thought-forms which underlie the acts of Spirit. Spirit comes into its own when it consciously appropriates and understands these thought-forms as a system. In the Philosophy of Nature, we return to the objective world in which we find the categories of the Logic 'embodied'. The Philosophy of Spirit will show the 'emergence' from nature of Spirit, whose nature is to negate nature, to build a human world – and ultimately to come to consciousness of itself and write *The Phenomenology of Spirit*. See also **Absolute Knowing; Christianity; concrete universal; consciousness; Logic; 'master–servant dialectic'; phenomenology; science; self-consciousness; Spirit**.

philosophy and the history of philosophy (*die Philosophie; die Geschichte der Philosophie*)   For Hegel, philosophy is the highest form of Absolute Spirit. Absolute Spirit is Spirit knowing itself, and its two other forms are art and religion. In both artwork and religious worship, Spirit is confronting itself – though the individual human beings who engage in these activities may not realize this. Artwork is always an expression of our own nature, and Hegel regards religion (pre-eminently Christianity) as, in essence, a mythic representation of Spirit's role in actualizing Idea in the world. However, philosophy is 'higher' than art and religion, because neither of these is able to give an account of itself; i.e., they are incapable of true self-understanding. Philosophy is able to reveal the 'inner truth' of art and religion because philosophy is able to know the Idea directly, rationally and conceptually. Both art and religion are, in effect, groping to achieve something that can only be achieved by philosophy. Art and religion fail to deliver true self-knowledge, for they utilize 'picture-thinking': images, metaphors, stories, myths, etc. Hegel believes that true self-knowledge is possible only through conceptual thought.

Hegel also refers to philosophy as Absolute Knowing, and as speculation. In the *Phenomenology of Spirit*, Hegel refers to his philosophy as a 'System of Science' (with the *Phenomenology* as its first part). *The Phenomenology of Spirit* argues that Absolute Knowing is, in a sense, the goal or summit of all forms of human Spirit. Everything that human beings do in some way aims at self-awareness – a goal which can only truly be satisfied by Absolute Knowing. Thus, for Hegel, the achievement of philosophy is, in a sense, the consummation of human life itself. In fact, philosophy constitutes the completion or perfection of the world, because it is through the thought of the philosopher that existence comes to consciousness of itself.

For Hegel, the most fundamental form of philosophy (First Philosophy, one might say, borrowing a term from Aristotle) is Logic. In Hegel's Logic the human mind deals only with pure concepts and conceptual necessities – not with information derived somehow from observation of the world. The categories of the Logic constitute a complete conceptual whole capped by Idea itself, which overcomes the distinction between subjectivity and objectivity. Idea is, in effect, the conceptual anticipation of concrete, human self-knowledge, in which the subject becomes object to itself, and the object becomes the subject. Philosophy of Nature and Philosophy of Spirit are, in a sense, 'applied logic' for Hegel (he states this explicitly in EL § 24

philosophy and the history of philosophy

A-2; Geraets, 58). Philosophy of Nature depicts how the categories of the Logic display themselves in the forms of the physical world, and how those forms all approximate to self-knowledge, to the embodiment of Idea. In the Philosophy of Spirit we discover how nature gives rise to human beings, who alone are capable of true self-consciousness. Humanity therefore constitutes the self-consciousness of nature – which is fully actualized when we come to awareness of the fundamental structure of reality itself, a structure revealed in the Logic. With the Philosophy of Spirit (and specifically with Absolute Spirit) Hegel's philosophy thus comes full circle. Hegel's *Encyclopedia of the Philosophical Sciences in Outline* constitutes his sketch of this philosophical system.

We can see from the foregoing that philosophy, for Hegel, is at one and the same time self-knowledge and knowledge of the whole. Thus, it satisfies the two classical Greek definitions of wisdom. For Hegel, as for Plato, there can be no knowledge of the self without a knowledge of the greater whole of which the self is a part. Hegel is able to make this claim in much stronger terms, owing to his doctrine of internal relations (in the simplest terms, the idea that all things are connected or inter-related; thus nothing truly stands alone as a bare individual or unit). Further, Hegel holds that the categories of thought studied in the Logic are simultaneously the categories of being. Hence, philosophy in its most fundamental form (as Logic) is both self-knowledge and knowledge of the whole.

Many philosophers today distinguish between philosophy and 'the history of philosophy' (often dismissing 'historians of philosophy' as non-philosophers). For Hegel, there is no distinction between the two. Philosophy just is the history of philosophy, for the true understanding of philosophy's history reveals it to be not simply a riot of different and incompatible standpoints, but the progressive articulation of *the truth*. In a fragment preserved by Hegel's biographer Karl Rosenkranz, Hegel states 'From the true cognition of [the principle of all philosophy], there will arise the conviction that there has been only one and the same philosophy at all times. So not only am I promising nothing new here, but rather am I devoting my philosophical work precisely to the restoration of the oldest of old things, and on liberating it from the misunderstanding in which the recent times of unphilosophy have buried it.'[19] All the different philosophers, each in his own way, articulated some aspect of the truth. All the very different approaches to philosophy – rationalism and empiricism, for example – each assert something that is true, but only within certain limits. Regardless of the differences between thinkers, philosophy has always had the two ultimate aims mentioned earlier: self-knowledge and knowledge of the whole, which together constitute 'wisdom'. To put things in the simplest possible terms, Hegel demonstrates how philosophy as a whole displays itself in time, in the person of the different philosophers, progressively realizing those two aims. The ultimate consummation of the love of wisdom occurs when, as discussed earlier, self-knowledge and knowledge of the whole become one and the same in a philosophy that demonstrates that self-knowledge is the purpose of existence itself.

Of course, an implication of this claim is that Hegel's system constitutes, in a real sense, the end of philosophy. Although Hegel does not say this outright, he makes remarks which come close to it, and such a claim is a clear implication of his thought. Another way of putting the foregoing, therefore, is to say that Hegel understands the entire history of philosophy as a series of partial, inadequate approaches to his own standpoint. Such a view may seem like colossal arrogance, but in fact it is a position that has been taken by other philosophers. Aristotle, for example, usually begins discussing an issue by reviewing what his predecessors had to say about it, and then demonstrates that each, in his own way, grasped part of the truth only fully grasped by himself. Furthermore, Hegel's argument for this position (like Aristotle's) is actually quite persuasive. What must be emphasized about this approach is that Hegel believes that philosophy underwent a necessary process of historical development. He believes that it would have been impossible, for example, for Plato to have grasped the whole truth in his own time. In order for philosophy to have reached Hegel's standpoint, certain historical changes had to take place (for example, the rise of Christianity), which could not have been anticipated and understood by Plato. Thus, in a sense all philosophy is a product of its time. Hegel, however, believes he is unique in that he lives in a time in which he is able to survey the history of philosophy and see that it has, in a sense, achieved its ultimate aims.

Hegel's account of the history of philosophy is to be found in remarks throughout his works, but the principal source for it is his *Lectures on the History of Philosophy*. Hegel taught this course nine times in his career: once in Jena in 1805–06; twice in Heidelberg in the period 1816–18; and six times in Berlin from 1819 to 1829. At the time of his death in 1831, he

Philosophy of Right

had just begun to teach the course for a tenth time. After Hegel's death the lectures were published in three volumes, for the first time in 1833–36. The material has since been heavily re-edited by different scholars, and re-issued several times. See also **Absolute Knowing**; **Absolute Spirit**; *Encyclopedia of the Philosophical Sciences in Outline*; **history and Philosophy of History**; **Logic**; **Philosophy of Nature**; **Philosophy of Spirit**; **picture-thinking**; **relation**; **science**; **speculation**; **system**.

***Philosophy of Right* (or *Elements of the Philosophy of Right; Grundlinien der Philosophie des Rechts*)**   Printed in 1821, *The Philosophy of Right* was the last book Hegel published in his lifetime. He had lectured on the subject matter of the work first in Heidelberg in the academic year 1817–18, then again in Berlin in 1818–19, where he would offer his course four more times. In the autumn of 1831 he lectured on *The Philosophy of Right* once more, but died a month after the course had begun. In short, Hegel lectured on this topic a total of seven times in the last fourteen years of his life. It is thus reasonable to conclude that it was of great importance to him, and it is easy to see why. The *Philosophy of Right* is Hegel's ethical and political philosophy. In it he sets forth his views on the nature of ethical life, the nature of society, and the purpose of government. In addition, he also deals with such matters as international law and the meaning of world history.

Hegel begins the *Philosophy of Right* with an attack on idealism in politics. Consider, for a moment, the Philosophy of Nature. Wouldn't it have been peculiar if Hegel, in addition to describing the fundamental forms of nature, had also legislated the ways in which nature ought to be different? This would be more than peculiar (ridiculous, even) because nature is a product of forces beyond our control, and it is futile to try and think of how nature could be otherwise. Wouldn't it be much wiser to try and see some inherent reason (or wisdom) in why nature is the way it is? This is, of course, precisely the approach Hegel does take with nature – and, surprisingly, he takes exactly the same approach with the human world of society and the state. For Hegel, it makes about as much sense to 'critique' society as it does to 'critique' nature. The human world – the world of Spirit – has its laws too. It is the task of the philosopher to discern what these laws are, not to legislate new ones. Human society as we know it is the product of thousands of years of historical evolution, in which there may be a profound wisdom at work. It is sheer hubris, Hegel believes, to look at this product and to reject it, dreaming of something 'better'.

Infamously, Hegel states that 'What is rational is actual; and what is actual is rational' (Nisbet, 20). The actual is an expression of Idea, and as a result the actual comes more and more to be a recognizable expression of the rational working itself out in time. It is up to us to discern the inherent rationality in what is. Further, Hegel tells us that philosophy always comprehends its own time, and cannot overstep its time. However, Hegel believed that his own time was unique because in it certain historical and philosophical trends had reached their natural conclusion, and that an absolute (as opposed to relative) truth could now be discerned.

To come now to a more basic issue, what does Hegel mean by 'right'? *The Philosophy of Right*, in fact, covers much of the same territory as what is termed 'Objective Spirit' in the *Encyclopedia*. 'Subjective Spirit', which precedes it, deals with the 'psychology' of the individual, including such matters as unconscious drives, perception, will, imagination, memory and the passions. In fact, it is a kind of bridge between nature and the human. Objective Spirit covers the world that humans have built themselves, which stands both in opposition to and dependence upon the natural order. At a basic level, we can call this the sphere of 'right' because the social world we have built is an expression of our sense of what 'ought' to be. This 'ought' is the human response to nature's bare 'is', and the expression of this ought is uniquely human. Further, as Hegel demonstrates, it is only within a concrete social context that our sense of 'right' develops.

In his Introduction, Hegel tells us that the idea of right is freedom, and later he remarks that the sphere of right encompasses all of ethical, social and political life, including history. In fact, Hegel shows how the development of these aspects of right is the development of will. The reason for this is that it is only in a social setting that my will becomes determinate and truly free. Hegel is careful to tell us that true freedom does not mean what he calls 'arbitrary will': doing whatever one likes. (This amounts to allowing ourselves to be led by our passions – but these are not things I have freely chosen!) Nor does freedom simply mean lack of constraint. Many things constrain me – both aspects of myself, and the society in which I live. Freedom as 'lack of constraint' simply doesn't exist. For Hegel, true freedom consists in affirming or 'willing' the ways in which we are determined. I may not have any control over the constraints placed on me by my society, but if

Philosophy of Right

I can come to understand the reasons behind these things, and the ways in which they make me and my sphere of action possible, then in a way they become 'mine'. Having made them mine in this fashion, I remove the sense of being constrained or oppressed by them. Oddly enough, true freedom for Hegel thus consists in choosing to accept our determination. For him, we must identify ourselves with the world in which we find ourselves, or feel forever oppressed by it.

Hegel divides *The Philosophy of Right* into three major sections: 'Abstract Right', 'Morality' and 'Ethical Life'. These are the three major spheres, as it were, in which right (and freedom) plays itself out dialectically. In these sections, we see how the will comes to determine itself, or to allow itself to be determined, in progressively more and more adequate forms. To put it a different way, in these sections Hegel treats different, dialectically-related ways of conceiving the sphere of right, culminating in a fully adequate conception. What follows is a very brief account of the argument of *The Philosophy of Right*, each of the major divisions of which is treated under separate entries in this volume.

Abstract right is essentially the 'classical liberal' view of society as founded upon a contract, made for the benefit of individuals who are each pursuing their own self-interest. In a society founded upon abstract right, the primary relations between individuals (outside the family) are property relations, and government exists to protect property. Abstract right is, in fact, built around the most primitive form in which freedom expresses itself: the claim that this or that is *mine*. The trouble with such a society is that there is really nothing that binds people together aside from self-interest – nothing that creates a true sense of community. It is through Hegel's discussion of *wrong* that we actually discover how the dialectic passes beyond abstract right. Wrong (or injustice) typically involves coercion of some kind, which amounts to a refusal to recognize others as rights-bearing individuals like ourselves. This fundamental contradiction brings to light something positive: a universal principle of right or justice. It is out of a recognition of this principle, in fact, that we demand wrong-doers be punished. (Hegel's discussion of punishment is one of the most famous parts of *The Philosophy of Right*. See the separate entry on this topic.)

Punishing wrongdoers in the name of right, however, requires impartial judges able to set aside their individual interests and to judge according to universal principles. But in the sphere of abstract right we concern ourselves with the rules for purely selfish reasons. Hegel therefore argues that abstract right cannot be self-sufficient, because its self-maintenance requires a *moral standpoint* which it does not itself foster. Aside from enjoining us not to restrict the liberties of others, abstract right also provides us with no guidance in determining just *what* the universal principles of right might be. As a consequence, the dialectic passes beyond abstract right – right considered in its external or objective manifestation – to morality, which deals with right as it develops itself in the subjective, inner life of the individual.

In morality (a term which Hegel uses here in a special sense) we look to conscience, feelings, sentiments, or to abstract moral principles we have derived ourselves and chosen autonomously – a further form in which freedom realizes itself. But how precisely is the subject supposed to derive principles from his or her 'inwardness'? Hegel's discussion of morality is a profound critique of ethical theories such as Kant's, which base morality on abstract rules 'legislated' by individual conscience or reason. The dialectic turns, therefore, from morality to ethical life.

Hegel's account of ethical life shows that what ethics requires, in fact, is a social setting in which individuals are tutored in concrete moral traditions, and in which their faculty of moral judgement is honed and refined. Essentially, Hegel argues that individuals do not learn to be ethical through the absorption of abstract rules. Instead, they develop ethical attitudes as a result of finding themselves situated within a social whole, and realizing their place vis-à-vis others. In other words, it is within a social whole – in my relations to others – that I am led to rise above a narrow concern with the satisfaction of my personal impulses and desires and to become aware of higher duties and obligations. Ethical life, for Hegel, has three moments which constitute the three most basic such 'social wholes', the institutions of family, civil society and the state.

The family is the simplest and most 'natural' of these. Marriage is an ethical institution because husband and wife subordinate their individual, subjective wills to the good of the marriage and the family they create together. 'The good' becomes the good of the family itself. We do not hold this in the form of an abstract principle, but simply through the feeling of love. Through love we subordinate individual feelings and desires to the good of the whole. Of course, the children eventually leave home and enter into what Hegel calls civil society. This is, in effect, the 'business world' of

Philosophy of Right

strife and competition, the antithesis of the loving family. Still, it is through civil society that individuals acquire a determinate sphere in which they can realize who they are and exercise others sorts of freedom. Freedom actualizes itself in civil society mainly through the choice of occupation, and ethical development is made possible by membership in what Hegel calls 'corporations' (guilds, unions and professional associations). Membership in a corporation encourages co-operation and fellow-feeling. Through participation in civil society, we come to see society itself as a condition for the possibility of our freedom. Under the heading of 'Administration of Justice', Hegel deals with how disputes over property or violations of property rights are protected in civil society. Here Hegel discusses how civil society promulgates certain basic principles of justice, such as the idea that everyone is equal before the law.

The public-spiritedness engendered by civil society is, however, motivated largely by self-interest. Therefore, Hegel argues that there must be some still greater whole in society that serves to bind people together; something that transcends individual self-interest. This is the state, which unites people by embodying the spirit of the nation: its traditions, mores and customs. In ethical terms, the state is an advance on civil society because it creates a sense of common citizenship and obligation to the whole. The state not only unifies the people, it safeguards and supports the spheres of family and civil society. These more or less 'private' spheres are made possible by a public, legal order which protects and regulates them. The state preserves and protects the different sorts of freedoms we have seen expressing themselves in family and civil society. Further, it makes a place for the freedoms we found under abstract right and morality: freedom expressing itself through property claims, and through the conscience of the individual. It is obvious from what has been said so far, however, that for Hegel the state is not merely 'government': an apparatus of laws, departments and authorities. The state is 'Objective Spirit' and it provides a people with a reflection of itself. As noted earlier, Hegel argues in *The Philosophy of Right* that freedom is truly realized only through identifying ourselves with our community. What this really means is that true freedom only comes about through membership in the state.

Hegel's state is a constitutional monarchy. The role of the monarch, as he conceives it, is simply to be the final authority. The King is advised by his officials, and his job is to make their recommendations the policy of the state. Should there be disagreement among the officials, it is the King who decides. Such a 'decider' is a practical necessity, and Hegel believes that society needs to see the 'spirit of the nation' embodied in a single personality. The simplest and most unproblematic way to 'select' such an individual is through hereditary succession. Aside from the role of the sovereign, Hegel also discusses the 'executive branch' of government (in which he includes the judiciary). Public opinion has its say in the legislative branch, though Hegel tells us, wisely, that the state must both respect and distrust public opinion. Hegel's legislature consists of two houses: the upper house consists of the landed aristocracy, and the lower house is essentially made up of representatives of the business class.

The Philosophy of Right ends with a sketch of international relations and of world history. If we ask how different states (or different nations) exist in relation to one another, essentially Hegel asserts that they exist in a state of nature. Because there is no authority (no 'world government') to which the individual states are subject, their relations are fundamentally lawless. As a result, periodic conflicts are inevitable. However, Hegel does not see war as unqualifiedly bad. States, like individuals, have a lifespan. Wars often have the effect of ending outworn ways of life, or societal structures. Wars also galvanize people and cause them to feel a greater sense of national solidarity.

History, for Hegel, reveals the coming-into-being of the modern state, which recognizes the inherent dignity and rights of all individuals, making a place for public opinion to speak its mind while never losing sight of the fact that citizens must be educated and guided in the making of sound judgements. The 'ideal form' of the state is displayed in *The Philosophy of Right*. Hegel's state is not identical with any form of government existing in his time, though here and there it bears similarities to many. It is completely false and ridiculous to say, as some have, that it is simply a carbon copy of the Prussian state under which Hegel was then living and working. Instead, Hegel's state is an ideal which has revealed itself in the modern world, and the modern, Western states are approximations to it. It is not an ideal like Plato's city in the *Republic*, or like Marx's communist utopia: it is an ideal that is embodied to one degree or another in different places. See also **abstract right; civil society; ethical life; family; freedom; history and Philosophy of History; morality; Objective Spirit; 'owl of Minerva'; punishment; 'real is the rational. . .'; right; state; wrong.**

Philosophy of Spirit

Philosophy of Spirit (*die Philosophie des Geistes*) The Philosophy of Spirit is the third division of Hegel's system, after Logic and Philosophy of Nature. (It is also the third division of *The Encyclopedia of the Philosophical Sciences in Outline* – the only complete overview of the Philosophy of Spirit Hegel produced.)

The categories of Hegel's Logic constitute a conceptual account of the fundamental nature of reality, culminating in Idea itself, which transcends the distinction between subjectivity and objectivity. The Philosophy of Nature interprets nature in terms of the categories of the Logic, and shows how all natural forms approximate to the embodiment of Idea: to the transcendence of the subject-object distinction achieved in *self-consciousness*. Individual animals or plants are 'specifications' of the Idea, but each living thing expresses the universal in its own limited and one-sided way. Furthermore, each dies. (Individual living things are thus 'overcome', in a manner analogous to how specific definitions of the Absolute are overcome dialectically in the Logic.)

In Spirit, in human nature, the Idea finds a more adequate expression. In self-aware Spirit, the Idea implicit in nature has become explicit, or for-itself. Human beings are, of course, natural beings; yet they transcend the merely natural through their unique form of consciousness. It is human beings alone who are capable of true self-consciousness, and who are thus the true embodiment of the self-related thought that is Idea. With the Philosophy of Spirit, therefore, Hegel's philosophy comes full circle back to Logic, for it is in the terms of the Logic, fundamentally, that we achieve what is simultaneously self-knowledge, and knowledge of existence itself. Indeed, one can say that humanity constitutes the self-awareness of existence. Through us, existence turns back upon itself and knows itself. Through us, it achieves closure and completeness. Hegel tells us that Spirit achieves an experience of a world which is 'merely an apprehension of itself', and that 'the aim of all genuine science is just this, that Spirit shall recognize itself in everything in heaven and on earth. An out-and-out other simply does not exist for Spirit' (Wallace, 1; PS § 377 A).

Hegel divides the Philosophy of Spirit into Subjective Spirit, Objective Spirit and Absolute Spirit. In Subjective Spirit Hegel deals with the 'psychology' of the individual, including such matters as unconscious or preconscious feelings and drives, perception, will, imagination, memory and the passions. In Subjective Spirit, Spirit is not yet in possession of itself;

not yet truly self-aware. The aspects of ourselves discussed in this section are just as much an 'other' to us as is the external world. Our task is to make the material of Subjective Spirit our own, which means to bring it under the control of the conscious self, and to understand it. Objective Spirit is humanity expressing or 'objectifying' its nature in the world through culture, tradition, moral order, government, law, and world history. Humanity is not, however, always aware that these are a projection of its own nature, and may attribute them to external factors. Thus, while Objective Spirit is one way in which humanity confronts itself, it does not do so with full consciousness. (Much of the material of Objective Spirit is covered far more thoroughly in the 1821 *Philosophy of Right*, Hegel's last book.) Absolute Spirit, by contrast, is Spirit come to full consciousness of itself through art, religion and, pre-eminently, philosophy. Hegel's lectures on Aesthetics, Philosophy of Religion and the History of Philosophy can be considered his fullest elaboration of Absolute Spirit, which is covered only very briefly in the *Encyclopedia*.

The Philosophy of Spirit must be understood as distinct from the similarly-titled *Phenomenology of Spirit*. The first major division of Subjective Spirit is 'Anthropology', the data of which do not appear in the *Phenomenology*, even though we know that Hegel was working on this material in the Jena period. The *Phenomenology* presupposes the ego and, for the most part, excludes from consideration subconscious or unconscious processes (which are covered in Hegel's treatment of Subjective Spirit). In the 1807 *Phenomenology* Hegel narrows his scope and presents only the material on Spirit which is needed for his primary aim: an account of Spirit in a number of different forms, showing how each form is merely a stopping point on the way to Absolute Spirit. The reader is intended to work his way through each stage, abandoning each as inadequate to achieve the ultimate goal of wisdom. Hegel does repeat a certain amount of material from the *Phenomenology* in the Philosophy of Spirit, primarily in a subsection entitled 'Phenomenology'. This material is presented, however, in the context of Hegel's scientific account of human conscious faculties, and eschews the educative, initiatory function of the 1807 *Phenomenology*. Thus, the *Phenomenology* and Philosophy of Spirit, despite certain commonalities, should be seen as very different works, differing not only in content but in intent. See also **Absolute Spirit**; ***Encyclopedia of the Philosophical Sciences in Outline***;

physics

Objective Spirit; phenomenology; *Phenomenology of Spirit*; Spirit; Subjective Spirit.

phrenology (*die Schädellehre*) Hegel's famous discussion of phrenology occurs in *The Phenomenology of Spirit*, in the first subsection of Division C (AA.) Reason. Phrenology is the 'science' of determining a person's character by means of the bumps or indentations on the head, which differ from person to person. It was developed by Franz Joseph Gall (1758–1828) and is generally considered today to be a pseudo-science. This is essentially Hegel's take on the matter, and he discusses it in the *Phenomenology* in connection with a similar pseudo-science, the physiognomy of Johann Kaspar Lavater (1741–1801), which purported to reveal an individual's character through the shape of the body. Hegel attacks both of these as forms of what would today be called 'reductive materialism': the belief that everything about human personality can be understood in terms of bodily features, organs and processes. Hegel maintains that the true expression of a person's character is to be found in his acts, not in his bodily shape or bumps. In a fundamental sense, Spirit is not a thing: Spirit is the world of things come to consciousness of itself. Yet the reductive materialist wants to treat himself simply as one material thing among many. This approach simply cannot account for Spirit's freedom – its capacity to negate and transform the given, including itself. Freedom cannot be found in the bumps on our head – or, we might add, in the cells in our brain and their inter-relations. Had Hegel lived today, he might well have attacked neurophysiology (and much of 'philosophy of mind') as pseudo-scientific, given its reductive materialist assumptions. See also **freedom**; *Phenomenology of Spirit*; **Spirit**.

physics (*die Physik*) The Philosophy of Nature consists of three main stages or moments: 'Mechanics', 'Physics' and 'Organics'. Mechanics treats the 'external aspect' of matter, dealing with the actions of one thing upon another. With physics we turn to the interiority of matter. We discover not only that the individual material body must be understood as containing within itself an order and structure, but that the relations between bodies are affected by that interior structure and are capable of altering it.

In the 'Physics of Universal Individuality,' Hegel discusses the nature of the solar, planetary, lunar and cometary bodies and their relations –

followed by a treatment of another quaternity, the four elements of earth, air, fire and water. Along the way there occurs a highly significant discussion of light, which Hegel describes as the 'universal self' of matter, because in light everything reveals itself. Further, because light unifies things without physically affecting them, it is a kind of 'spatial' reflection of the Idea.

In the 'Physics of Particular Individuality', Hegel deals with the characteristics of material objects through which their individuality is determined. Cohesion, for example, constitutes a 'will toward individuality' in its most primitive form. But what coheres can, of course, come loose. The direction Hegel is moving in here is to show that matter possesses a fatal flaw which will always frustrate its 'drive' to be individual, self-sustaining and self-determining.

In the 'Physics of Total Individuality', Hegel deals with forces or processes which can, in differing ways, serve to involve separate material bodies in totalities greater than themselves. Magnetism is the first such phenomenon Hegel treats. This attracting force is answered by a repulsing force: electricity. Hegel treats electricity figuratively as the lashing out of bodies against each other. Chemical process is the 'unity of magnetism and electricity' (Miller, 233; PN § 326). It is capable of effecting the highest type of fusion or totality encountered thus far, because in chemical process different matters interact with one another in such a way that their fundamental natures change. They can even become the ingredients in the production of an entirely new being. In this latter case, the individuality of the ingredients is thoroughly obliterated. Hegel's discussion of chemical process covers alloys, galvanism, combustion, formation of salts, and chemical affinity. The intrinsic flaw in chemical process, however, is that it is effected only through the intervention of an external agent.

Hegel's reflections on the processes of mechanics and physics show how these must be understood in terms of the production of individuality and wholeness. What is, in a sense, anticipated in those reflections is an individual which is a complex whole of parts, and which can effect its own chemical and other processes without the continual intervention of external forces. Obviously, this is a description of a living being, and so Hegel passes from physics to organics. See also **light**; **matter**; **mechanics**; **nature and Philosophy of Nature**; **organics**.

picture-thinking (*die Vorstellung;* or *das vorstellende Denken*) Hegel sometimes uses the term 'picture-thinking' to describe the tendency of most people to conceive of ideas in terms of images. ('Picture-thinking' is a widely-used translation of Hegel's *Vorstellung*, a word which in other German authors is often translated as 'representation'.) This is a common tendency in unphilosophical people (and even in some philosophers) and is closely associated with what Hegel calls the understanding. For Hegel, philosophy demands that we completely eschew picture-thinking. His Logic requires a new form of conceptual thought that even avoids 'applying' concepts to real-word examples, striving instead to understand concepts and their relations in as pure a manner as possible.

Religion, for Hegel, is the truth grasped in picture-thinking. Philosophy speaks of the Absolute and gives a purely rational, dialectical account of its nature. Religion speaks instead of God and uses images and myths to reach an understanding of it. Though Hegel regards religion as a legitimate (and necessary) expression of Spirit, in another way he sees philosophy as approaching the truth more adequately, precisely because he believes that rational, conceptual thought always proves more adequate to the expression of the truth than picture-thinking. See also **commonsense; Logic; religion and Philosophy of Religion; understanding**.

place and motion See **space and time**.

psychology (*die Psychologie*) Hegel divides his treatment of Subjective Spirit into 'Anthropology', 'Phenomenology' and 'Psychology'. Anthropology deals with 'the soul': that aspect of our selves that is still mired in nature and is not a function of the conscious mind. Phenomenology, on the other hand, deals with 'consciousness' and 'self-conciousness', in which the ego or selfhood appears. The content of the soul in effect becomes an 'other' for ego, which it must take control of. In 'Reason', the final division of Phenomenology, a form of conscious thought is attained which is intersubjective, rather than being merely personal. Psychology, the final major section of Subjective Spirit, deals with much that would be termed 'theory of knowledge' today. This is especially the case in the first division of psychology, 'Theoretical Spirit', where Hegel covers such topics as the nature of sensation, attention, intuition, memory, imagination, judgement, logical reasoning, etc. It would be impossible to do justice to this material here. At every step, Hegel is treating theoretical spirit as an effort to make the object its own – to annul the subject-object distinction – in thought. For example, in recollection the object becomes 'mine' because I can call it to mind at will. In imagination it becomes still more my possession, because I can alter my recollection of it however I please. Full 'possession' of the object comes with its integration into our theoretical account of the whole. Full possession means full understanding.

'Practical Spirit', the second subdivision of psychology, involves a very different way in which we attempt to reshape the object. This time it is not through observation or understanding or theory-building, but through concrete practice. The most primitive form this takes is that of feeling: feelings such as agreeableness and disagreeableness tell us how the world 'ought' to be. The world, of course, frustrates our feelings, and so feelings issue in desires, impulses or yearnings, which are largely unreflective 'plans' for going about in the world. Of course, this approach to things cannot produce ultimate satisfaction. It cannot negate the otherness of the other; reality keeps resisting, and so happiness remains always just out of reach. With 'Phenomenology' we passed into the sphere of ego-controlled activity, but it is clear that our passions and drives are not chosen by us. Not only does a world stand opposed to me, but so does much that is mine: my sensations, memories, emotions, drives, impulses, etc.

'Free Spirit', the third subdivision of 'Psychology', involves the subject understanding all that has gone before as the necessary condition of its development. It does not suddenly become free of its unchosen impulses, but it learns to understand them. Thus, no part of Spirit is alien to itself. Nevertheless, it would be impossible to rise to the level of Absolute Spirit and the philosophical standpoint if our feelings, drives and impulses went unchecked. Only civilized society can force us to sublimate and channel our drives in such a way that we may eventually realize our full human potential. Hegel turns, therefore, to the level of Objective Spirit. See also **anthropology; Objective Spirit; phenomenology; Philosophy of Spirit; Subjective Spirit.**

punishment (*die Strafe*) Hegel's discussion of punishment occurs in the section on 'Wrong' in *The Philosophy of Right*, within the subdivision 'Abstract Right'. Hegel tells us that punishment (or righting the wrong) is a negation of the negativity of crime. ('The criminal act is not an initial

quality, quantity, measure

positive occurrence followed by the punishment as its negation, but is itself negative, so that the punishment is merely the negation of the negation,' Nisbet, 123; PR § 97 A). To negate a negation is to restore the positive that was negated in the first place: not (not x) = x. To negate *in*justice is thus to restore justice. Hegel's theory of punishment is one of the most famous and controversial parts of *The Philosophy of Right*, mainly because he asserts that it is the criminal's *right* to be punished.

In so far as criminals are capable of looking beyond the narrow frame of reference they call their 'self-interest', and are capable of thinking in rational (i.e., universal) terms, they will see that what they have done is a negation of justice, and so must be put right. The negation must be negated through a just punishment. And so, at some level, criminals *will* their own punishment. Furthermore, Hegel tells us that insofar as we give criminals their just punishment, we honour reason in them. The punishment is what criminals could see to be justified – *if* they were able to see the situation objectively and rationally. (Hegel is not so naive as to imagine that all criminals will actually exercize such cool-headed judgement!) And so, by giving them what they themselves *ought* to see as just, we honour their own rational judgement, their own wish. We might respond to Hegel that perhaps our aim should be to 'rehabilitate' criminals, not to punish them. Hegel, however, says that this is to treat criminals as if they were dumb animals in need of better conditioning. The humane thing to do is not to rehabilitate but to punish, because at least in punishing criminals we are recognizing their humanity: their rational nature. See also **abstract right**; *Philosophy of Right*; **wrong**.

quality, quantity, measure (*die Qualität, die Quantität, das Maß*) The Doctrine of Being, the first major division of Hegel's Logic, is divided into three main sub-sections: 'Quality', 'Quantity' and 'Measure'. In order to fully understand the argument of the Doctrine of Being, one must go through the dialectic of categories within these sub-sections. However, a brief overview is possible.

If we make a first stab at defining what being is we might say that to be is to be some *sort* of thing or other – to possess this or that characteristic. In short, we might identify being with quality: to be is to possess certain definite qualities. This is a perfectly valid assertion, but it is incomplete. Beings certainly do possess qualities, but they always do so in some degree or amount. To take a simple example, let's say that something is red. How red? Red all over? We must, therefore, supplement quality with quantity. Everything that exists, in fact, is a qualitative quantum. Hegel states that, 'Quantum is the way that quality is there [i.e., exists; *ist das Dasein*] . . .' (Geraets, 161; EL § 101 A). Nevertheless, qualities may not exist in any quantity. For example, if a man grew tall enough to bump his head on the moon we actually wouldn't consider him a mere man any longer. Everything has quality in some quantity, but if one is changed the other may be changed also. Therefore, something must determine a quantitative range in which the qualities of something can exist. This notion of a limit to quantity leads us to the final division of the Doctrine of Being – 'Measure'. The realization of the necessity of measure, in turn, will point beyond being to the Doctrine of Essence, to the inner 'nature' of something, which must determine its limits. As Hegel puts it in the *Encyclopedia Logic*, 'essence is being as shining within itself [*als Scheinen in sich selbst*]' (Geraets, 175; EL § 112). See also **Being, Doctrine of**; **determinate being**; **Logic**; **measureless**.

quantum (*das Quantum*)   In the Logic, Hegel first treats being as having to do with quality: to be is to possess this or that quality or characteristic. However, beings always possess qualities in some degree or amount. Therefore, Hegel passes from a consideration of quality to quantity. A quantum is simply a limited or circumscribed quantity: quanta result when a quantity is broken up into distinct units by the imposition of a limit. A quantum is distinct from other quanta and is delimited by them – not unlike how determinate being (under the division 'Quality') is delimited by other determinate beings. The difference, however, is that a determinate being is delimited by something qualitatively different from itself. Quanta, however, are not distinguished from one another in virtue of any qualitative *or* quantitative differences. The quanta possess the characteristics of the whole (the quantity) from which they were derived, and they are quantitatively identical. Quanta are thus indistinguishable 'units', and Hegel argues that it is the derivation of quanta which forms the basis of number. When quanta are collected together into 'sums' we have the basis for enumeration. See also **Being, Doctrine of**; **being-for-self**; **determinate being**; **number**; **quality, quantity, measure**.

— R —

'real is the rational . . .'   Notoriously, in the Preface to *The Philosophy of Right*, Hegel states that 'What is rational is actual; and what is actual is rational' (*Was vernünftig ist, das ist wirklich; und was wirklich ist, das ist vernünftig*, Nisbet, 20; often glossed as 'The real is the rational, and the rational is the real'). Then and now, many readers have understood him as trying to justify or excuse the status quo. More specifically, he has often been accused of trying to legitimize the existing political order of his time. In short, these famous lines have often been taken as an expression of a reactionary tendency in Hegel, at least in his later years. However, this is largely a misunderstanding of what Hegel intended.

In his lectures, Hegel expressed the same idea *dynamically*, stating that 'What is actual becomes rational, and the rational becomes actual.'[20] For Hegel, the Idea of the Logic considered in itself has no *actual* existence, but all that does actually exist can be understood as an expression or realization of it. Thus, despite false starts and wrong turns, the actual comes to be discernible more and more as an expression of the rational working itself out in time. It is our task to see this inherent rationality in what is. However, this is not the same thing as coming to see everything as 'good'. What it does mean is that we come to understand that things are as they are for a reason, and that they may perhaps be that way because there is an end or purpose towards which things are working. And so, later in the Preface, Hegel enjoins us to discern 'the rose in the cross of the present' (Nisbet, 22). Further, Hegel tells us that philosophy always comprehends its own time, and cannot transcend its time. This sounds like an expression of radical historicism – but Hegel believed that his own time was unique, in that in it certain historical and philosophical trends had reached their natural conclusion, and that an absolute (as opposed to relative) truth could be discerned. See also **actuality; history and Philosophy of History; 'owl of Minerva';** *Philosophy of Right*; **'rose in the cross of the present'**.

reality   See **actuality**.

reason (*die Vernunft*)   Reason is one of the most important concepts in Hegel, and a term he often uses. Hegel's conception of reason as distinct from and 'higher' than understanding, is something he takes over from Kant. In Kant's philosophy, understanding is the faculty that judges and interprets the appearances of objects in space-time according to certain *a priori* categories. Our 'commonsense' view of the world is therefore the product of understanding, and science is founded upon the same categories. For Kant, reason is the faculty of the mind that strives to, in a sense, go beyond the understanding by attempting to effect higher-level syntheses of knowledge. For example, when science strives to understand not this part of nature or that, but to arrive at a total understanding of the 'complete series of conditions' in nature, it is reason that is at work, pushing the mind to think beyond the here-and-now. According to Kant, we can never arrive at such total knowledge, but reason strives for it nonetheless, as a kind of 'regulative ideal'. This is the positive function of reason. It functions negatively when it hypostatizes such ideals and imagines that it can arrive at knowledge of transcendent objects (e.g., God or the soul) through 'pure reason' unaided by the senses. Kant attempts to demonstrate the futility of such metaphysical ambitions through his 'transcendental dialectic', which purports to show that there are equally good arguments on both sides of metaphysical issues (the so-called 'antinomies').

Hegel adopts but radically transforms this distinction between reason and the understanding. Hegel claims that the dialectic of reason can be a means to actually achieve the higher-level syntheses of knowledge that Kant believes to be impossible, and he introduces his own distinction between negative and positive aspects of reason (quite different from Kant's distinction). The negative aspect is just dialectic, which (for Hegel) has the function of demonstrating that there are contradictions inherent in the understanding's views on any matter. Dialectic sets up antitheses, but

recognition

what Kant failed to see is that these antitheses can be transcended through speculation, the positive aspect of reason. It is speculation that is able to see how antithetical ideas may be reconciled or overcome in a further idea, a third moment which cancels the opposition of the first two. Hegel's concept of the understanding is similar to Kant's, insofar as he sees the understanding as the faculty that interprets experience according to set categories. But Hegel's treatment of understanding is almost always negative, because he believes it is unable to think beyond those set, i.e., fixed and rigid, categories. In particular, it is prone to thinking in terms of inflexible dichotomies. (Because Hegel sees this tendency at work in Kant's treatment of the antinomies, and other matters, he regards Kant, for all his genius, as a philosopher of the understanding.) Reason, as Hegel conceives it, is essentially the faculty that transcends the either-or thinking of the understanding.

Although Hegel, like Kant, treats reason as a faculty of the mind, unlike Kant, Hegel also believes that there is an objective reason inherent in the world itself. For Hegel, the world is the Idea unfolding itself in time, according to an objective dialectical process that parallels the dialectic of the Logic. Thus, it is possible for Hegel to discern a rational process at work in history (in addition to nature), and to speak of the 'cunning of reason'. See also **'cunning of reason'**; **dialectic**; **Kant, Immanuel**; **reflection**; **speculation**; **understanding**.

recognition (*die Anerkennung*)   In *The Phenomenology of Spirit*, in the section on 'Self-Consciousness', Hegel argues that self-consciousness can only occur when we encounter ourselves in the responses of another human being who sees us as like himself. We must, in short, be *recognized* by that other. Furthermore, we don't desire this recognition just from certain people. We desire to be recognized – to be affirmed as what we are – by *everyone*. Therefore, Hegel argues that ultimately we can be satisfied only by universal recognition.

Hegel claims that the desire for recognition is of such importance to human beings that they are willing to risk death in order to gain recognition from others. In fact, our willingness to risk our lives for ideals like recognition is what makes us distinct from animals. In the *Phenomenology*, Hegel presents a vivid picture of what he takes to be the first and most primitive form in which human beings sought recognition from one another: the so-called 'master–servant dialectic'. Imagine two individuals who each fight to be recognized by the other. Suppose one yields to the other. He would become what Hegel calls the 'servant' (*Knecht*), whereas the victor would be the 'master' (*Herr*). The master is recognized by the servant, but not vice versa. To the master, the servant is subhuman: an individual who valued mere life over honour (or recognition). Nevertheless, the servant's recognition can hardly be satisfying to the master, since it is the recognition of an inferior. In truth, neither is satisfied.

The next stages of the dialectic follow out the transformations of the servant's consciousness, as it seeks recognition (and freedom) through other means. Freed from physical labour by the servant, the master loses himself in pleasure and becomes dissipated. The servant fares better, for he actually develops as an individual and achieves greater self-knowledge through his work. In fact, Hegel argues that the servant creates culture – including science, technology and the arts – while the master simply stagnates. Hegel discusses 'stoicism', 'scepticism' and 'the unhappy consciousness' as forms in which the servant tries – and fails – to win freedom and recognition (of a kind) through *thought* alone.

For Hegel, in fact, all of human history can be understood as the struggle for universal recognition. This is finally achieved only through membership in the modern state, which affirms the freedom and dignity of all of its members. In other words, it is only when the distinction between masters and servants is annulled that freedom and universal recognition are achieved.[21] See also **freedom**; **history and Philosophy of History**; **'master–servant dialectic'**; ***Phenomenology of Spirit***; **self-consciousness**.

recollection, imagination, memory (*die Erinnerung, die Einbildungskraft, das Gedächtnis*) Hegel discusses the psychological functions of recollection, imagination and memory in his account of Subjective Spirit. Recollection is the capacity to retain an intuition and call it to mind at will. First, we have a sensory intuition of an object in space and time. Then, through recollection, we are able to recall this intuition within the privacy of our own minds. In imagination we can alter the image at will. We can, for example, recall an image of someone's face, but imagine them with a moustache, or wearing a different tie. Whereas recollection and imagination involve images, in memory (as Hegel defines it) we are freed from images through language. Human language is a system of symbols which frees us from exclusive concern with the individual and momentary, and allows us to conceive the universal. Memory involves our ability to retain words and what they mean, and to recall them and use them when need be. All three of these processes in a sense involve the subject overcoming the otherness of the object, and making the object its own conscious possession.

Hegel also employs the term 'recollection' in the final section of *The Phenomenology of Spirit*: Absolute Knowing. There, Hegel uses the term several times to describe what has occurred in the foregoing text. At one point he hyphenates the German word as *Er-Innerung*, suggesting an interpretation of 'recollection' as a 'going within' of the subject (*inner* has the same meaning in German as in English, and *Innerung* has the sense of 'innering' or 'inwardizing').[22] The *Phenomenology* is, in fact, a recollection of Spirit's development by Spirit itself. It is Spirit going within itself, recollecting itself, and writing its autobiography – not in the sense of a literal history, but instead the *natural* history of its manifestations. See also **Absolute Knowing; 'owl of Minerva'; Phenomenology of Spirit; psychology; Spirit; Subjective Spirit.**

reflection (*die Reflexion*)   In the Doctrine of Essence of the Logic, Hegel explains that 'The term "reflection" is primarily used of light, when, propagated rectilinearly, it strikes a mirrored surface and is thrown back by it' (Geraets, 176; EL § 112 A). Something similar is going on when we say that we reflect on something or think it over. First, we consider it just as it appears. Then thought, as it were, 'bounces back' from the surface and tries to consider it in terms of underlying reasons or grounds which explain why the thing appears as it does. Reflection thus demarcates things into appearance and (underlying) essence. Hegel shows how the standpoint of reflection usually involves thinking in terms of conceptual pairs, each member of which is what it is only in relation to its other: e.g., appearance and essence, form and matter, thing and properties, whole and parts, force and its manifestation, etc. Typically, these conceptual pairs always involve a distinction – founded upon the fundamental distinction between appearance and essence – between what is given immediately, and what is mediated. To take one example, for reflection the manifestation of a force is given immediately, as a phenomenon in the physical world – but our awareness of the underlying force is mediated by the appearance of its manifestations (i.e., the manifestations are known directly, the force indirectly).

Hegel regards reflection as a necessary and valuable form of thought, though he also sees it as extremely limited in what it can accomplish. Reflection reaches its zenith in the Kantian philosophy, where it is essentially an attempt to think beyond the immediate surface appearance of things and to understand how that appearance is mediated by factors or conditions that do not themselves appear. Considered in itself, Kantian reflection is most certainly an advance on earlier sorts of philosophy. However, reflection erects a dichotomy between appearance and reality (or essence) and holds to this opposition rigidly. In general, reflection makes progress in philosophy by discerning the necessary dependence of certain concepts or structures on others, but it tends to hold fast to these conceptual relations or oppositions, and proves incapable of thinking beyond them. (This is essentially the problem with what Hegel calls the understanding – making reflection and understanding closely-related terms in Hegel.)

In Kantian reflection, the opposition of subject and object is rigidly maintained, with the subject's awareness confined to phenomena (or appearances) and forever unable to penetrate beyond them to things-in-themselves (or things as they *really* are). Speculative philosophy (the standpoint of Hegel) overcomes the dichotomy of subject and object by conceiving of a human activity in which subject becomes object, and vice versa: Absolute Knowing. Hegel also overcomes Kant's appearance/reality dichotomy by understanding appearance as the unfolding of reality itself: appearances or phenomena *just are* the Absolute displaying itself in all its myriad forms, apart from which the Absolute (or 'the real') is an empty posit. Hegelian speculation thus allows us to transcend reflection and its insistence on hard and fast conceptual dichotomies.

Hegel refers to the standpoint of the Doctrine of Essence as that of reflection, and he refers to the categories of essence as 'categories of reflection'. In the Doctrine of Essence, a series of appearance/reality dichotomies is set up: the 'inner truth' is always the *antithesis* of the outward show or appearance. However, just as they are in Kant, these antitheses are ultimately false. Thus, as Hegel makes clear, the standpoint of Essence is false (in the sense of being partial or one-sided) and must be

relation

overcome by the Doctrine of the Concept. Reflection gives us *part* of the truth, but Hegel shows us this truth in the process of its own self-overcoming. See also **Absolute Spirit**; **dialectic**; **Essence, Doctrine of**; **Fichte, J. G.**; **Kant, Immanuel**; **Logic**; **reason**; **speculation**; **understanding**.

relation (*die Beziehung; das Verhältnis*) Hegelian philosophy distinguishes between two basic sorts of relation. Items are *externally related* to each other when the removal or alteration of one makes no difference to the being of another. For example, in the statement 'x and y' it makes no difference to either term if we reverse the order and make it 'y and x'. Also, if x were simply eliminated, it would not alter y. An example drawn from ordinary life would be the items on the table in my kitchen. They are a knife, a dish towel and a corkscrew. These items are related to each other in virtue simply (and solely) by being on the table. However, if I remove the knife and put it elsewhere, normally we would not think that the other items have somehow been changed. The understanding tends to view all relations as external. It views the world essentially as a collection of externally related particulars. The modern mechanistic-materialist view of nature (one of Hegel's frequent targets) exemplifies this view. In philosophy, probably the starkest example of this mentality is to be found in Bertrand Russell's theory of 'logical atomism' (which he consciously formulated as a response to the neo-Hegelian 'holism' championed by authors like F. H. Bradley).

By contrast, Hegel sees the world as a whole of *internally related* terms. His position is often glossed as maintaining that 'everything is related to everything else', and this position was in fact emphasized by later British and American Idealists like F. H. Bradley (1846–1924) and Brand Blanshard (1892–1987). (Blanshard is reputed to have introduced this idea to students by tossing a piece of chalk over his shoulder and declaring, 'I have just altered the coastline of China'.) For Hegel, each thing derives its meaning and being from its place within the whole, and each thing is what it is in *not* being others. Therefore, a change in one thing has the potential to affect myriad others. A simple example would be the body: disease in one organ has the potential to affect the functioning of all the others.

Contemporary Hegelian philosophers like Errol E. Harris have emphasized that the understanding's tendency to see only external relations is at the root of much of the mischief modern people have done against the environment. Implicitly believing things in nature to be related only externally, we have destroyed ecosystems and driven species to extinction, heedless of the consequences. If we believed, as Hegel does, in the principle of holism (which presupposes a doctrine of internal relations) we would be much more wary about tinkering with this or that part of nature. See also **coherence**; **identity and difference**; **mechanism, chemism, teleology**; **nature and Philosophy of Nature**; **understanding**; **whole, the**.

religion and Philosophy of Religion (*die Religion; die Philosophie der Religion*) Hegel's Philosophy of Religion is central to his thought, however he did not publish a Philosophy of Religion in his lifetime. Instead, he lectured on the topic in Berlin in 1821, 1824, 1827 and 1831. Editions of these lectures were published after his death.

According to Hegel, each of the forms of Absolute Spirit – art, religion and philosophy – constitutes a manner in which humanity puts itself into relation with the whole, and confronts itself through the whole. Hegel tells us that the content of both religion and philosophy is identical: both concern themselves with God. 'God is the one and only object of philosophy' (LPR I, 84; VPR I, 3). However, philosophy calls God the Absolute or Absolute Idea: the self-knowing thought that is the apex of existence. For Hegel, this exists only as embodied by self-knowing human minds, capable of philosophical reflection. Aside from their esoteric or mystical offshoots, however, religions typically do not recognize this, and conceive the divine as a transcendent other. Partly this is due to the fact that religion, like art, expresses itself in sensuous form: in images, metaphors and stories. Religion is humanity groping toward true self-understanding, but unable in the end to truly arrive at it precisely because of the limitations of the sensuous image. True self-awareness, in fact, may only be found in philosophy: the purely conceptual grasp of truth, unfolding in dialectical form.

In *The Philosophy of Right* Hegel states that 'The content of religion is absolute truth, and consequently the religious is the most sublime of all dispositions' (Nisbet, 292; PR § 270). Speculative philosophy, Hegel insists, is not hostile to religious belief. In fact, philosophy affirms that religion on its own, without the 'assistance' of philosophy, is absolute truth. Hegel states

religion and Philosophy of Religion

that 'religion is precisely the true content but in the form of picture-thinking, and philosophy is not the first to offer the substantive truth. Humanity has not had to await philosophy in order to receive for the first time the consciousness or cognition of truth' (LPR I, 251; VPR I, 159). Humanity, then, *can* receive the truth through religion alone, without the need for philosophy. Religion is for everyone, Hegel claims, unlike philosophy which is for the few.

Hegel believes that religious belief and religious practice will never cease to exist as human activities because people need to encounter the truth in 'sensuous form' – though philosophy still constitutes a more adequate articulation of the truth. Nevertheless, it would be a mistake to think that Hegel firmly dichotomizes religion and philosophy. It is true that there is a huge difference between religious belief, with its reliance on the image, and philosophy's reliance on the pure, abstract language of thought-determinations. Still, there are passages in Hegel that suggest that he regards philosophy as, in a sense, a higher form of religion. For instance, Hegel tells us that 'philosophy *is* theology, and [one's] occupation with philosophy – or rather *in* philosophy – is of itself the service of God [*Gottesdienst* – which can also be translated as 'worship']' (LPR I, 84; VPR I, 4).

Hegel believes that the truth has always been an unconscious possession of mankind. At various times and in the person of various thinkers, it has expressed itself in different forms, and in different degrees of adequacy and completeness. The philosopher 'recollects' this unconscious wisdom in a form that can fully, and finally, express it. This interpretation is supported by Hegel's remarks in *The Lectures on the Philosophy of Religion*, where he refers to religions as 'sprouting up fortuitously, like the flowers and creations of nature, as foreshadowings, images, representations, without [our] knowing where they come from or where they are going to' (LPR I, 196; VPR I, 106). Hegel states that 'Religion is a begetting of the divine spirit, not an invention of human beings but an effect of the divine at work, of the divine productive process within humanity' (LPR I, 130; VPR I, 46).

Hegel does not, however, regard all religions as equally adequate expressions of eternal truth. In the *Lectures*, Hegel presents a kind of taxonomy of religions past and present, which he changed greatly over the years. His presentation of this material is highly idiosyncratic, and reflects the very rudimentary nature of contemporary scholarship on ancient and non-Western religions. This material is grouped by Hegel under the heading

'Determinate Religion' (i.e., determinate forms taken by the religious impulse). This section is then succeeded by 'Absolute Religion', which refers exclusively to Christianity. Hegel states elsewhere that 'God has revealed Himself through the Christian religion; i.e., he has granted mankind the possibility of recognizing his nature, so that he is no longer an impenetrable mystery' (Nisbet, 40; VIG, 45).

In Christianity the very idea or concept of religion itself has become a religion. In other words, in Christianity the relation of the human to the divine becomes the central element of the religion. Through Jesus Christ, the distinction between man and God is understood to be literally overcome. Hegel claims that the three parts of his system – Logic, Nature, Spirit – correspond to the three persons of the Christian Trinity: Father, Son and Holy Spirit. In general, he sees in Christianity a kind of allegory depicting the central truths of his own philosophy. Hegel takes issue with Christian theologians and clergy who hold that mankind cannot know God, or who consider the attempt to know God as impious or hubristic. Hegel claims not only that such knowledge is possible, but that it is our highest duty to obtain it. Knowing God is our highest duty because, for Hegel, God only fully comes into being in the community of worshippers. Hegel holds that 'The concept of God is God's idea, [namely,] to become and make himself objective to himself. This is contained in God as Spirit: God is essentially in His community and has a community; he is objective to himself, and is such truly only in self-consciousness [so that] God's very own highest determination is self-consciousness.' Beforehand, God is 'incomplete', Hegel says (LPR I, 186–87; VPR I, 96).

Hegel does not consider his views to be so 'speculative' as to be alien to the ordinary believer, however. In fact, he holds that his way of looking at God and religion are much closer to real religion than to what was called in his time 'rational theology'. We have seen that Hegel does not believe religion to be dependent on philosophy, but he does claim the reverse, that philosophy depends on religion. He writes that 'It is the distinctive task of philosophy to transmute the content that is in the picture-thinking of religion into the form of thought; the content [itself] cannot be distinguished' (LPR I, 333; VPR I, 235). The philosopher first encounters the content of absolute truth in religion. Indeed, Hegel holds that, before Christianity arrived on the scene, it would have been impossible for philosophy to present absolute truth in a fully adequate or complete form. Speculative

religion of art

philosophy cannot be done in a vacuum: it requires a certain social, historical and religious context to make it possible. See also **Absolute Spirit**; **Boehme, Jacob**; **Christianity**; **God**; **Idea**; **mysticism**; **picture-thinking**; **theology**; **Trinity**.

religion of art (*die Kunst-Religion*)   Hegel's discussion of the 'Religion of Art' is found in *The Phenomenology of Spirit*, in Subdivision III (CC): Religion, which falls within the larger section he designates as Division C. His discussion is chiefly concerned with the religion of the Ancient Greeks, in which we find the divine expressed primarily in representations of the human body. By contrast, natural religion – which Hegel discusses just prior to the religion of art – depicts the divine in natural, animal or monumental forms. Since religion, for Hegel, is typically an unconscious projection of Spirit into something exalted beyond the human, he regards the Greek depiction of the divine in human form as a major advance. In worshipping their gods, Hegel believes the Greeks were essentially worshipping themselves, and approaching self-awareness.

Implicit in Hegel's discussion is a distinction, later made explicit by Nietzsche, between the Apollinian (or Olympian) and Dionysian aspects of Greek religion. In terms of the Dionysian, Hegel discusses the mysteries of Demeter and Dionysus, through which the initiate knows himself to be at one with the divine secret. This reflects a different sort of conception of the unity of the human and the divine – but one in which Spirit loses possession of itself in religious ecstasy. Hegel also treats the Greek athletic festivals as religious celebrations in which the athlete figures as 'an inspired and living work of art' (Miller, 438; PG, 473); i.e. as an expression of the divine. He also discusses the epic, tragic and comic forms, in which the individual is progressively coming into his own, achieving consciousness of his individual character. Nevertheless, though the religion of art constitutes an advance in religious consciousness, it still only imperfectly conveys the unity of the human and the divine. For Hegel, the perfect (religious) expression of that unity is to be found only in Christianity, or revealed religion: the Word made flesh. See also **art and Philosophy of Art**; **Christianity**; **classical art**; **natural religion**; *Phenomenology of Spirit*; **religion and Philosophy of Religion**.

repulsion and attraction (*die Repulsion; die Attraktion*) In the Logic, Hegel discusses repulsion and attraction under 'Being-for-self', within the subdivision of the Doctrine of Being designated as 'Quality'. In being-for-self we encounter a conception of a being that is a whole, possessing its qualities through an internal self-differentiation. Being-for-self is a whole of distinct 'parts'. This means, Hegel points out, that being-for-self has two aspects: it is both one and many, unity and multiplicity. There is thus a basic tension within being-for-self. Hegel uses the concepts of repulsion and attraction to make this tension clearer. The coherence of the parts or 'oneness' of the one is the 'attracting' moment, while the differentiation of the parts, of the many, is the 'repulsing' moment.

If we attempt to conceive the unity of being-for-self as distinct from its parts, the unity becomes purely abstract and contentless (unity *of what*?), and indistinguishable, Hegel tells us, from *the void*. (Hegel is here openly alluding to the ideas of the ancient Atomists and Epicureans.) As to the parts, these are the many, related to each other as determinate beings. Nevertheless, each is, as it were, an image of the one or whole: each is itself *a one*, a unity. If we emphasize the negative relation of each 'one' to every other we can see that what results here (conceptually) is a kind of infinite repulsion and reduplication of 'ones'. Consider it: if each of the parts of the one is itself a one, and each of those ones is a unity of parts/ones, and each of those ones is a unity of parts/ones, and so on, we generate an infinity of 'ones', as each unity reverts to its opposite, to multiplicity, and back again.

Hegel's discussion of one and many and attraction and repulsion marks the end of his treatment of 'Quality'. We can see that what has occurred here is that the infinite reduplication of 'ones' is completely indifferent to their qualitative character. Once we make this shift from concern with the qualitative nature of being to the external relation of *beings* considered without regard for their qualities, we have in fact shifted to a consideration of *quantity*. See also **Being, Doctrine of**; **being-for-self**; **determinate being**; **quality, quantity, measure**; **relation**.

revealed religion See **Christianity**.

right (*das Recht*) Near the beginning of The Philosophy of Right, Hegel tells us that 'The idea of right is freedom' (Nisbet, 26; PR § 2 A). A little later he states that 'The basis of right is the *realm of the Spirit* in

right

general and its precise location and point of departure is the *will*; the will is *free*, so that freedom constitutes its substance and destiny and the system of right is the realm of actualized freedom, the world of Spirit produced from within itself as second nature' (Nisbet, 35; PR § 4; italics in original). Essentially what we are being told here is that 'right' covers the same territory as what is termed Objective Spirit in the *Encyclopedia*. Subjective Spirit (which precedes it) covers the 'psychology' of the individual, including all those aspects of our selves which are unconscious or preconscious. (In fact, Subjective Spirit is on the cusp between the natural and the truly human.) Objective Spirit refers to the social, cultural world that humans have created, which stands in opposition to, yet in dependence upon, the natural world.

Hegel's account of the sphere of right (or Objective Spirit) will show that it constitutes the self-development of the human will. The true nature of the will is freedom, but this freedom is only actualized under certain conditions. This development of the will's freedom is simultaneously the development of our sense of 'rightness'. Our will creates the human world by transforming nature according to what we believe *should* be. No other animal has ideas about 'rightness'; animals concern themselves only with 'is', never with 'ought'.

Das Recht (which is cognate with the English 'right') can refer to justice, to law, and to a 'right' in the sense of a claim of entitlement (e.g., the 'right to property'). Hegel's use of the term involves all of these meanings. Philosophers prior to Hegel typically used 'right' to refer to positive (social) law and to legal institutions, and distinguished it from 'morality' (*Moralität*; the ethics of individual human actors) and from 'ethical life' (*Sittlichkeit*; the ways in which ethics is grounded in social institutions and practices). In *The Philosophy of Right*, however, Hegel understands right much more broadly, as subsuming these other two areas. Right, for Hegel, involves three moments: abstract right, morality and ethical life. Abstract right essentially gives an account of how freedom expresses itself in property claims, and thus deals with the 'objective' (or external) aspect of right. Morality deals with the development of personal ethics, and is thus 'subjective'. In ethical life, the objective and subjective spheres of right are sublated in an account of how the social institutions of family, civil society and state ground rights claims, concretize personal morality (otherwise empty and abstract), and make possible the fullest expression of human freedom.

Therefore, if one wants to know about Hegel's 'ethics', his 'politics' and his theory of social justice, these are all to be found in his account of right. Unlike other philosophers, however, Hegel does not treat these as separate matters. Indeed, like Aristotle, he regards ethics as fundamentally a political inquiry, and rejects the idea that ethics is a matter of following abstract principles or rules, divorced from a social context. This does not mean, however, that Hegel regards morality or social justice as culturally relative. He believes that our nature consists of being self-aware and self-determining (i.e., free). History, for Hegel, is the long process of our coming to consciousness of what we are. Therefore, societies may be judged in terms of the degree to which they recognize human nature for what it is, and the degree to which self-awareness and self-determination flourish within them.

Nevertheless, freedom is always freedom within a specific social context. It is only in society that we are able to express the myriad aspects of our nature. Society opens certain avenues up to us – but also necessarily closes others and constrains us. For Hegel, paradoxically, true freedom consists in affirming or 'willing' the ways in which we are limited or determined. I may have little control over the constraints placed on me by my society, but if I can come to discern the ways in which they make me and my own sphere of freedom possible, then in a way I am able to own them. Having made them mine in this way, I remove the feeling of being constrained or oppressed by them. For Hegel, we must learn to identify with the world in which we find ourselves, or feel forever oppressed by it.

Right in the sense of some principle of 'justice' governing human relations becomes thematic in *The Philosophy of Right* through Hegel's discussion of 'wrong', which in German is *Unrecht* (un-right, or injustice). Wrong always involves coercion in some form, and coercion always amounts to a refusal on the part of the wrongdoer to recognize others as free beings like himself. This fundamental contradiction brings to light something positive: a universal principle of right or justice, which has been violated by the wrong. It is out of a recognition of this principle that we demand wrongdoers be punished. The attempt to articulate this principle leads Hegel to his discussion of morality, and then to ethical life. See also **abstract right; ethical life; freedom; morality; Objective Spirit; Philosophy of Right; wrong.**

romantic art (*die romantische Kunst*)   Hegel's Philosophy of Art distinguishes between different art forms in terms of how well they harmonize the ideal 'content' of the artwork with its material medium. In 'symbolic art', the meaning of the artwork is so abstract that it cannot find adequate expression in material form. In 'classical art', on the other hand, a perfect harmony is achieved between content and form – as in Greek sculpture. 'Romantic art' is, for Hegel, essentially the art of the Christian world. Romantic art recognizes the essential falseness of the attempt to portray Spirit statically. Greek sculpture may be beautiful but it is rigid and still. Spirit's true nature, on the other hand, is to be continually negating and overcoming its limitations, constructing itself, and searching for an adequate medium of self-reflection.

The attempt to express the infinity of Spirit in romantic art is inevitably a failure, however, for no material medium can be truly adequate to Spirit's self-expression. Thus, while romantic art conceives of Spirit correctly, it can never fully express Spirit, essentially because of the sensuous limitations of art itself. Hegel identifies poetry, painting and music as the primary forms of romantic art, though poetry is probably the best exemplar here. The poet uses language to try to capture the nature of Spirit. However, because this language is metaphor – the written equivalent of the image expressed in painting and sculpture – it can never truly mirror Spirit back to itself. (This can happen, ultimately, only through a very different use of language: the philosopher's conceptual grasp of the whole, which is the consummation of Absolute Spirit, Spirit confronting itself.)

Classical art is perfect art for Hegel; it is the most beautiful and aesthetically pleasing form of art. However, romantic art may be understood as 'higher' if we are thinking solely in terms of the place of art in the realization of Idea through Absolute Spirit. This is because romantic art provides the dialectical transition beyond art altogether, from the aesthetic to the religious. In romantic art we most truly confront the fact that all *material* forms fail to adequately express Spirit. See also **Absolute Spirit**; **art and Philosophy of Art**; **classical art**; **symbolic art**.

'rose in the cross of the present'   In the Preface to the *Philosophy of Right*, Hegel attacks political idealism, employing a now-famous metaphor: 'To recognize reason as the rose in the cross of the present and thereby to delight in the present – this rational insight is the *reconciliation* with actuality which philosophy grants to those who have received the inner call *to comprehend* . . .' (Nisbet, 22). In the *Lectures on the Philosophy of Religion* of 1824, Hegel employs the same metaphor: 'in order to pluck reason, the rose in the cross of the present, one must take up the cross itself' (LPR II, 248, note 45). In a review essay published in 1829, Hegel acknowledges that this image is a reference to the mystical society of the Rosicrucians, which was known for its reactionary, anti-Enlightenment politics.[23] When Hegel lived and worked in Berlin, the reigning king was Friedrich Wilhelm III. His predecessor had been Friedrich Wilhelm II (1744–1797), a member of the Rosicrucian Order whose cabinet included several powerful ministers who were also Rosicrucians.

Though Hegel's choice of this image is certainly strange, its meaning is fairly clear. Throughout the Preface, Hegel attacks revolutionary or utopian politics, which despise the present and look towards a future 'perfected' state. Hegel enjoins us, instead, to see what exists in the present as 'rational': as part of the process of Idea expressing itself in time. This is the meaning of his famous claim (also in the Preface) that 'What is rational is actual; and what is actual is rational.' The image of the rose in the cross is essentially that of the rational blooming forth from history, the great 'way of despair'. See also **Philosophy of Right**; **'real is the rational . . .'**; **'way of despair'**.

— S —

scepticism   See **stoicism, scepticism, unhappy consciousness**.

Schelling, F. W. J. (1775–1854)   Friedrich Wilhelm Joseph Schelling was the son of a prominent Lutheran pastor. At the age of fifteen he was admitted to the theological seminary at Tübingen, where he became friends with Hegel and Hölderlin, who were both five years older than he. Schelling quickly earned a reputation as a young genius. At the age of seventeen he wrote a dissertation on the book of Genesis, and at twenty he published 'On the Ego as Principle of Philosophy'.

Schelling is notorious for having frequently changed his views over the course of his career, so much so that Hegel famously quipped that he was

Schelling, F. W. J.

'educating himself in public'. Schelling began his philosophic career as a follower of Fichte, however he significantly modified Fichte's system, and eventually abandoned it entirely. It was Fichte's belief that the Kantian system could be 'completed' through the elimination of the thing-in-itself, and the demonstration of how all of experience (indeed, all of the world) could be deduced from the activity of an Absolute Ego. Fichte makes it clear that the Absolute Ego is not to be identified with our finite personality or selfhood. Indeed, it transcends the subject-object distinction itself and is the *source* of that very distinction (the division between subject and object always being made *within* the experience of a subject). But why, Schelling objects, should we call something that is beyond subject and object an 'Ego'? After all, this seems to imply subjectivity. Schelling uses the term 'the Absolute' to describe that which transcends subject and object. The Absolute is not only beyond this distinction but all others: it is (in his words) 'the indifference point' (and in the words of classical mysticism 'the coincidence of opposites').

In his *System of Transcendental Idealism* (1800), Schelling argues that there are two philosophical approaches to this Absolute: transcendental idealism and philosophy of nature. The former looks very much like Fichte's system – but Fichte never argued for a philosophy of nature, and indeed says almost nothing about nature. For Fichte, the objective world is simply a field of moral achievement. We put our stamp on it; we change the real to bring it into accord with the ideal. In short, nature for Fichte is really nothing more than raw material for human use. By contrast, Schelling looks at nature and asks if we might somehow discover ourselves within it – not by changing nature, per se, but by understanding it. Indeed, we find ourselves in nature everywhere. This is most obvious in the things we have in common with animals. But Schelling makes a stronger point: we must understand nature teleologically, as a great chain of being leading up to mankind and to human self-consciousness.

For Schelling, transcendental idealism begins with subjectivity and asks how an object comes to be for it. In other words, it follows Kant in asking in virtue of what are things given to us as objects: what are the structures of subjectivity which can make this possible? The difference is that for Schelling and for Fichte there is no thing-in-itself, which means that in some sense objects are understood to be *wholly* an expression of subjectivity. Philosophy of nature, on the other hand, begins from the side of the object, from nature, and asks how subjectivity comes to be *within* it. In other words, in philosophy of nature, Schelling begins with the recognition that human subjects show up as natural objects, and as members of a hierarchical, developmental order. He then argues that the end or goal of nature is subjectivity itself: all of nature constitutes a kind of approximation to human subjectivity, which is characterized principally by the capacity for self-reflection. Thus, we may say that for Schelling the end of nature is nature's coming to consciousness of itself through humanity.

In both transcendental idealism and philosophy of nature we approach the Absolute: the Indifference Point that is beyond subject and object. In philosophy of nature, the subject, which seems to stand opposed to the world of objects, is shown to be the highest expression and *raison d'être* of nature (or objectivity) itself. Transcendental idealism has the same result, but starting from the other end: it shows how beginning with the subject we can show how a world of objects comes to be for the subject *so that the subject may become object to itself*. Subject, in short, becomes object.

Thus, both of these sciences – transcendental idealism and philosophy of nature – in a certain way 'concretize' the Absolute (again, as Indifference Point of subject and object): they make it real. However, they make it real, in a sense, only in theory. Schelling insists that there must also be something which makes the Absolute concretely real in an experience which is satisfying to the whole person, not just to the intellect. He provides us with a clue as to what this is early on in the *System of Transcendental Idealism*: 'The objective world is simply the original, as yet unconscious, poetry of the spirit; the universal organon of philosophy – and the keystone of its entire arch – *is the philosophy of art*.'[24] The two parts of the arch held up by the keystone are, of course, transcendental idealism and philosophy of nature. But why is philosophy of art the keystone? The reason is that in artistic production of any kind the distinction between subject and object is, in a way, transcended. The artist takes material found in nature – material that is wholly other or objective – and refashions it according to his own artistic ideals. Thus, in the artwork the object is refashioned into an expression of the subject; the subject 'objectifies' itself or its ideals. Further, the artist works according to principles that cannot be fully defined, and yet seem necessary. When we contemplate the finished artwork a kind of 'transcendental satisfaction' is experienced. We feel that through the artwork we've 'got something', and (if it is successful as a piece of art) that it is 'just

Schelling, F. W. J.

right'; that some indefinable principle has been satisfied. In essence, Schelling holds that in artistic experience we are intuiting the Absolute: the perfect coincidence of subject and object, ideal and real, not in theory but laid before us in concrete, sensible reality.

But why does Schelling call the philosophy of art the 'universal organon of philosophy'? ('Organon' simply means 'instrument'.) The reason is that Schelling believes that ultimately the only way to explain why an objective world exists is on analogy with artistic production. The artist, recall, creates according to rules, but the rules are not fully definable; they seem 'right' and 'necessary' but cannot be made fully clear or rational. In the same way, objects appear to a subject according to rules that are ultimately indefinable. In Transcendental Idealism, as I have said, Schelling attempts to show how a world of objects is constituted by transcendental subjectivity. It is possible, as Kant did, to describe the most basic, necessary structures of subjectivity that make objects possible – but how are we to explain why it is *these* objects that appear to us, and not others? In other words, the Forms of Intuition and Categories of the Understanding, and Schemata (to borrow some of Kant's terminology) can be shown to be conditions for the possibility of an object appearing to me – but why should that object be a tomato, with all the sensuous properties of a tomato? Why, in other words, does *this* world appear, with its unique and peculiar look and feel, its joys and its horrors, rather than some other?

Transcendental idealism cannot answer this question, but philosophy of art, in a way, can. It is as if at the root of reality itself, indefinable artistic principles are at work. Or, perhaps more aptly, it is as if artistic inspiration is at work. (It is at this point that one can't help drawing comparisons between Schelling's views and certain mystical doctrines – such as the Hindu view that the world is Brahma's dream.) The objective world, in short, is very much like a kind of playful, artistic production unfolding before us. As Schelling says, the world is 'the original, as yet unconscious, poetry of the spirit.' What unfolds it? The Absolute. And we are the vehicle of the Absolute's awareness of itself. We are the beings who come to be aware of the poetry of spirit (the poetry that is reality itself) *as* poetry. Or, as I have already said, we are the self-consciousness of nature. Still more to the point, we are the realization of the Absolute in time.

For a number of years, Hegel lived and worked in Schelling's shadow. In Jena, the two men co-edited the *Critical Journal of Philosophy*, though it was Schelling who was, at that time, by far the major figure. Hegel's first philosophical work was a defense of Schelling's thought (*The Difference Between Fichte's and Schelling's Systems of Philosophy*, 1801). Over the next several years, however, Hegel became increasingly critical of Schelling's approach. For all intents and purposes, he announced his break with Schelling in the Preface to *The Phenomenology of Spirit* (1807), through an Attack on Schelling's conception of the Absolute. Famously, Hegel characterizes Schelling's Absolute as 'the night in which all cows are black' (Miller, 9; PG, 13), meaning that it is simply empty talk to say that the Absolute is 'beyond all distinctions', or that in it 'all is one'. This makes of the Absolute simply a blank, devoid of content. Hegel revolutionizes the concept of the Absolute in the *Phenomenology*, and in his tripartite philosophical system, by understanding it not as a 'beyond', but rather as reality itself, conceived as an internally differentiated, systematic whole, continually 'specifying itself' into the many things that exist, and coming to consciousness of itself in human thought.

For his part, Schelling was wounded by Hegel's criticism, and the two men were not on friendly terms for many years. As Hegel's star ascended, so Schelling's seemed to burn itself out. Schelling felt that Hegel had stolen many of his ideas, in effect simply revamping them and reorganizing them into a 'new system'. However, it is about as true to say that Hegel stole Schelling's ideas as it is to say that Schelling stole Fichte's (grafting them onto a re-tooled Spinozism), or that Fichte stole Kant's. The truth is that there is much in Hegel's system that was originally said by Schelling, but in Hegel the ideas have been given not just a new, systematic, dialectical structure, but also a depth and argumentative rigor that is often lacking in Schelling.

It is impossible here to summarize the entire course of Schelling's philosophical development after the period of his association with Hegel in Jena (and unnecessary, since in this context we are primarily interested in Schelling as an influence on Hegel). In any case, the once-prolific Schelling never published anything after the 1809 *Essay on Freedom*. In 1841, ten years after Hegel's death, Schelling was called to Berlin to lecture, some contending that this was to combat the lingering influence of Hegel and his followers. Schelling's lectures – on a philosophy of mythology – began auspiciously, with large audiences (among those attending were Mikhail Bakunin, Friedrich Engels and Søren Kierkegaard). But the exceedingly obscure lectures proved a disappointment, and after a while Schelling discontinued them. He died in 1854, outliving Hegel by twenty-three years. See also **Absolute**; **Fichte, J. G.**; **Hölderlin, Friedrich**; **Kant, Immanuel**; **'night in which all cows are black'**; **Spinoza, Benedict**.

science (*die Wissenschaft*)   One of Hegel's terms for his philosophy is 'science'. The full title of Hegel's first major work, *The Phenomenology of Spirit* (1807), was *System of Science: First Part, The Phenomenology of Spirit*. This choice of words will seem odd to English speakers, as we do not customarily think of philosophy as a science. However, the German *Wissenschaft* has a broader meaning than our 'science'. *Wissenschaft* is derived from *Wissen*, which means simply 'knowledge'. *Wissenschaft* essentially refers to any attempt to understand some aspect of existence in a manner that is rational, systematic and methodical. Biology studies life in such a manner. Physics does the same with matter, and the laws governing the behaviour of material bodies. Astronomy does the same with the planets and stars – and so on.

Unlike these other disciplines, however, philosophy does not deal with a specific *part* of existence – it deals with existence considered as a totality. It is concerned with, in Hegel's words, the whole. This is the fundamental difference between philosophy and what we commonly refer to as 'science'. Nevertheless, philosophy deals with the whole in a manner that is rational and systematic. Therefore, it can accurately be described as *Wissenschaft*.

Still, there is a further, important difference between philosophy and the other sciences. I described such fields as biology and physics as dealing with their subject matter in a way that is systematic, rational and *methodical*. Hegel, however, explicitly rejects the idea that there is a philosophical 'method'. The reason for this has to do with Hegel's insistence that philosophy must be a *presuppositionless* science. All other sciences operate with certain presuppositions that usually go entirely unquestioned. For example, physicists never (at least, in so far as they are physicists) entertain the philosophical question 'Do we know that an objective world exists at all?' Instead, physicists presuppose that this question has been answered in the affirmative and proceed to study the fundamental physical properties of that world. This does not point to a failing on the part of physicists: if they were to ask such fundamental 'meta-questions', physics itself would never get off the ground. Further, each of the natural and social sciences presupposes the validity of certain methodological considerations. The nature and validity of the scientific method itself is an issue raised by the *philosophy of science* – but not within science proper. Thus, the sciences themselves are incapable of providing proof of their most basic presuppositions. They are not, in short, self-grounding.

Philosophy, on the other hand, must be a self-grounding science. This is because, again, Hegel conceives philosophy as a science of the whole. In order to grasp the whole faithfully, we cannot simply assume the truth of certain ideas or a certain methodology. Philosophy is the most fundamental science of all because the presuppositions of all the other sciences are interrogated by philosophy. Thus, philosophy itself may have no determinate presuppositions, for there is no science more fundamental than it that could provide justification for those presuppositions. Hegel's philosophy, therefore, attempts to be self-grounding and self-justifying. It accomplishes this by beginning (in the Logic) literally with an indeterminate nothingness, the path to which is provided by *The Phenomenology of Spirit*.

Hegel's philosophy is thus 'scientific' not because it applies pre-existing standards of rationality, systematicity and method. Rather, Hegel's philosophy actually generates or determines the idea of rational, conceptual, systematic order itself, through the dialectic. This might lead one to think that the dialectic is in fact the 'method' that Hegel employs, and commentators often speak of it this way. Nevertheless, Hegel maintains that the 'form' of the dialectic is inseparable from its 'content'. (As a result of this, all the attempts that have been made over the years to formalize 'dialectical logic' are, if Hegel is right, completely misguided.)

Hegel's philosophy is quite literally a super-science, which can not only comprehend all other sciences (and their systematic relationship to each other), but which also generates its own form, its own rules, and even its own subject matter (for the Absolute is, in fact, 'actualized' in the activity of our comprehending the science). See also **Absolute; dialectic; Logic; philosophy and the history of philosophy; system; whole, the**.

Science of Logic, The   See **Logic**.

self-consciousness (*das Selbstbewußtsein*)   In the first major division of *The Phenomenology of Spirit* – 'Consciousness' – Hegel

self-consciousness

discusses certain fundamental ways in which the subject seeks to know objects. But how do we make ourselves into an object, how do we achieve self-consciousness? Somehow, our focus must switch from awareness of objects to awareness of the self. This comes about, Hegel argues, not through *knowing* objects but through *acting* on them – acting to change or to overcome them. In the following section, 'Self-Consciousness', Hegel introduces the term *desire* to describe a primal, human will to alter objects in order to bring them into accord with the subject's wishes. (The human will to know objects is also, implicitly, a will to overcome the opposition of the object. Thus knowledge too involves something like what Hegel calls desire. Here, though, he concerns himself with action – the *transformation*, not the understanding, of the world.)

It is important to understand that desire is a kind of negative force – a will to annul otherness. For Hegel, human nature in its germinal form is a kind of pure, desiring nothingness which negates and transforms being. But how is this negativity the key to self-consciousness? The answer is fairly simple. When we desire we are always aware of ourselves desiring. My hunger, for example – my desire to gobble up edible objects – makes me aware of myself. Further, the world resists our desires; it does not immediately acquiesce to them (a decent restaurant, for example, may be hard to find). The opposition of the world to our desires causes us to turn within, to regroup, to reflect on our desires and our manner of trying to satisfy them. As the mystic Jacob Boehme (an influence on Hegel) stated in one of his works, 'Nothing is revealed to itself without opposition.'

Animals, too, exhibit something like what Hegel calls desire, though in them we find it expressed in very primitive, and limited forms. The crucial difference between human and animal desire is not only that human desire seems to be a limitless, Faustian striving, but that human beings do not just direct desire on inanimate or non-human objects. They direct it on other humans, and what they desire from other humans most of all is *recognition*. In the final analysis we only achieve self-consciousness in interaction with other human beings who reveal us to ourselves – who recognize and affirm us as human. We desire to be recognized as what we are by others like ourselves. Furthermore, we don't desire this recognition just from this person or that, but from all persons. Hegel argues, therefore, that ultimately we cannot be satisfied by anything less than a universal recognition.

Hegel goes so far as to claim that this desire is of such importance to human beings that they are willing to risk death in order to win (or to compel) recognition from others. For animals, nothing is more important than biological survival. What makes us human is precisely our willingness to fight for certain ideals at the risk of our lives, and recognition is the most basic such ideal. Hegel tells us that the first form taken by the desire for recognition is the attempt to force it from others. In such a contest, one will typically yield to the other. The victor becomes what Hegel calls 'master' (*Herr*) and the vanquished becomes 'servant' (*Knecht*). The master puts the servant to work for him. Superficially, it may seem as though the master is in the better position, but Hegel argues that this is not the case. Freed from the necessity of labour, Hegel tells us that the master loses himself in enjoyment. The master had previously transcended the natural in fighting for an ideal – for recognition – but now he becomes immersed in pleasure and passion; i.e. in the natural and less-then-fully-human aspects of ourselves. Meanwhile, the servant works to transform nature in the service of the master. As we have seen, Hegel argues that this transformation of nature, of the objective world, is one of the primary means to the achievement of self-consciousness. Thus, in service to the master the servant actually begins to advance in self-consciousness, while the master stagnates. In the process of working for the master, the servant creates science, technology and the arts. Still, this does not mean that the servant is fully satisfied in working for the master. His fundamental human desire for recognition remains unfulfilled. He is seen by others as subhuman and, to a great extent, he internalizes this and regards himself as an inferior being. Hegel shows how the consciousness of the servant therefore undergoes a series of transformations in which he seeks, in one way or another, freedom and recognition by other means. Specifically, Hegel deals with 'stoicism', 'scepticism' and 'the unhappy consciousness'.

What is crucially important to understand is that these transformations of the servant's standpoint are all stages of *thought*. The servant, in other words, is seeking freedom not in fact but in idea. Stoicism aims at freedom through detachment from the world. Ultimately, it is unsatisfying because it is really just talk, not actual freedom. The dialectic turns from stoicism, therefore, to scepticism, an outright denial of the reality of the world. The servant becomes 'free' because the world in which he is enslaved is but an illusion. However, scepticism contains a fundamental contradiction. The sceptic continues to work and live in the 'unreal world'. His actions, in other words, contradict his philosophy. The unhappy consciousness is essentially the Christian teaching seen as a kind of 'slave morality' (to borrow Nietzsche's term). It involves a yearning for recognition by a transcendent God, and for freedom in the afterlife. In relation to God, the biggest Master of all, we are all servants – and thus all equally unfree. Obviously, this simply recapitulates the master–servant antithesis on a new level. However, the unhappy consciousness is nevertheless a true advance (and Hegel's judgement of Christianity is ultimately quite positive). In the stage of the unhappy consciousness we attempt to place ourselves into accord with the universal, indeed to subordinate our particular wishes and desires to it. But it is not a *thinking* subordination, and is bound up with the myth, mystery and dogma of religion. In the next major section of the *Phenomenology*, 'Reason', we begin to relate ourselves to the universal or to cognize the universal in rational, conceptual forms. See also **Absolute Knowing; Boehme, Jacob; consciousness; desire; 'master–servant dialectic';** *Phenomenology of Spirit;* **stoicism, scepticism, unhappy consciousness**.

self-estranged Spirit (*der sich entfremdete Geist*)   In subdivision '(BB) Spirit' of *The Phenomenology of Spirit*, Hegel describes a certain type of mentality which feels alienated from nature and the society in which it finds itself. This is 'self-estranged Spirit', which has the conviction that it must remake nature and society in order to remove their opposition to itself, and to 'perfect' them. This is the sort of mentality one often finds in revolutionaries and political idealists, but it is also the quintessence of modernity itself. In fact, this section of the *Phenomenology* actually consists of a sustained critique of modernity, with sometimes open, sometimes veiled allusion to such features of modern history as the Enlightenment, and the French Revolution. Hegel takes up the critique of 'self-estranged Spirit' elsewhere, and one can find echoes of it in the Preface to the later *Philosophy of Right*. See also **absolute freedom and the Terror; Enlightenment;** *Phenomenology of Spirit; Philosophy of Right*.

sense-certainty (*die sinnliche Gewißheit*)   Sense-certainty is the first form of Spirit discussed by Hegel in *The Phenomenology of Spirit* (under the first division of the text, 'Consciousness'). If we ask ourselves to identify the most basic, primitive form of consciousness, we would probably say that it is our direct, immediate awareness of objects: for example, I seem to have a direct awareness of this keyboard in front of me, and this cup of coffee to my right. This is what Hegel means by sense-certainty. We tend to believe, in fact, that in this form of awareness we really grasp the object *just as it is*, in an unmediated fashion. It is easy to show, as Hegel does, that this standpoint is naive and cannot accomplish what it aims at. As Hegel puts it, our awareness of an object in sense-certainty is of a *this*. However, once we say anything more about the object we have actually transcended the level of sense-certainty. This object in front of me is a *this*, but once I designate it a 'coffee cup' I have passed beyond the level of bare sensory immediacy. Why? Because I have now situated it within a network of concepts and an entire world of objects. I call this thing 'a cup' – a term that has an application beyond *this here* object to others similar to it. I describe it more precisely as a 'coffee cup', and now the object is made to refer beyond itself to another sort of thing entirely: coffee, which may or may not even be present to sensory awareness (depending on whether the cup is empty or full). Thus, the moment we begin to say or think anything *about* the object, we are immediately carried beyond the level of bare, sensory givenness. Indeed sense-certainty is, in fact, an empty and artificial perspective, not the one from which we normally experience objects. Ordinarily we experience objects as situated within complex lines of relation to others, and in terms of whole networks of concepts. Indeed, one of the major points of Hegel's philosophy is to argue that objects are only grasped as they truly are when we achieve a perspective that allows us to understand them in relation to the whole. The dialectic of consciousness thus quickly leaves sense-certainty behind. See also **consciousness**; **perception**; *Phenomenology of Spirit*.

'slaughter-bench of history'   Hegel writes in *The Lectures on the Philosophy of World History*: 'But even as we look upon history as a slaughter-bench [or 'altar'; *Schlachtbank*] on which the happiness of nations, the wisdom of states, and the virtue of individuals are sacrificed, our thoughts inevitably impel us to ask: to whom, or to what ultimate end have these monstrous sacrifices been made?' (Nisbet, 69; Werke 12, 35). Hegel answers his own question by telling us that the ultimate end of history is the achievement by human beings of self-awareness, which is simultaneously the achievement of freedom. This process is the 'reason' –

space and time

the rational pattern or order – behind all that occurs, and it has always been at work in history, though human beings are usually unaware of it. At the time that events are occurring, they may seem unqualifiedly bad and senselessly irrational, but in the grand scheme of things that is world history, every event can be seen as being used by 'the cunning of reason' to bring about the ultimate realization of the universal aims of World Spirit. See also **'cunning of reason'; history and Philosophy of History; 'rose in the cross of the present'; world-historical individuals; World Spirit**.

soul   See principally **anthropology**. See also **actual soul; feeling soul; natural soul; Subjective Spirit**.

space and time (*der Raum, die Zeit*)   Hegel's Philosophy of Nature opens with a discussion of space and time (under the subdivision entitled 'Mechanics'). Space, Hegel tells us, is the idea of externality as such. That this should be the first category of the Philosophy of Nature is hardly surprising. The Absolute Idea – the final category of the Logic (which precedes the Philosophy of Nature) – transcends space and time. As an 'other' to Idea what must chiefly characterize nature is the very notion of one thing being external or physically opposed to another. Pure space is analogous to pure being – the first category of the Logic. We understand (or think we understand) what both terms mean, yet they are virtually ineffable. It is perfectly sensible to talk about the being of things, even though on examination it turns out to be a completely empty category. Similarly, we understand perfectly what it means for one thing to be external to another or to be in space, yet this concept is so primitive to our understanding of the physical world that it is hard to define or to explain in a non-circular manner.

Hegel characterizes space as 'pure quantity': it is actual or existent quantity, only the idea of which was given in the Logic. Hegel speaks of time as the 'truth' of space, because he regards time as the 'self-transcendence' of space; space overcoming its own spatiality. In the whole of the Philosophy of Nature, this must be one of Hegel's most obscure claims. Space 'breaks up' into distinct points, lines and planes, which constitute the 'parts' of space. This division of space is accomplished through things which possess three dimensions. Without things external to one another, externality, and thus spatiality itself, make no sense. The negation of space consists in a change in the position of these mutually external things: thing A at point 1, moves into point 2 and thereby, in the absence of A, point 1 'vanishes' as a determinate space. Time *just is* this negation. Hegel writes that time is not a container in which things exist, instead it is the idea or abstraction of their negation or overcoming in space: 'time itself is the *becoming*, this coming-to-be and passing away, the *actually existent abstraction*, Chronos, from whom everything is born and by whom its offspring is destroyed' (Miller, 35; PN § 258). Time is not a 'thing', it is a kind of ideality that we experience as *there*: as all around us in the world, but intangibly. In The Phenomenology of Spirit, Hegel states that 'Time is the Concept itself that is there' (*Die Zeit ist der Begriff selbst, der da ist*) (Miller, 487; PG, 524). Hegel calls time the Concept because time is the expression in the spatial world, or nature, of the determinate negation we find in the Concept's dialectical self-specification. Things are overcome in time because they are finite, and this negation of finitude points to the infinite and the eternal. Time itself, this 'Chronos', is infinite and eternal. Hence, time is the existent Concept.

There is thus a close correspondence between being-nothing-becoming in the Logic, and space, time and what Hegel calls 'place and motion' (*der Ort und die Bewegung*) in Mechanics. Space and time are both 'empty', just as being and nothing proved to be empty. Further, time negates space, just as nothing negates being. Yet in their identity – in the identity of space and its negation – we find a positive third term: motion (from place A to B), which is concrete or actual becoming. What is implicit in the foregoing, however, is that all of these mechanical concepts presuppose the concept of matter (*Materie*). Without material objects there is no 'externality', and no motion through space in time. At this point, Hegel therefore passes to a discussion of matter. See also **being, nothing, becoming**; **Concept, Doctrine of the**; **matter**; **mechanics**; **nature and Philosophy of Nature**.

speculation (*die Spekulation*)   Hegel refers to his philosophy as 'speculation' (and as 'speculative philosophy'). Unsurprisingly, he does not use this term in the usual way; it has nothing to do, for instance, with guesswork or conjecture.

'Speculation' has a long history in philosophy. The term was used by the scholastics; and by mystics like Nicholas of Cusa (1401–1464), who

speculation

associated it with the Latin *speculum*, which means mirror. *Speculatio* referred to knowing God through His creation – which is, as it were, a mirror reflecting God. Thus, speculation originally meant an attempt to reach beyond the appearances of things in order to know the divine. Kant uses 'speculation' to refer to rationalist attempts to know the transcendent, which he decisively rejects. Schelling and Hegel, however, picked up the term and both use it in a positive sense, because both believe that it is possible to overcome Kant's restriction of knowledge to mere appearances.

Hegel contrasts speculation to the understanding, which tends to think in terms of rigidly held dichotomies or pairs of opposites. Speculation, by contrast, thinks beyond dichotomies. It looks for ways to reconcile oppositions, usually by finding a third term that has been overlooked (often one which encompasses the antitheses), or by demonstrating the fundamental identity of opposed terms. Speculative thinking, for Hegel, is animated by a sense of the greater whole to which things belong. It therefore involves the overcoming of limited or partial standpoints, which restrict themselves to this part of the truth or that, in order to articulate a complete account of the whole itself. Interestingly, Hegel states that this approach makes speculation 'the same as what used in earlier times to be called "mystical" [*Mystische*], especially with regard to the religious consciousness and its content' (Geraets, 133; EL § 82 A). Hegel here has in mind precisely the thought of figures like Cusa, who sought knowledge of God through an overcoming of dichotomous, either-or thinking.

In Hegel, the terms speculation, dialectic and reason are closely linked. Hegel will, at various times, use all of these words to describe the type of philosophy he is engaged in. Speculation, in fact, is reason in its 'positive' aspect. In Kant, reason is the part of the mind that attempts to arrive at a higher synthesis of knowledge – higher than the understanding can provide. Hegel essentially takes over this use of 'reason', though obviously his estimation of it is far more positive than Kant's. Dialectic, for Hegel, is reason in its 'negative' aspect: it identifies contradictions inherent in the understanding's view of things. What is involved in speculation, again, is insight into the whole – which is what actually makes possible the supersession of opposing terms, and of one standpoint (e.g., a definition of the Absolute) by a more adequate one. See also **dialectic; mysticism; negation; reason; system; understanding; whole.**

Spinoza, Benedict (1632–1677) Spinoza was a Dutch–Jewish philosopher who is considered one of the great rationalists. His controversial views led him, at the age of 23, to be excommunicated from the Jewish community, after which he adopted the Latin name Benedictus (which, like his given name Baruch, means 'blessed'). For the rest of his life Spinoza worked as a lens grinder, and set out his ideas in a series of treatises. Spinoza's philosophy would prove controversial to Christians as well, and for many years to come.

Spinoza's *Ethics* (*Ethica Ordine Geometrico Demonstrata*, 1677) was published after his death, and is the principal work upon which his reputation rests. The style of the work is quite off-putting, as Spinoza decided to organize it like a geometrical system, with axioms, definitions, postulates, and so forth. (Presentations of Spinoza's ideas often do not follow him in this.) The Ethics is divided into five parts, which deal in turn with God, the mind, the emotions, and the related issues of human bondage and human freedom. Spinoza refers to God as substance, and defines substance as that which exists necessarily: it is the cause of itself. God, furthermore, is absolutely infinite and possesses infinite attributes. In contrast to philosophers who treat God as transcendent, as existing apart from the world, Spinoza argues that God's infinity requires that there be nothing outside him which could in any fashion function as a limitation. Thus, he claims that whatever exists exists *within God*. This is perhaps Spinoza's most radical thesis.

Traditional theology had drawn a sharp contrast between God and the world, claiming that whereas God is perfect, the world is quite imperfect. Some even made the claim that God is *infinitely* different from (and more perfect than) the world. Spinoza, however, claims that the physical universe exists within God, as one aspect of God's being. This has at least three important implications. First, it means that Spinoza regards God as, at least in one respect, material. Part of God's being is to be materially embodied. Second, by equating nature with God, Spinoza has jettisoned the traditional claim that nature is 'imperfect'. Since nature is an expression of God – indeed, we might say, 'the body of God' – it is truly perfect, regardless of how it may appear to us, or how we may feel about it. Finally, Spinoza also clearly maintains that God without nature or embodiment is 'incomplete'. This is, in fact, the most radical implication of Spinoza's position, for traditional theology had claimed that God's perfection entails that he not only must exist independently of creation, but would have lost nothing had the world never come into being at all.

Spinoza's position has long been glossed as 'pantheism', the thesis that everything is God, but it is more accurately described as *panentheism*, the claim that everything is *in* God. Though God possesses an infinity of attributes, only two of them – thought and extension – are apparent in the world of our experience. An implication of this is that although nature is within God, God is infinitely greater than nature. Spinoza also holds that nothing can be conceived apart from God: since everything exists within God, everything is ultimately intelligible only in terms of its place within him; nothing is intelligible in isolation from the whole that is God. This is the reason Spinoza opens the *Ethics* not with anything that looks traditionally like ethics, but with theology. Human nature, and human ethics, like everything else, must be understood in terms of the whole.

God may be understood as within time, or as temporal, insofar as he includes nature. However, the natural order is, as noted already, only one aspect of God. Insofar as he transcends nature, God is atemporal and eternal. Time, for Spinoza, is of infinite duration. In time all the different possibilities in nature will become actualized, for all such possibilities are within God, and God is continually unfolding his nature without end. God is continually acting, but there is nothing outside him which causes him to act. Everything within God/Nature, however, is subject to the causal influence of other beings. This means that God, in fact, is the only truly free being.

For Spinoza, there is such a thing as human freedom, but it consists in the mind's capacity to understand itself and the world. Spinoza deals at length with the passions and their destructive power, and argues that passions can be neutralized through forming a clear understanding of them. In general, he believes that we cannot eliminate the forces that act upon us and (if unchecked) limit and constrain us – but we can to some extent rise above them through understanding their nature and how they affect us. The ultimate aim of all our efforts at understanding is, in fact, knowledge of God, for true knowledge of the causes acting upon us would consist in knowledge of the entire causal nexus; i.e., knowledge of the whole, or of the divine.

Spinoza's philosophy was important for Hegel, as well as his schoolmates Hölderlin and Schelling. Hölderlin's Tübingen poetry (1788–93) exhibits a kind of 'pantheistic paganism' which seems to have had its origin in his study of Spinoza. Hölderlin inscribed the Greek 'pantheist' motto, *hen kai pan* ('one and all' – i.e., the many is one), in Hegel's yearbook of 1791. The phrase *hen kai pan* itself was taken from *On the Teaching of Spinoza in Letters to Mr. Moses Mendelssohn* (1785), by Friedrich Heinrich Jacobi (1743–1819). In this work, Jacobi records Lessing as having said, 'The orthodox concepts of the deity are no longer for me. *Hen kai pan*, I know no other.' This book was principally responsible for the Spinoza revival of the late eighteenth century, which exercized a profound influence on many thinkers of the day. Thanks to Jacobi, pantheism became, as Heinrich Heine would put it in the following century, 'the unofficial religion of Germany'. (Actually, it was not Jacobi's intention to create a revival of Spinozism: by exposing Lessing's interest in Spinoza – who was understood by many as a secret atheist – he hoped to discredit one of the heroes of the Enlightenment.) According to Hegel's biographer Karl Rosenkranz, Hegel, Schelling, and others at the Tübingen seminary, all read Jacobi's book. Schelling in particular developed an enthusiasm for Spinoza which would last for some years. In a letter to Hegel from February 1795, Schelling writes, 'For us [as with Lessing] the orthodox concepts of God are no more . . . I have in the interim become a Spinozist! Do not be astonished. You will soon hear how. For Spinoza the world, the object by itself in opposition to the subject, was *everything*. For me it is the *self*.'[25]

One of the reasons Hegel, Schelling and Hölderlin embraced Spinoza was that they thought his philosophy might provide some way to bridge the gulf Kant had created between the realm of 'phenomena' (things as we know them) and that of 'things as they are in themselves' (which we can never know). As noted above, Spinoza made thought and extension (or mind and nature) different aspects of the same being – God. All things are within God, and understanding them ultimately means understanding their place within God – knowledge which Spinoza held to be attainable. In short, an implication of Spinoza's position seems to be that we *can* know things as they are in themselves, or, we might say, what things *really* are: things are really God, who is (at least in theory) knowable.

In any case, leaving aside Schelling and Hölderlin, there is much in Hegel's philosophy to remind us of Spinoza's. Like Spinoza, Hegel claims that nature is part of the being of God: Hegel's philosophy of nature demonstrates how the natural world is an expression or externalization of

Spinoza, Benedict

the Idea, which is God 'in himself'. Further, both men conceive of God as infinite, and understand this to mean that there are no beings existing outside God that would limit him. Thus, the finite must be contained within the infinite. This is Hegel's concept of the 'true infinite', and it would seem to owe something to Spinoza's theology. For both Hegel and Spinoza, the true is the whole. Spinoza claims that because all things are within God, to know anything means to know it in relation to God. Hegel essentially claims the same thing, maintaining that true knowledge is knowledge of the whole. Further, like Spinoza, Hegel does not believe that we can completely rid ourselves of all that constrains and determines us. However, through coming to understand those factors and, especially, through coming to see how they make us what we are and open up to us certain determinate possibilities, we can nullify the sense of being constrained by them. Like Spinoza's freedom, Hegel's is one that is won through understanding.

Hegel's principal criticisms of Spinoza are directed at what he sees as Spinoza's thorough-going monism: his insistence that there is one and only one substance, and that everything is (or is in) this substance. Superficially, it might seem that Hegel and Spinoza agree on this, but Hegel charges that Spinoza's God or nature is simply a block universe in which all is, in effect, actual at once, without life or dynamism. Hegel sees Spinoza's God/Nature as static, whereas Hegel makes his God dynamic: God unfolds himself in the world through a constant process of determinate negation (or dialectic). Further, in Spinoza's universe the human, or what Hegel calls Spirit, is simply one of the finite beings within God. Hegel, of course, claims that it is through Spirit that God is truly actualized. In the *Encyclopedia Logic*, Hegel states that 'God is certainly necessity or, as we can also say, he is the absolute matter [*Sache*], but at the same time he is the absolute *person*, too. This is the point that Spinoza never reached' (Geraets, 226; EL § 151 A). For Spinoza, God requires nature to be complete. For Hegel, God requires nature *and* Spirit, and achieves true actualization when Spirit 'returns to the source' in its philosophical understanding of the systematic structure of the real.

In his *Lectures on the History of Philosophy* of 1805, Hegel makes the following remarks about Spinoza, and oddly enough compares him unfavourably to the German mystic Jacob Boehme: 'His [Spinoza's] philosophy is only fixed substance, not yet Spirit; in it we do not confront ourselves. God is not Spirit here because he is not the triune. Substance remains rigid and petrified, without Boehme's sources. The particular determinations in the form of thought-determinations are not Boehme's source-spirits which unfold in one another.'[26] Hegel is here charging that whereas Boehme gives a quasi-dialectical account of the attributes of God, Spinoza simply posits that God is internally differentiated into attributes, without giving any account of that internal differentiation and how it unfolds. See also **Boehme, Jacob**; **Hölderlin, Friedrich**; **infinity**; **Kant, Immanuel**; **Schelling, F. W. J.**

Spirit (*der Geist*)   Spirit is perhaps the most important term in Hegel's philosophy, and one of the most widely misunderstood. Many students of the history of philosophy have the vague impression that Hegel's Spirit is something otherworldly or ghostly: some sort of supernatural being that pulls the strings in this world. (It doesn't help matters that the German word *Geist* is related to the English 'ghost'.) The truth is that Spirit for Hegel is actually something quite worldly and familiar to us. However it *is* also ultimately 'supernatural', though not in the usual sense of that word.

Spirit means for Hegel something close to what we mean by 'human nature'. In the past, scholars routinely translated Hegel's *Geist* as 'mind', but mind is actually only part of what the term means. Spirit refers to the unique form of consciousness possessed by human beings. Unlike all other animals, human beings are capable of self-consciousness or self-awareness: we are the beings who are able to know ourselves. In common with other animals, we possess instincts and drives – but the difference is that we can reflect upon these, understand them and, to some extent, curb them. We are also capable of reacting against those drives, even disavowing or stifling them (as in the case of individuals who choose a life of voluntary celibacy). In fact, to a great extent human beings choose to be what they are – they choose their own nature through the act of self-understanding or self-discovery. In essential terms, this is what human freedom consists of.

However, Hegel recognizes that the achievement of self-conscious Spirit is something that takes time. As individuals, we all start off as small children in a more or less animal state: ruled by our drives and needs, and unreflective. Maturation consists in large measure in the process of learning to think critically about ourselves, and achieving a degree of self-awareness. But all of this is also true of the human race as a whole. As a race we began, Hegel believes, in an infantile state and were ruled by childish beliefs – myths and

Spirit

superstitions. We were actually the authors of these, but we were not self-conscious enough to realize it. Because we were unself-conscious, we lacked freedom for we could not see the degree to which we could change the ideas we lived by and therefore shape our own nature. For Hegel, history is in fact the story of our gradual achievement of self-consciousness, which is simultaneously the realization of our freedom, our capacity for self-determination. With this achievement, which truly occurs in the modern period, human Spirit is fully realized.

Hegel's philosophy treats the different aspects of Spirit. *The Phenomenology of Spirit* is, in essence, a sketch of many of the different forms in which Spirit shows itself to us. Some of these forms are higher than others. For instance, our most basic psychological drives are a part of Spirit – a part of human nature or human consciousness – though a very rudimentary part since they are unself-conscious. Spirit also displays itself in the social institutions and laws of society, since these are the creation or projection of human consciousness. However, human beings frequently do not realize this and believe instead that the laws and forms of their society are written in nature, or ordained by God. The highest form of Spirit, for Hegel, is Spirit fully aware of itself – which means, in essence, Spirit able to speak the truth about itself. This is precisely what Hegel thinks philosophy is. Socrates said that the goal of philosophy was self-understanding, and that 'the unexamined life is not worth living'. Through philosophy, Hegel asserts, Spirit actually realizes itself in its highest form – it achieves a kind of 'absolute self-consciousness'. However, Hegel believes that only a philosophy that understands the historical development of Spirit can achieve that 'absolute' status.

'The Philosophy of Spirit' forms one of the three major divisions of Hegel's philosophy. The others are Logic and Philosophy of Nature. One way to look at the Logic is that it is a system of ideas that constitute the fundamental categories or forms of existence as such. Nature, for Hegel, embodies these categories. Spirit is the being that is capable of achieving awareness of the fundamental categories of existence, and of how they are displayed in nature, and in human nature. Human Spirit thus emerges as something that begins in nature (we are, after all, animals), but that raises itself out of the merely natural through reflection on nature and on itself. Interestingly, Hegel draws a parallel between the three parts of his system – Logic, Nature, Spirit – and the three persons of the Christian

Trinity: Father, Son, and Holy Spirit. Hegel sees this Christian doctrine as a kind of mythical anticipation of the fundamental forms of his system, and he sees in the traditional idea of God an image of his conception of Spirit. See also **Absolute Spirit; God; history and Philosophy of History; Objective Spirit;** *Phenomenology of Spirit;* **Philosophy of Spirit; Subjective Spirit; Trinity**.

'spiritual animal kingdom' (*das geistige Tierreich*)   This unique image appears in *The Phenomenology of Spirit*, Division C. After discussing the problematic individualism of the life of self-indulgence and the 'law of the heart', Hegel turns to 'The spiritual animal kingdom and deceit, or the "matter in hand" itself' – a highly obscure portion of the text, to say the least. Essentially, Hegel is dealing here with a further development of individualism within the sphere of reason. What he seems to have in mind is the modern world of super-specialization, in which individuals pursue extraordinarily narrow activities, often without any sense of *why* they do what they do, or of the larger significance of their acts. In part, Hegel seems to be commenting upon the state of modern academic research in which scholars and scientists pursue their interests in extraordinarily narrow subjects, oblivious to the larger context which might confer meaning on their work, and unconcerned with its relevance to life.[27] They may even be fundamentally unconcerned with whether what they produce is *true*. The situation is reminiscent of what Thomas Kuhn described as 'normal science': continued specialization and research within a paradigm which may, in fact, have already shown itself to be defective. It is research carried on for its own sake, and it is a false form of reason, disconnected from the higher purposes of Spirit. See also **law of the heart;** *Phenomenology of Spirit*.

state (*der Staat*)   In Hegel's *Philosophy of Right*, the 'State' is the third division of 'Ethical Life', which describes the different institutions necessary for human beings to become fully developed, free and responsible individuals. Essentially, Hegel argues that individuals develop ethically as a result of recognizing their situatedness within certain social wholes. In each case, they come to recognize that they are what they are, and can do what they wish to do, only as a result of belonging to the whole. Therefore, they learn to subordinate their personal interests to its interests.

The family is the first such social whole examined by Hegel. This is the most basic ethical institution, because it is in the family that individuals typically first learn what it means to live for the whole, rather than exclusively for their own personal desires. In civil society, the antithesis of family, individuals relate as competitors. Nevertheless, they come (ideally) to develop a sense of public spiritedness, and civil society helps to foster this through its various guilds, unions and professional organizations. However, in civil society these ethical sentiments are largely motivated by self-interest.

Hegel argues, therefore, that there must be something in society that binds people together by completely transcending individual self-interest. This role is played by the state, which brings a people together by embodying its traditions, mores and customs: the spirit of the nation. The state represents an 'ethical advance' on civil society because it creates a sense of common citizenship and obligation to the whole. The state also reconciles the two opposed moments of family and civil society. Through the state, individuals are united in a bond that, as in the family, transcends personal self-interest, while at the same time securing a sphere in which they may pursue their own private, selfish ends. The state not only unifies the people, it safeguards and supports the spheres of family and civil society, which are made possible by a public, legal order which protects and regulates them. It should be clear from what has been said so far, however, that Hegel's state is not merely 'government'. The state is 'Objective Spirit' because it provides the people with a reflection of itself.

Contrary to what is often claimed, Hegel's state is not 'totalitarian': it does not nullify the individual. Hegel writes that 'The right of individuals to their *particularity* is . . . contained in ethical substantiality, for particularity is the mode of outward appearance in which the ethical exists' (Nisbet, 197; PR § 154). (This is an application of a fundamental Hegelian principle: that the whole, the concrete universal, has being only in and through its parts.) Nevertheless, Hegel argues in *The Philosophy of Right* that freedom is truly realized only when we will or affirm the conditions that make our freedom possible. These conditions are largely social: society provides us with determinate spheres in which we exercise freedom of choice; without these, our 'freedom' would be merely empty and abstract. Since the state is, in fact, the larger social whole which makes possible the different ways in which we can express our freedom, Hegel claims that true freedom only comes about through membership in the state.

Turning now to the details of Hegel's state, when he refers to its 'constitution' he does not mean a written document. Constitutions may be written (as in America) or unwritten (as in England). However, Hegel does not believe that they may simply be 'invented'. Instead, constitutions evolve over time, and are the living expression of the spirit of a people. The three branches of Hegel's state are the legislative, executive, and sovereign (which correspond, in his Logic, to the categories of universal, particular, and individual).

Hegel is an advocate of constitutional monarchy, and as he conceives it the function of the monarch is to be the 'final word'. The legislative branch concretizes universal ideals or ethical principles in the form of law. The executive branch makes recommendations about courses of action to the King, and it is the King's job to make these recommendations official state policy. Where there may be a difference of opinion among his advisors, the King's role is to make the final decision. Modern readers, however, may wonder why this role must be played by a King. Why not a Prime Minister or a President? First of all, it must be noted that whatever we call the individual who makes the final decision, there must, in fact, be such an individual, for purely practical reasons. Why this individual should be a hereditary monarch, however, is more complex. Hegel believes that although the state is the embodiment of the spirit of a people, as such it is an abstraction. The people need to see their nation embodied in a concrete, single personality: someone they can look to as, in effect, the father (or mother) of the country. Such a person should not be a politician, since in order to serve as a national symbol *for everyone*, they must be above political factions. This is why 'the sovereign' cannot be a Prime Minister or a President (where this is understood to be an elected individual, known to be aligned with some particular faction). But why make the sovereign hereditary? Why not let the people choose the sovereign? Again, this would bring factions into play and any sovereign chosen in such a manner could serve as a national symbol only to those on the winning side (which would defeat the purpose of the sovereign serving as a 'unifying' figure). The simplest procedure, and the one least likely to lead, in the worst case, to political upheaval or revolution, is to make the position of sovereignty hereditary. This neatly eliminates any problems of 'selecting' a sovereign and reduces factionalism: with the position of sovereign open only to members of a certain family, there is no question of who the next sovereign is to be, and no struggle for power.

state

Hegel's executive branch interprets and executes legislation and the edicts of the monarch. Therefore Hegel insists that it must include the judiciary (which interprets the law) and the police (who execute or enforce the law). These posts are not elected: they are within the gift of the sovereign and his advisors. Government for Hegel is largely an activity carried out by civil servants, and he insists that they must be educated in such a way that they see their jobs as public service. In short, civil servants must be trained to keep in mind the interests of the whole of society. Hegel thinks that government is, in general, a matter calling for expertise, and so should primarily be staffed by individuals who have been well-educated and trained to govern. To simply select officials by lot or by democratic vote is, from Hegel's point of view, a foolish and dangerous way to form a government. Hegel tells us that 'To know what one wills, and even more, to know what the will which has being in and for itself – i.e., reason – wills, is the fruit of profound cognition and insight, and this is the very thing which "the people" lack' (Nisbet, 340; PR § 301). Hegel's civil servants will be drawn from the middle class, because this is the educated class (the upper and lower classes having no need of education). Further, an ethic of industriousness (the so-called 'Protestant work ethic') has been instilled into the members of this class. Therefore, it is Hegel's belief that the middle class has the education and character best suited for officialdom.

The legislative assembly is where public opinion has its voice, and here the spirit of the nation can express itself and codify itself in the form of laws and resolutions. However, Hegel regards public opinion as something that 'deserves to be *respected* as well as *despised*' (Nisbet, 355; PR § 318). It must be respected because it is capable of giving voice to the universal, to what is right, and to the people's spirit. But the voice of public opinion is also the voice of unfounded prejudice, superstition and half-baked notions of all kinds. Most people don't think deeply or consistently about issues, and so to an extent public opinion must be distrusted. It cannot rule.

The legislative assembly consists of two houses. The upper house is made up of the landed aristocracy – an 'agricultural class' of gentleman farmers, equivalent to the British House of Lords (as it once was). Hegel believes those who have inherited their property are ideally equipped for a political role because they are 'equally independent of the resources of the state and of the uncertainty of trade, the quest for profit, and all variations in property' (Nisbet, 345; PR § 306). The lower house is made up primarily of the business class – merchants, manufacturers, etc. – who are characteristically less able to perceive the good of the whole, precisely because of their concern with personal profit and the short term. It can easily be seen that it is the members of what Hegel refers to (in his discussion of civil society) as the 'estate of trade and industry' that would make up the lower house. Hegel holds that what he calls 'corporations' (guilds, unions and professional associations) arise within this estate, and police themselves. Presumably these corporations would appoint or elect representatives to the legislature.

Hegel is often accused of deifying the state, and indeed he does refer to it as 'the march of God in the world', and as 'this actual God' (Nisbet, 279; PR § 258 A). He also says at one point that 'we should venerate the state as an earthly divinity' (Nisbet, 307; PR § 272 A). Hegel understands 'God' as religion's way of talking about the Absolute or Idea: the whole of reality understood as an internally related system which reaches closure through Absolute Spirit, the self-consciousness of reality itself. Objective Spirit is another form in which Idea expresses itself – but Hegel actually introduces Objective Spirit in the *Encyclopedia* by telling us explicitly that it is merely Idea 'existing in itself' (*nur an sich seiend*) (Wallace, 241; PS § 483). Therefore, we can say that the state, the highest expression of Objective Spirit, is God – but only God in social form, not in the form of Absolute Spirit. Another way to put this is to say that the state may be an 'earthly divinity', but it is only an *earthly* divinity. The state is the greater social whole with which we identify ourselves, and thus, in a sense, it is a kind of microcosm of the Absolute: the all-encompassing whole which includes society and everything else. Hegel should not be understood as claiming that people should *literally* bow down and worship the state. He holds, furthermore, that one of the functions of the state is to safeguard religion – but he does not claim that the object of religious worship is the state. Hegel is also frequently accused of having specifically deified 'the Prussian State' – whereas in fact the state he describes in *The Philosophy of Right* is quite different in many respects from the one under whose auspices he taught in Berlin. See also **abstract right; civil society; ethical life; family; freedom; morality; Objective Spirit;** *Philosophy of Right*; **universal, particular and individual.**

stoicism, scepticism, unhappy consciousness (*der Stoizismus, der Skeptizismus, das unglückliche Bewußtsein*)

This sequence of concepts occurs in the 'Self-Consciousness' section of *The Phenomenology of Spirit*, after the famous 'master–servant dialectic'. Hegel shows how in the primal struggle for recognition, the servant is the one who yields, making the other master. The master is recognized by the servant, but not vice versa. The master, of course, regards the servant as subhuman, as an inferior being (and we might also observe that for precisely this reason, the servant's recognition can hardly be fully satisfying to the master). The master puts the servant to work satisfying his needs. Though it may seem that the master is better off, in fact Hegel argues that, freed from the necessity of labour, he becomes a servant to his own passions and pleasures. The servant, on the other hand, discovers himself and develops as an individual through his work, through transforming nature. Still, the servant can hardly be satisfied given that he is regarded as an inferior being and has thus not won the recognition of others. The next stages of the dialectic follow out the transformations of the servant's standpoint, as he attempts to achieve freedom and recognition by different means.

The first such attempt is stoicism, in which the servant aims at freedom through detaching himself from the world and from his own predicament, achieving peace of mind through mental aloofness and self-control. Historically, stoicism has been a standpoint of both masters and servants: the Roman Emperor Marcus Aurelius (121–180 AD), and Epictetus (55–135 AD), who was a slave. It is a standpoint both of submission or resignation (to that which we cannot change), and self-mastery. What it achieves, however, is not real freedom, but only the empty idea of freedom. In scepticism – which Hegel regards as the inner truth (or, perhaps, ultimate consequence) of stoicism – Spirit simply denies the reality of this world, but its deeds belie its words: it continues to live and work in the 'unreal' world. Scepticism is thus an internally contradictory position. In the 'unhappy consciousness', we find a position that is, in fact, explicitly characterized by contradiction: the opposition of Spirit to a transcendent ideal, from which it desires a kind of recognition, and with which it imagines it would enjoy freedom after death. The unhappy consciousness simply recapitulates the master–servant distinction on a new level. We are servants to the great world-master, God.

Hegel's discussion now involves him in giving an interpretation of the Trinity, given that he understands Christianity as a form of the unhappy consciousness. The Father represents God as inaccessible to finite consciousness. The Son is a tentative reconciliation of the two, but realized in only one person. Spirit is another attempt at reconciliation, this time through a community of those who worship together. This last moment does not, however, fulfill the desire for recognition, for adequate recognition only occurs when human beings are recognized in their true nature. In the form of the 'unhappy consciousness', men define themselves insofar as they stand opposed to an empty, abstract ideal which they have projected into the heavens. There is a dearth of self-knowledge here, and recognition exists only in the intercourse of beings who are truly self-knowing. Instead of seeing itself as the being that in a sense creates its own world, at this point Spirit projects its true nature into a transcendent ideal from which it remains alienated. All of these elements are, as one would expect, taken up and transformed in the final result of the dialectic. The tripartite God will remain, but its third moment will be just this world-creating humanity – i.e., Spirit – which, at this point in the dialectic, Spirit itself cannot recognize. See also **Christianity**; **desire**; **God**; **'master–servant dialectic'**; *Phenomenology of Spirit*; **recognition**; **self-consciousness**; **Spirit**; **Trinity**.

Subjective Spirit (*der subjektive Geist*)   Subjective Spirit is the first division of Hegel's Philosophy of Spirit, the other two being Objective and Absolute Spirit. Hegel's only published account of Subjective Spirit is to be found in *The Encyclopedia of the Philosophical Sciences*.

The Philosophy of Nature understands nature in terms of the categories of the Logic, demonstrating how all natural forms approximate to the embodiment of Idea; i.e., to self-related thought. The individual natural being (e.g. plant or animal) is a 'specification' of the idea, but all such specifications are finite and limited. Each living thing expresses the universal in its own limited and one-sided way, and each perishes. In Spirit, in human nature, the Idea finds a better medium of expression. In human thought, the Idea implicit in nature has become explicit, or for-itself. Human beings are, on one level, natural beings, yet they transcend the merely natural through the unique type of consciousness they possess. It is human beings alone who are capable of true self-consciousness. Thus, human beings are the true embodiment of the self-related thought that is Idea.

Subjective Spirit

However, there is much more to human nature than self-consciousness. Furthermore, an individual requires a lengthy process of development before true self-consciousness and self-possession are achieved – and so does an entire culture. (For Hegel, history itself is the story of humanity's progressive achievement of self-understanding.) Thus, when Hegel's system makes its transition from the Philosophy of Nature to the Philosophy of Spirit, it is to Subjective Spirit that it first turns. Subjective Spirit can be said to deal, broadly speaking, with what we would call the 'psychology' of the individual. Hegel deals with all those aspects of our selves which are unconscious or preconscious, as well as such matters as perception, will, imagination, memory and the passions. He divides Subjective Spirit into 'Anthropology', 'Phenomenology' and 'Psychology'.

Anthropology, Hegel tells us, deals with 'soul', which is Spirit still mired in nature: all that within us which precedes our self-conscious mind or intellect. Hegel further subdivides his treatment of soul into 'natural soul', 'feeling soul' and 'actual soul'. In the formation of human personality, lower levels of the psyche must be brought under the control of the higher levels and, to a great extent, mastered. If this does not take place the higher forms of Spirit cannot emerge. Hegel contends that it is primarily through the development of *habit* that the 'natural' part of the self is tamed, thus freeing the higher levels of the mind for other activities, including philosophy. This achievement constitutes the development of actual soul.

In 'Phenomenology' Hegel revisits some of the same ground covered in the 1807 *Phenomenology of Spirit*. Just as in that work, Hegel's discussion begins with 'Consciousness', in which the distinction between subject and object first emerges. (What Hegel calls the soul is not yet truly aware of a distinction between itself and another.) 'Consciousness' is succeeded by 'Self-Consciousness', in which we find the first glimmerings of a sense of self-identity. In 'Reason', the final subdivision of 'Phenomenology' (at least so far as Subjective Spirit is concerned), a form of conscious thought is achieved which is intersubjective, and therefore 'objective' instead of being merely personal.

Finally, 'Psychology', deals with a great deal that would be categorized as epistemology (or 'theory of knowledge') today. Hegel discusses, among other things, the nature of attention, memory, imagination and judgement. Hegel is treating subjectivity in all its forms as a progressive attempt by the subject to annul the otherness of the object, and make it its own. (Full 'possession' of the object would mean full understanding: the philosophical understanding of the object in terms of its place within the whole.) 'Practical Spirit' (the second subdivision of 'Psychology') shows how concrete practice, in addition to observation or theory-building, is another way we attempt to possess the object. For example, our feelings tell us how the world 'ought' to be and induce us to try and change it, but the world continually frustrates these feelings. Practical spirit thus cannot truly negate the otherness of the other.

'Free Spirit', the third and final subdivision of 'Psychology', involves the subject understanding all the preceding as the necessary condition of its development. This does not mean that it becomes free of its unchosen feelings, drives and impulses, but it does learn to understand them. Still, it would be impossible to rise to the level of Absolute Spirit and philosophy if these went unchecked. Only civilized society can compel us to sublimate and channel our drives in order that we may realize our human potential. Hegel's dialectic therefore turns from Subjective Spirit to Objective Spirit. See also **actual soul**; **anthropology**; **feeling soul**; **habit**; **natural soul**; **phenomenology**; **psychology**.

subjectivity, objectivity, idea (*die Subjektivität, die Objektivität, die Idee*)   In *The Science of Logic*, Hegel divides the Doctrine of the Concept into three sections: 'Subjectivity', 'Objectivity' and 'the Idea' (in the *Encyclopedia Logic* these are given as 'the Subjective Concept', 'the Object', and 'the Idea'). In the Concept, we have transcended the categories of being and essence. To put the matter very succinctly, though the categories of being and essence deal with what is objective, they are also categories of thought, or concepts. In the Doctrine of the Concept, Hegel treats the nature of the Concept *as such*. Thus, in this portion of the Logic, Hegel in effect deals with ideas about ideas.

Subjectivity involves thinking about the most basic forms taken by thinking: concepts (universal, particular and individual), judgement forms and the syllogism. In this section Hegel gives a speculative account of the different forms studied by traditional logic. In the section on objectivity, he turns to an examination of the most basic ways in which we may conceive objects, or the 'objective world': mechanism, chemism, and teleology. These appear to foreshadow the Philosophy of Nature's mechanics, physics,

subjectivity, objectivity, idea

and organics (and indeed they do), but Hegel understands them as 'styles of thinking' which have application to more than just observable natural phenomena. In teleology we conceive objects as self-differentiating, self-sustaining wholes which are, in effect, images of what is to come: the Idea, the concrete universal subsuming the whole system that is the Logic. In the concept of teleology, therefore, thought confronts itself in still another way, and discovers that the true end of objectivity is thought finding itself objectified within the world.

Idea has three moments: life, cognition and willing, and Absolute Idea. What follows is an attempt to give the gist of some extremely involved and difficult passages. The transition to life is via teleology. Again, the true paradigm for the self-differentiating, self-sustaining systems described by teleology is the Logic itself. However, the examples most ready-to-hand would be living organisms. Hegel therefore calls life 'the immediate idea': the idea that is *there*, expressed or embodied concretely, but not aware of itself. In living things, cognition is really a process of bringing the objective world 'inward'. Cognition duplicates the world in subjectivity; through it the objective becomes subjective, or inwardized. Animals, of course, are not aware that they are doing this, but in higher-level human cognition we can become aware of it. Willing, on the other hand, does not cognize things in the world, it *transforms* things into what the subject thinks they ought to be. Cognition and willing are both processes of inwardizing the object, or bringing it into conformity with the subject, but we are not explicitly aware that this is what is happening.

In Absolute Idea we reach the standpoint where the subject recognizes itself in the object explicitly. Absolute Idea is literally idea of idea, or 'thought thinking itself' (which is Aristotle's description of God, quoted by Hegel in this context). In it subject has become object and vice versa. However, in order to understand how, in concrete terms, we come to recognize ourselves in the object, we must go beyond the Logic. In the Philosophy of Nature, we find the entire conceptual scheme of the Logic reflected in nature itself. We come to see the world as intelligible only as a kind of approximation to the self-thinking thought of human beings, the 'structure' of which is delineated in the Logic. See also **Absolute Idea; Concept, Doctrine of the; Idea; judgement; mechanism, chemism, teleology; syllogism; universal, particular and individual.**

sublation (n. *die Aufhebung*; or v. 'to sublate', *aufheben*) Hegel frequently uses the separable verb *aufheben* in his writings. This word is notoriously difficult to render into English, but in recent years the seldom-used English term 'sublation' has become a popular translation (though its use in translations of Hegel actually dates back to Stirling's 1865 *The Secret of Hegel*). Hegel explains the meaning of *aufheben* in his *Science of Logic*: '*Aufheben* . . . constitutes one of the most important concepts in philosophy. . . . *Aufheben* has a two-fold meaning in the language: on the one hand it means to preserve, to maintain, and equally it also means to cause to cease, to put an end to. . . . It is a delight to speculative thought to find in the language words which have in themselves a speculative meaning; the German language has a number of such' (Miller 106–7; WL I, 101). Thus, *aufheben* essentially means to cancel or abolish, and to preserve or retain. *Aufheben* can also mean to 'raise up', which Hegel makes clear elsewhere. Hegel's use of *aufheben* often connotes *all* of these meanings simultaneously. He frequently employs *aufheben* when speaking of transitions in the dialectic, and the meaning of this term is a key to understanding the dialectic itself.

To take one example, in *The Philosophy of Right* the dialectical sequence family – civil society – state appears. The family is 'sublated' by civil society in the sense of being 'cancelled': civil society, in which adult individuals compete with one another, is the antithesis of the family, which is characterized by the bond of love. In the state, the divisive relations of civil society are also sublated in the sense of being cancelled: the state binds people together as civil society never can. However, at the same time, in the idea of the state we find the world of distinct, competing individuals preserved or retained. Further, we find that in a sense the state has not only preserved the family in providing a means to secure and protect it, the state has also in effect created a higher type of 'family' in which individuals are able to overcome their differences and achieve fellow-feeling through identifying themselves with the nation. Thus, in the concept of the state, the family and civil society are not only 'cancelled' (in the sense of being conceptually overcome), but also raised up and preserved. Starker examples are to be found in Hegel's Logic, where, for example, being and nothing are cancelled, raised up, and preserved in becoming. See also **being, nothing, becoming**; **dialectic**; **ethical life**; **negation**.

'substance becomes subject'   Hegel claims in *The Phenomenology of Spirit* that his philosophy demonstrates that 'what seems to happen outside of [the self], to be an activity directed against it, is really its own doing, and Substance shows itself to be essentially Subject' (Miller, 21; PG, 28; often glossed as 'substance becomes subject'). 'Substance' is an important concept in the history of both ancient and modern philosophy. Substance (Latin *substantia*) translates the Greek *ousia* or being, which Aristotle held was the object sought by the most fundamental sort of philosophy. Aristotle identified *ousia* with God and argued that all of reality derives its being from its approximation to God, a being which transcends nature. Further, Aristotle described God as a mind which is pure self-consciousness: it thinks only of itself. When Hegel refers to 'substance' he has in mind not only Aristotle, but also Spinoza, who defined God as an absolute substance that contains all finite particulars within itself.

Hegel's Logic culminates in Absolute Idea, a purely self-related concept. Absolute Idea may be likened to Aristotle's ideal, transcendent God or substance, and Hegel encourages this identification, referring to Absolute Idea as 'thought thinking itself'. Hegel argues, however, that Absolute Idea is still *merely* idea, and refers to the Logic as a whole as a 'realm of shadows'. Self-related Idea has true reality only as embodied in the self-thinking (self-aware) *thought* exhibited by human beings, and pre-eminently in philosophy. From the Logic, Hegel turns to the Philosophy of Nature. He understands nature as a scale of forms, each of which approximates to the self-relatedness that is finally only exhibited in human thought – treated by the Philosophy of Spirit. Thus, we come to understand that Spirit is the ultimate purpose of reality – the meaning of reality itself. Hegel writes in the Philosophy of Spirit that 'the aim of all genuine science is just this, that Spirit shall recognize itself in everything in heaven and on earth' (Wallace, 1; PS § 377 A). Thus, in Hegel's philosophy substance (or being) becomes subject (or Spirit). See also **Absolute Idea; Absolute Spirit; Aristotle; God; Logic;** *Phenomenology of Spirit*.

syllogism (*der Schluß*)   In the third and final division of the Logic – the Doctrine of the Concept – thought has achieved true self-relation. This first reveals itself in what Hegel dubs 'Subjectivity', a subdivision within which he considers the most basic forms of thought: the concepts, judgements and inferences that have been catalogued in the past by traditional (pre-Hegelian) logic. A syllogism is a deductive argument consisting of two, and only two, premises. For example:

All men are mortal.
Socrates is a man.
Therefore, Socrates is mortal.

This is a categorical syllogism, and it consists of three terms. 'Mortal' is the major term; 'Socrates' is the minor term; and 'man/men' is the middle term, which links the two premises and makes possible the inference from the two premises to the conclusion. The syllogism was for many years the basic argument form studied by traditional logic, a discipline pioneered by Aristotle. The three statements that make up all syllogisms are judgements, and Hegel's discussion of the syllogism follows his discussion of the various forms of judgement.

Just as he does with the judgement forms, Hegel sees past the mundane uses of the syllogism and recognizes in it an attempt, ultimately, to express the nature of the whole. The different judgement forms are ways of relating Universal, Particular and Individual terms. For example, 'Socrates is mortal' relates an individual, Socrates, to the universal 'mortality'. Hegel argues that judgements like this really assert that the meaning of the individual is to be found in the universal – its being is its relation to, or place within, the whole. However, in the different judgement forms, the whole is, in a sense, dividing itself or expressing its different aspects. The judgement 'Socrates is mortal' merely relates an individual to a larger conceptual whole – mortality – which is itself part of a larger conceptual whole. Because the syllogism relates or brings together judgements – each of which identifies some part of the truth – it aims, in a sense, at a restoration of the whole.

This strange claim can be made more intelligible in the following simple way. A judgement like 'Socrates is mortal' is essentially saying 'The individual is universal'. But consider what happens when this judgement appears as the conclusion in the syllogism given earlier. In arguing that Socrates is a mortal, *because* he is a man and all men are mortal, we are relating the individual to the universal *through* the particular; i.e., it is because the individual is a man (a particular of a given kind) that he is mortal. Thus, while judgements merely assert, in essence, that 'the

symbolic art

Individual is Universal', syllogisms such as this one tell us that 'the individual, as particular, is universal', thus unifying all three conceptual moments.[28] It is obvious that when Hegel understands traditional deduction as aiming (unconsciously) at the whole, he is seeing it as a kind of imperfect approximation to the 'true deduction' (if one may call it that) exemplified by his dialectic.

Hegel claims, in fact, that 'everything is a syllogism'. Everything is an individual, belonging to a particular species, subsumed within a larger universal (or genus). Universal, particular, and individual are the three moments of the Concept, and Hegel tells us that 'Everything is a *concept*, and the way that the concept is there [i.e., the way it exists] is the distinction of its moments, in such a way that its *universal* nature gives itself external reality through *particularity*, and in this way . . . the concept makes itself into the *individual*' (Geraets, 257; EL § 181). Hegel sees his entire philosophy as a syllogism, and thus all of reality as a syllogism as well. Logic, Nature and Spirit are the three 'terms'. Nature can be seen as the middle term linking Logic and Spirit – if we understand nature not only as that which embodies Idea, but also that which Spirit must differentiate itself from in order to achieve conscious possession of Idea. However, the 'syllogistic' nature of the Hegelian system can be understood in two other ways. Logic may be understood as the middle term linking Nature and Spirit: the Logic is simultaneously the 'formal structure' of nature as such, and the formal structure of human thought. Finally, we may understand Spirit as the middle term insofar as Idea only has true reality as expressed in the self-thinking thought of Absolute Spirit, and Nature is only intelligible (or meaningful) as an approximation to Spirit. See also **Concept, Doctrine of the**; **judgement**; **Logic**; **subjectivity, objectivity, idea**; **universal, particular and individual**.

symbolic art (*die symbolische Kunst*)   Hegel's Philosophy of Art discusses different art forms in terms of how well the ideal 'content' of the artwork and its material medium are brought together. In great art, a complete or perfect harmony is present. Hegel lists three major forms of art: the symbolic, the classical and the romantic. In symbolic art the meaning of the artwork is so abstract that it cannot find adequate expression in material form. Spirit is struggling to express itself in symbolic art, but it expresses itself in a way that is wholly indefinite and mysterious. The meaning gets lost in the form, and the result is that the artwork stands as a riddle.

Hegel identifies monumental architecture as the primary form of symbolic art, and he uses the ancient Egyptians as one of his chief examples of this. In the Sphinx we have an artwork in which the massive, stone medium has completely overwhelmed the message: it stands (for us and, Hegel seems to have believed, the Egyptians themselves) as simply a riddle. Humanity still 'confronts itself' through such an artwork (which is, after all, a human product), but it does so inadequately. The move from symbolic art to classical is essentially the move beyond the expression of strange, indefinite ideas, to the expression of concrete, human individuality. In classical art a perfect harmony of content and medium is achieved. See also **art and Philosophy of Art**; **classical art**; **natural religion**; **romantic art**.

system (*das System*) The word system derives from the Greek *sustema*, which refers to a whole of parts. A whole is not the same thing as a mere collection, such as the items one finds in one's desk drawer. On the contrary, a whole is, in a sense, an individual something that is articulable into parts. The human body is a system in this sense. Needless to say, for an individual to be truly individual and possess unity, there must be some principle (broadly construed) according to which the parts hang together to form a whole. The Ancients regarded nature itself as such a *sustema*. However, they did not seem to apply the term to thought or knowledge. In the early modern period, however, the word 'system' came to be much more widely employed, and books began appearing with titles like 'System of Logic', 'System of Rhetoric', 'System of Grammar', 'System of Theology', 'System of Physics', etc.[29] The Greek philosophers probably would not have regarded their activity as 'systematic' because they saw themselves as describing a reality which was itself a *sustema*.

Hegel's use of the term system falls within this modern tradition of 'system building', while at the same time recovering the ancient meaning of the term. This is because Hegel's system is not merely a systematic organization of concepts: it is an account of reality as a whole, revealing it to be a system itself. Hegel sees philosophy as Plato did, as knowledge of the whole, and he is quite explicit about this. As noted, a whole is not a collection, but an ordered system of parts. Therefore, true philosophy (for

system

Hegel) captures the whole in speech by displaying it as an ordered system, and by revealing the principle of order involved.

In the *Phenomenology of Spirit*, Hegel states not only that 'the true is the whole', but that 'the true is actual only as system' (Miller, 14; PG, 18). In the *Encyclopedia Logic*, he describes the system as follows:

> Each of the parts of philosophy is a philosophical whole, a circle that closes upon itself; but in each of them the philosophical Idea is in a particular determinacy or element. Every single circle also breaks through the restriction of its element as well, precisely because it is inwardly [the] totality, and it grounds a further sphere. The whole presents itself therefore as a circle of circles, each of which is a necessary moment, so that the system of its peculiar elements constitutes the whole Idea – which equally appears in each single one of them. (Geraets, 39; EL § 15).

The primary such circle, however, is the Logic, which is essentially an ontology (a theory of being) articulating the fundamental nature of reality in terms of a system of ideas or categories. The Logic is a *system* of categories because Hegel demonstrates that each is what it is in its relations to the others. In other words, the Logic is an internally related totality of concepts. The principle of order governing the Logic as system is simply that each category is a 'provisional definition' of the whole, or Absolute. Each, starting with the very first and most basic, 'pure being', is shown to be in effect an attempt to express what is only truly expressed by the final category of the Logic, Absolute Idea. Further, Hegel's dialectic demonstrates how the inadequacies of each category cause them to be superseded by further categories. In other words, each category is supplanted or augmented by the others in a progressive definition of the Absolute. When we finally do arrive at Absolute Idea we find Hegel claiming that in a sense all the preceding categories are 'contained' within it. They are, as it were, the 'filling' of Absolute Idea, seen as a self-differentiating whole. Furthermore, Hegel tells us that Absolute Idea is, in fact, the idea of idea. Through Absolute Idea, therefore, the system of ideas comprehends itself and reaches closure. The Logic is, in short, a self-comprehending and self-grounding system. No other 'system' with which we are familiar can claim this. Thus, the Logic is not just a system – but the very ideal of system itself.

Hegel makes it clear that Absolute Idea, however, is merely idea. What we find in the Logic is an almost Platonic account of objective idea. Yet in the end Hegel is more true to Aristotle, insisting that idea 'in itself' is something ghostly and irreal: idea must be 'actualized' in nature. Hegel's Philosophy of Nature demonstrates how the system of the Logic can be used to make nature itself intelligible. And, indeed, the Logic forms the template of Hegel's philosophy: he draws upon it in making sense of all else. (Thus, one may argue that the Logic is the core of Hegel's philosophy, and the branch of it that is rigorously systematic in the strictest possible sense.) Hegel understands Nature to be a scale of forms which seems to approximate to a realization of the 'self-relatedness' anticipated 'abstractly' in Absolute Idea. This self-relatedness, however, only truly achieves actuality through human self-consciousness (the subject matter of the Philosophy of Spirit). Through Absolute Spirit (art, religion and philosophy) the system that is reality reaches closure: reality, in the person of mankind, achieves awareness of itself. Hegel believes that he has therefore demonstrated that the world is a kind of specification or 'embodiment' of the system of the Logic, culminating in active, self-related thought: the incarnation, as it were, of the self-related Idea that is the climax of the Logic. At the end of his Introduction to the *Encyclopedia Logic* Hegel gives the structure of his system as follows:

I. The Logic, the science of the Idea in and for itself.
II. The Philosophy of Nature, as the science of the Idea in its otherness.
III. The Philosophy of Spirit, as the Idea that returns into itself out of its otherness. (Geraets, 42; EL § 18)

Hegel's early presentation of his system (c. 1802–03) consisted of four parts: 'Logic and Metaphysics', 'Philosophy of Nature', 'System of Ethical Life' and theory of the 'Absolute Idea' (art, religion and philosophy). In the summer of 1804, Hegel radically altered the structure of his system: he shortened it from four major divisions to three. The new tripartitite structure combined the last two divisions into a 'Philosophy of Spirit', with 'System of Ethical Life' becoming 'Objective Spirit'. However, in his lectures from the winter of 1806, Hegel reintroduced a fourth division: a 'Phenomenology of Spirit'. At the time, Hegel was writing his book of the same name, which he would publish the following year. *The Phenomenology of*

theology

Spirit was conceived as an introduction or propaedeutic to the tripartite system of Logic-Nature-Spirit. See also **Absolute, the**; **dialectic**; **Logic**; **nature and Philosophy of Nature**; **Philosophy of Spirit**; **science**; **truth**; **whole, the**.

— T —

teleology   See **mechanism, chemism, teleology**.

theology (*die Theologie*)   In the *Encyclopedia Logic*, Hegel states that both philosophy and religion hold that, 'God and God alone is the truth' (Geraets, 24; EL § 1). In Hegel's manuscript for *The Lectures on the Philosophy of Religion* (1824), he writes that 'God is the one and only object of philosophy . . .' and that 'philosophy is theology' (LPR I, 84; VPR I, 3–4). Hegel holds that philosophy is theology, but that is not the same thing as stating that philosophy is religion.

For Hegel, philosophy and religion have the same object. Religion calls it God; philosophy calls it the Absolute or Idea. Philosophy expresses itself in purely conceptual and rational terms. Religion, on the other hand, employs what Hegel calls 'picture-thinking': myths, images and metaphors. Because religion expresses itself in this way, it cannot give a rational, conceptual account of itself and its inner truth. Nevertheless, religion is a form of Absolute Spirit, and a necessary element in human life (as is art, another form of Absolute Spirit). In fact, religion is the way that most individuals approach the ultimate truth of existence, whereas philosophy is for the relatively few.

The concept of religion stated above is obviously not given from the religious standpoint. It constitutes the result of reflection upon religion, and religion's treatment of its subject matter. Such reflection constitutes theology: an attempt to give an account of the true meaning of the myths, images, and dogmas of religion, without using myths and images and without making dogmatic claims. Theology is the *logos*, the study or account, of God (*theos*) and the truths of religion. But Hegel claims that the results of theology (true theology) turn out to be indistinguishable from those of philosophy: God is revealed to be the Absolute, and the Christian Trinity to be a figurative way of speaking about the three moments of the Absolute: Logic (or the account of the Absolute Idea), nature and Spirit. In essential terms, this is the reason why Hegel can claim that 'philosophy is theology'. Hegel states in the *Lectures*: 'Philosophy is only explicating itself when it explicates religion, and when it explicates itself it is explicating religion' (LPR I, 152–53; VPR I, 63).

Hegel's entire philosophy may be understood to be theological, and as an expression of the inner truth of all religions. However, Hegel claims that he did not arrive at his philosophy simply through reflection on religion. In fact, he claims that his philosophy is without any presuppositions whatsoever, and that he arrived at it by beginning (in the Logic) with 'pure being' (which is equivalent to nothing), and allowing the truth (the Absolute) to display itself dialectically. Therefore, Hegel's philosophy is *not* theology if theology is taken to mean a field which simply presupposes some religious tradition, and than proceeds to develop some deeper understanding of it. Rather, Hegel holds that philosophy is theology because the truth of philosophy *coincides* with the (inner) truth of religion.

Still, it would be inaccurate to say that Hegel believes it is *merely* a coincidence that his philosophy happens to express truths also expressed by religion. He believes that religion in and of itself is absolute truth: it is one form – the primary form, in fact – in which human beings encounter the truth. Indeed, the philosopher himself encounters truth first in the form of religion. Hegel holds that Spirit has undergone a necessary process of historical development, and that before Christianity appeared philosophy could not have presented absolute truth in a fully adequate form. This leaves us with a troubling question: how can one square this claim about philosophy's dependence on religion with Hegel's claim that his philosophy is 'presuppositionless'?

The answer is fairly simple. In the Logic, thought begins without any *determinate* presuppositions, meaning it does not begin by holding this or that idea to be true or 'given' or beyond doubt. However, the thought that thinks in this presuppositionless manner and generates the Logic is a determinate thought, which has undergone historical development. In other words, the thought that thinks the Logic is the thought of modern man shaped by Christianity, and much else. Had Plato begun without determinate presuppositions and thought in the manner Hegel suggests, his 'logic' would have turned out quite differently, because his thought was the product of an earlier time. He would not, in fact, have arrived at the whole truth, precisely because Spirit had to undergo its encounter with Christianity in order to know the whole. Does this mean that Hegel makes all thought relative to historical circumstances? Yes, it does. But Hegel also believes that his historical circumstances have allowed him to arrive at a philosophy which he can demonstrate to be fully adequate and complete. See also **Absolute Spirit**; **Christianity**; **God**; **picture-thinking**; **religion and Philosophy of Religion**.

thesis, antithesis, synthesis   These terms are frequently used to describe the stages of Hegel's dialectic – though their use has fallen out of favour in recent years. Hegel scholars rightly point out that in discussing his dialectic, Hegel himself never uses these terms. Furthermore, there are several problems with this manner of characterizing the dialectic. First, the term 'synthesis' is highly misleading. What moves the dialectic is the opposition of categories antithetical to each other (hence, 'thesis' and 'antithesis' are relatively unproblematic terms). This opposition is then overcome by a further term, but the manner in which it does so varies in Hegel's system and is almost never a 'synthesis', if this is taken to mean a literal combination or conjoining of ideas.

Second, at a very basic level the formula thesis-antithesis-synthesis implies precisely that there is a 'formula' to the dialectic. In fact, as just noted, there are many different ways in which oppositions are reconciled or overcome in the Hegelian system. Hegel insisted that form and content are inseparable in his philosophy, and thus it is fundamentally wrongheaded to speak of a 'method' or 'formal structure' of dialectic. Further, thesis-antithesis-synthesis implies that the dialectic is necessarily triadic. Though it does often seem to be that everything in Hegel comes in threes, he makes it clear that the real nature of dialectic is not triplicity but negation: what moves the supersession of one category by another is that it is always found to be, on its own terms, incomplete. Thus, it 'overcomes itself' and requires supplementation by a further idea. See also **dialectic**; **negation**; **triads**; **understanding**.

'topsy-turvy world'   See **'inverted world'**.

triads It is often asserted that everything in Hegel comes in threes. In recent years this has been vigorously denied by some Hegel scholars, who insist that it is one of the 'myths' about Hegel that caused his system to fall into disrepute. Nevertheless, a cursory glance at any diagram of the Hegelian system certainly seems to show abundant triadicity, and Hegel makes statements which indicate that he consciously employed the triadic form. In *The Phenomenology of Spirit*, for example, Hegel says that with Kant triadicity was 'a lifeless schema', but it has since (presumably, with Hegel) been 'raised to its absolute significance . . . so that the Concept of Science has emerged' (Miller, 29; PG, 37). In one of the remarks in the *Encyclopedia Logic*, Hegel states that, 'Any division is to be considered genuine when it is determined by the Concept. So genuine division is, first of all, tripartite; and then, because particularity presents itself as doubled, the division moves on to fourfoldness as well. In the sphere of Spirit trichotomy predominates, and it is one of Kant's merits to have drawn attention to this' (Geraets, 298; EL § 230 A).

The dialectic is often characterized as a tripartite process of thesis, antithesis, synthesis – though scholars are correct to point out that Hegel himself never uses these terms, and that the third (synthesis) is misleading. Nonetheless, the dialectic typically involves the assertion of a category, which is then understood to lead to or to involve its opposite (or, at least, a conflicting category or claim). The two antagonistic categories are then 'resolved' in a third, which often identifies the underlying unity between the two. (How these antagonisms are resolved varies considerably in Hegel, and is one of the reasons why 'dialectical logic' is impossible to formalize.)

However, despite his conscious use of triadic form, Hegel makes it clear in the conclusion to the *Science of Logic* that in the final analysis it is inessential. What *is* essential is negativity, which is the engine of the dialectic. The categories of philosophy are generated through negation, and though it is convenient to group them into threes, they could also be grouped in twos, fours, etc. See also **dialectic; Logic; negation; thesis, antithesis, synthesis; Trinity.**

Trinity (*die Dreieinigkeit*) In the 'Revealed Religion' section of *The Phenomenology of Spirit*, in the Lectures on the Philosophy of Religion and elsewhere, Hegel presents a speculative understanding of Christianity and Christian doctrines. Most famous of all is his treatment of the Trinity of

Trinity

Father, Son and Holy Spirit. Indeed, Hegel's understanding of the Trinity is central to why he sees Christianity as the Absolute Religion. The Christian Trinity, for Hegel, is a kind of mythic representation of the three moments of speculative philosophy.

According to Christian teaching, the Father is the 'godhead', and the Son is Jesus Christ, God manifest or become flesh. The Holy Spirit dwells within the community of believers, uniting them and guiding them to true faith in God. Further, the three 'persons' of the Trinity are understood as mysteriously one, or 'consubstantial' (of one substance). This doctrine has been cast and interpreted in many different ways, and has been the source of many schisms within Christianity.

Hegel's speculative reading of the Trinity holds that the Father represents Idea 'in-itself', unmanifest, 'prior to creation'. The Father or Idea must 'freely release' himself (or itself) as otherness. This moment of otherness, God 'for-himself' (or Idea 'for-itself') is the second person of the Trinity, the Son. The Holy Spirit, of course, represents Absolute Spirit (self-aware humanity), which is God's 'other' come to consciousness of itself precisely as an expression of Idea (Idea 'in-and-for itself'). Thus, in Absolute Spirit we 'return to the Father'. Though this account may suggest that Hegel asserts a simple correspondence between Father, Son and Holy Spirit, and Logic-Nature-Spirit, the matter is actually more complex than this. Certainly, nature is an 'other' to Idea, and there are passages where Hegel does seem to identify nature with 'the Son'. For example, near the beginning of his discussion of the Philosophy of Nature in the *Encyclopedia*, Hegel states that 'God reveals himself in two different ways: as nature and as Spirit. Both manifestations are temples of God which he fills, and in which he is present. God, as an abstraction, is not true God, but only as the living process of positing his other, the world, which comprehended in its divine form is his Son; and it is only in unity with his other, in Spirit, that God is subject' (Miller, 13; PN § 246 A).

However, this should not be taken to mean that Hegel simply identifies Christ with nature, or understands him merely to be a symbol for nature. Rather, Christ represents the overcoming of the dichotomy between man and God: Christ is God, yet also a man. Christianity, Hegel holds, is the first religion to conceive (implicitly) of the idea of God realizing himself through humanity. In Hegel's philosophy, of course, the Absolute Idea is only 'actualized' through Absolute Spirit.

In the *Lectures on the Philosophy of Religion*, Hegel states that 'God [the Father] makes himself an object for himself [the Son]; then, in this object, God remains the undivided essence within this differentiation of himself within himself, and in this differentiation of himself loves himself, i.e., remains identical with himself – this is God as Spirit' (LPR I, 126; VPR I, 43). In other words, God/Idea objectifies himself/itself as nature but pre-eminently as man, who recognizes himself as one with Idea, or as Idea's concrete expression. Thus, we can say that through man God comes to know himself (Idea knows itself), which constitutes the self-completion or perfection of God. It is difficult not to see this interpretation of Christian doctrine as somehow 'mystical', and Hegel does not really dispute this. At one point in the *Lectures*, in fact, he quotes the medieval mystic Meister Eckhart (c. 1260–c. 1328): 'The eye with which God sees me is the eye with which I see him; my eye and his eye are one and the same. In righteousness I am weighed in God and he in me. If God did not exist nor would I; if I did not exist nor would he' (LPR I, 347–348; VPR I, 248).

Christianity therefore comes close, in Hegel's view, to realizing the truths of speculative philosophy. However, because it is religion and not philosophy of religion it cannot grasp the full import of what it teaches. See also **Christianity; religion and Philosophy of Religion; system; theology; triads**.

truth (*die Wahrheit*; adj. 'true', *wahr*) Hegel's conception of truth is very difficult to categorize in terms of the popular 'theories of truth' discussed in the recent literature of Anglo–American philosophy. To begin with, Hegel distinguishes between truth and mere 'correctness', and he does not treat truth as primarily a property of statements or assertions. A statement like 'the cat is on the mat' may be correct (if the cat is indeed on the mat), but for Hegel it is not 'true'. In the Logic Hegel defines truth as 'the agreement of a content with itself' (Geraets, 60; EL § 24 A). An example he uses to illustrate this is when we refer to someone as a 'true friend', meaning that their behaviour is in accord with the concept of friendship. However, no finite being is ever fully or completely in accord with its concept (or universal), and thus, in a sense, all finite beings are false. Just a few lines down from the last quoted passage, Hegel tells us that 'God alone is the genuine agreement between Concept and reality; all finite things, however, are affected with untruth; they have a concept, but their existence is not adequate to it.'

The foregoing gives us all we really need to understand Hegel's most famous statement about truth. In the Preface to *The Phenomenology of Spirit* he writes that 'the true is the whole' (*Das Wahre ist das Ganze*; Miller, 11; PG, 15). Everything, for Hegel, has its truth 'outside itself', as it were: in relation to the total system of reality of which it forms a part. Reality is a system in which things exist in organic relation to one another, mutually supporting and determining each other, each possessing its identity in its relation to the others. Thus, the 'truth' of something is in fact its place within the whole. If we seek to understand the ultimate significance of *why* the cat is on the mat – and the significance of cats and mats themselves, or of anything – we must adopt an approach which sees everything in its relation to the whole.

In short, Hegel's view of truth is somewhat similar to the so-called 'coherence theory'. However, one difference between Hegel and recent advocates of 'coherence' is that, again, Hegel is not particularly interested in the truth of statements or reports. For him, truth is really a property of concepts and of objects themselves. Reports are correct or incorrect, but the truth is something deeper and more significant than mere 'correctness'. It may be true to say (right now) that 'the cat is on the mat', but for Hegel all statements about finite things are, in a sense, false. To one degree or another, all such statements are (given that they concern finite things) only partial and incomplete; they may report only what is temporary, and present things only from one side. 'The cat is on the mat' is true only temporarily (until the cat gets off the mat), and concerns only *this* cat and *this* mat. Hegel looks at such statements – as well as reports concerned with what we would all agree are far weightier things – and finds no real *truth* in them at all.

All statements about finite things, in fact, are 'false' for Hegel because finite things *themselves* are 'false': they consist in only a partial representation of the whole, one small slice of it. (This is what Hegel means in the quote given earlier when he says that all finite things are 'affected with untruth'.) Similarly, each standpoint in Hegel's dialectic is 'false' because each, taken on its own, is only a part of the whole. Taken in abstraction from the whole, each part is, in a way, misleading. For instance, each category of the Logic is a 'provisional definition' of the Absolute. Each, on its own terms, is false as a definition – but each is part of the entire system of the Logic, which constitutes the complete articulation of the nature of the Absolute. Only the whole is true, and discovering the 'truth' of any finite object or idea consists in understanding its relation to the whole. See also **Absolute**; **coherence**; **system**; **whole, the**.

— U —

understanding (*der Verstand*)　　Hegel uses the term understanding in a special, technical sense to refer to a type of thinking inferior to reason. In his early essay, *The Difference Between Fichte's and Schelling's Systems of Philosophy* (1801), Hegel refers to the understanding as a 'faculty of setting limits'. Indeed, the understanding not only sets limits, but insists doggedly on the impossibility of thinking outside those limits. The understanding is chiefly characterized by a kind of 'either-or' mentality which insists on holding certain distinctions fixed and absolute. To take a simple example, commonsense insists that the concepts of 'being' and 'nothing' are polar, irreconcilable opposites. In Hegel's Logic, however, he argues that because being is really the emptiest category, devoid of all concrete determination, it is equivalent to nothing! This argument is a product of what Hegel calls speculation, which is the positive aspect of reason (dialectic being the negative aspect). Speculation involves the negation or transcendence of dichotomies. Hegel's philosophy works precisely by thinking beyond such dichotomies, usually by identifying their underlying identity, and/or cancelling them in a third position overlooked by the thinking that gave rise to the dichotomy in the first place. Incomprehension is the understanding's usual response to speculation: it cannot comprehend thought which thinks outside the dichotomies in which it has confined itself.

Speculation allows Hegel to solve many philosophical problems which remain insoluble for the understanding. For example, the understanding insists that the universe must be either finite or infinite, but cannot be both. However, as Kant demonstrated, there seem to be equally good arguments for either position. Hegel solves the dilemma by asserting that

understanding

the standard conception of infinity (as that which goes on forever) is false. Since the (false) infinite *excludes* the finite, it is actually limited by what it excludes, and thus cannot be infinite (or unlimited). The true infinite, for Hegel, has nothing 'outside' itself which could limit it, thus it must 'contain' or be composed by all that which is finite. This argument is impossible for the understanding to grasp, because it is incapable of adopting a critical standpoint about its most fundamental presuppositions. It is really for precisely this reason that Hegel regards the understanding as unphilosophical.

As Hegel argues in his Logic, philosophy must be a presuppositionless science, which holds no concepts as fixed or beyond question. This is the case even with the famous 'laws of logic': Identity (A is A), Non-Contradiction (A cannot be x and not x at the same time, in the same respect), and Excluded Middle (*either* x *or* not x, with no third possibility). Contrary to what is widely claimed, Hegel does not really reject these laws – but he does accuse the understanding of misapplying them. All the mistakes made by the understanding consist essentially in not recognizing that identity is a function of difference (A is thus, for Hegel, not not-A), *or* in failing to see an identity between apparently contradictory terms, *or* in failing to notice that sometimes apparent contradiction points to a third possibility (or some combination of these three). Those who think from the standpoint of the understanding often pride themselves on the 'rigor' of their thought – but their rigor is really the *rigor mortis* of a style of thinking that is extremely narrow and devoid of imagination. 'Commonsense', for Hegel, is a kind of lower level version of the understanding. Hegel tells us that commonsense is fine for everyday life, but it is useless for philosophy.

However, there are philosophers and scientists that are effectively 'caught' at the level of the understanding, and Hegel heaps justifiable scorn on their work. Hegel's distinction between understanding and reason is borrowed from Kant, who uses the terms in a somewhat different sense. For Kant, the understanding is the faculty of making basic judgements about experience according to certain fixed categories. As mentioned already, Hegel sees this function of the understanding as legitimate within certain contexts, but as leading to a kind of 'pigeon-holing' mentality. Reason, for Kant, is 'higher' than the understanding, for it seeks to synthesize knowledge and to find final answers, according to certain 'regulative ideals'. However, Kant holds that this faculty, while possessing a positive dimension, has the tendency to lead us into flights of metaphysical delusion. He illustrates this with the 'antinomies' of reason, such as the one mentioned earlier concerning the finitude or infinity of the universe: the universe cannot be both, yet there are good arguments for either position. For Kant, this means that the matter is simply insoluble by the human mind. Hegel, by contrast, sees Kantian reason and its antinomies as the dialectic in incipient form, and thus he assigns to reason a thoroughly positive role. What for Kant leads to delusion, for Hegel is philosophy itself and the path to truth. Despite his brilliance, Kant thus remains for Hegel a philosopher caught at the level of understanding. See also **commonsense**; **dialectic**; **Kant, Immanuel**; **reason**; **reflection**; **speculation**.

unhappy consciousness   See **stoicism, scepticism, unhappy consciousness**.

universal, particular and individual (*das Allgemeine, das Besondere, das Einzelne*)   In the third and final division of the Logic – the Doctrine of the Concept – thought has come to the point where it thinks itself. This reveals itself first in what Hegel calls 'Subjectivity', a subdivision within which he considers the most basic forms of thought: the concepts, judgements and inferences that have been catalogued in the past by traditional (pre-Hegelian) logic. Universal, Particular and Individual are the three moments of the Concept. Hegel tells us, in fact, that everything is a concept, and thus that everything can be understood in terms of these categories. Everything that exists is a universal that has specified itself into an individual of a particular sort. As he puts it, 'Everything is a *concept*, and the way that the concept is there [i.e., the way it exists] is the distinction of its moments, in such a way that its *universal* nature gives itself external reality through *particularity*, and in this way . . . the concept makes itself into the *individual*' (Geraets, 257; EL § 181).

A universal is a common character or nature we think in terms of when dealing with things: the 'manness' in men, the 'squareness' of square objects, etc. Things are understood as belonging to these universal categories when we disregard their individual differences and treat them as all alike, in virtue of their common character. When we treat things in this manner, they are understood as *particulars*: the universal 'manness' unites all the particular men, who are subsumed under or within it despite their

universal, particular and individual

myriad differences. (Some men are short, others tall, some blind, others sighted – but all are nonetheless the same in being men.) However, we understand that although we disregard differences in seeing things as particular instances of a universal, these differences are quite real. It is the differences that make things *individuals*, rather than simple particulars. In other words, though we see all men as the same insofar as they are men, we realize that in fact they are not simply the same: each is a unique combination of characteristics. Each is individual.

Hegel argues that these three concepts, though they seem quite distinct, are intimately bound up with each other. The understanding, however, does not see this and holds the three strictly separated. The understanding sees universals as externally related to particulars. In its extreme form, this may issue in an ontological separation between them, as in Plato's philosophy, where universals or 'forms' are held to exist in a different reality altogether separate from their particular exemplars. Hegel rejects any such approach, and shows how in a real sense it is quite impossible to think the universal, particular, and individual apart from each other. For instance, if the universal is thought to be absolutely separate from individuals, and unique in its own right, then isn't the universal an individual? Further, if an individual is understood as absolutely separate from universals, doesn't it become an empty abstraction (i.e., a kind of universal) without specific quality?

Hegel argues that the concepts of universal, particular and individual mutually determine one another. The universal may also be understood as particular – as one universal among many – and as individual, as a *distinct* universal among many. The particular is also universal, since the concept of particularity ranges over all the different instances of *any* universal. Further, the particular is also individual, given that it is one unique concept among many. The individual, finally, is universal, since the concept of 'individual' applies universally to all individuals – and the individual is also particular, as a particular universal among many. Hegel goes on to develop an account of the judgement forms and the syllogism, in terms of how they relate Universal, Particular and Individual terms. In fact, Hegel sees his entire system in these terms, where the Idea is the universal, nature is the particular, and Spirit the individual. See also **abstract and concrete**; **Concept, Doctrine of**; **concrete universal**; **judgement**; **relation**; **syllogism**; **understanding**.

— W —

war (*der Krieg*)   Hegel regards war as a necessary and ineradicable feature of international relations. He sees states as, in effect, super-individuals without any authority overarching them. Thus, while the individuals *within* nations co-operate and live under a legal authority, nations themselves exist in a state of nature. Hegel makes it clear in his *Logic* that an individual is what it is by not being other individuals. In other words, negation is inherent in the nature of an individual. Thus, as individuals, states will necessarily exist in antagonism with each other, and their interests will often conflict. Hegel writes that 'the state is an individual, and negation is an essential component of individuality. Thus, even if a number of states join together as a family, this league, in its individuality, must generate opposition and create an enemy' (Nisbet, 362; PR § 324 A). This makes war inevitable. However, though war may be inevitable, Hegel does not regard it as unqualifiedly bad. Like Heraclitus (who said that 'war is father of all and king of all'), Hegel sees war as playing a positive role in the world. As early as the *Natural Law* essay of 1802, Hegel claimed that war has a positive effect on the spirit of a nation. In times of protracted peace, citizens become preoccupied with their own personal affairs and tend to lose sight of their bond with the State. However, in wartime, citizens are called upon to keep the welfare of the State squarely in mind and to sacrifice, if need be, their own personal interests, or even their lives. This has the effect of creating a stronger bond between citizens, and between citizens and the State. 'Not only do peoples emerge from wars with added strength, but nations troubled by civil dissension gain internal peace as a result of wars with their external enemies' (Nisbet, 362; PR § 324 A). See also **'cunning of reason'**; **history and Philosophy of History**; **identity and difference**; **negation**; ***Philosophy of Right***; **'slaughter-bench of history'**; **World Spirit**.

'way of despair' (*der Weg der Verzweiflung*)   Hegel describes *The Phenomenology of Spirit*, in his Introduction, as 'the pathway of doubt, or more precisely as the way of despair' (Miller, 49; PG, 61). Hegel goes on to make it clear that his philosophy involves a radical form of doubt, in which the beliefs of commonsense must be ruthlessly interrogated – and left behind. Hegel's philosophy will not, in short, question commonsense ideas in order to justify them. Instead, philosophy involves a form of thinking that transcends the ordinary way of seeing things. To put this into Hegel's technical language, philosophy will involve transcending the understanding through speculative reason. This is a 'way of despair' because it is often very painful to abandon our cherished ideas about ourselves and the world. Indeed, it is too painful a path for many, who will remain wedded to commonsense. The image of the 'way of despair' is an allusion to the Biblical *Via Dolorosa*: the path taken by Jesus, carrying the cross, to the place of his crucifixion. Like Jesus, those of us who walk the path of *The Phenomenology of Spirit* are going to our own immolation, in which we will die to what we have formally been, but at the same time become who we truly are. At the very end of the *Phenomenology* Hegel again alludes to the crucifixion, when he refers to history as 'the Calvary [*Schädelstätte*] of Absolute Spirit' (Miller, 493; PG, 531). See also **commonsense**; **'foaming chalice'**; *Phenomenology of Spirit*; **science**; **speculation**; **understanding**.

whole, the (*das Ganze*)   Famously, Hegel states in the Preface to *The Phenomenology of Spirit* that 'the true is the whole' (*Das Wahre ist das Ganze*; Miller, 11; PG, 15). Hegel believes that all of reality is a system in which individuals exist in organic relation to one another; in which each is what it is by virtue of its relation to the others. Hence, the 'truth' of something is ultimately its place within the whole. Hegel also uses 'the whole' to refer, in effect, to the *idea* of the whole (or of wholeness) that is articulated in his Logic. For example, later in the Preface to the *Phenomenology* he states that the exposition of Science (*Wissenschaft*) 'belongs to Logic, or rather it is Logic. For the method is nothing but the structure of the whole [*der Bau des Ganzen*] set forth in its pure essentiality' (Miller, 28; PG, 35).[30] The Logic in effect lays bare the fundamental categories of the real, and it displays them as an interconnected system. Thus, the Logic is in effect the 'idea of the whole', or the idea of system itself.

The concept of the whole is, furthermore, crucial for understanding Hegelian dialectic. What is essential to the dialectic is not its apparent triadic form. One category supersedes another because what is being articulated through the dialectic is the whole itself. Each category in the Logic, for instance, is a kind of 'provisional definition' of the whole, but each proves inadequate and is negated by a further category. What moves this process is the immanence of the whole in each part – or, one might say, our sense of the whole, and the inadequacy of the part to fully express it. The interesting implication of this is that the dialectic involves the philosophical *recollection* of the whole. See also **Absolute; coherence; dialectic; recollection, imagination, memory; science; sublation; system; truth**.

whole and parts (*das Ganze und die Teile*) In the Doctrine of Essence of the Logic, Hegel discusses the relationship of whole and parts in a sub-section entitled 'The Essential Relationship'. This sub-section falls within a division of the Doctrine of Essence devoted to a treatment of 'Appearance'. What Hegel calls the essential relationship involves the distinction between surface appearance and inner essence (a distinction the entire Doctrine of Essence explores in one way or another). However, Hegel's treatment of the two demonstrates how they are internally related. By contrast, other philosophers have treated appearance and essence as externally related: as absolutely separate and distinct from each other. In the whole/part relationship the whole is seen as something 'essential', since it confers unity upon the parts: without the unity of the whole, the parts would not be parts at all. This gives the parts the status of an 'appearance' of the whole: in each of the parts, the whole, as unifying principle, is reflected. As an example, consider the human body. The body is made up of distinct parts or organs, yet these are what they are only in being unified within the greater whole that is the human organism. Thus, each part can be understood to be an 'appearance' of the whole, because each organ is always understood to be only an organ of the body. As Aristotle famously pointed out, a hand severed from the body is, in a sense, no longer a hand. The hand is nothing in itself – unless it plays a role within the larger whole that is the body. Thus, in the whole/parts relationship the whole seems to be primary.

However, it is also possible to consider things in such a way that the parts are given primacy. After all, the whole is not a whole at all without its parts. In truth, it is legitimate to see things either way: the whole is not a whole without the parts, and the parts are not parts at all unless members of a whole. Following out the logic of the Doctrine of Essence, which is always seeking some deeper or more essential explanatory term, Hegel passes beyond whole and parts to two other forms of the essential relationship before transitioning to the final division of essence: 'Actuality'. Nevertheless, the whole/parts distinction is important for understanding Hegel's system. Hegel regards reality itself as a systematic whole. The whole would not exist, however, without the 'parts' – the individual existents. However, these are what they are in terms of their place within the whole. Each can be considered an 'appearance of the whole' – but the reality of the whole consists precisely in these internally related 'appearances'. See also **actuality**; **appearance**; **concrete universal**; **Essence, Doctrine of**; **Logic**; **relation**; **whole**.

world-historical individuals, the (*die welthistorischen Individuen*) World-historical individuals are those whose personal goals and interests happen to involve or entail the advancement of Spirit to a further stage of development. This is one of the most famous concepts in Hegel's Philosophy of History. Oft-cited examples of such individuals would be Alexander the Great, Caesar and Napoleon. In these men, private passions and projects happen to coincide with the universal aims of Spirit. Hegel thus speaks of them as tools made use of by the 'cunning of reason' to bring about the realization of those universal aims. Much of Hegel's way of speaking about world-historical individuals is figurative, but many have succumbed to the temptation to take it literally. Thus, it is often asserted that Hegel believed in 'World Spirit' or reason as a kind of disembodied mind, which literally exhibits cunning in achieving its ends. In fact, all Hegel means is that human history itself has an inner logic and a goal: it is the coming to self-consciousness of the human race. World-historical individuals further the development of human self-consciousness by bringing about major changes in the organization of human society: bringing old forms of culture to an end, and inaugurating new forms. Through these changes, human beings discover new things about themselves, and are led to reflect on themselves and their potentialities.

In a sense, one can understand Hegel's theory of world-historical individuals as an application of Adam Smith's 'invisible hand' to history itself. According to Smith, when individuals in society pursue their own self interest they tend to promote the good of the community as a whole. For example, I open a drugstore merely to make a profit for myself, but in the process I make much-needed products available to my local community. However, world-historical individuals are those whose personal ends involve 'larger scale' interests and issues, and thus their actions dramatically impact whole peoples and civilizations. World-historical individuals may be largely oblivious to the fact that they are furthering the aims of Spirit, or they may be quite aware of the fact that they are actors on the stage of history. Napoleon, for example, seemed to have been well aware of his status as a world-historical individual, in precisely the sense described by Hegel. See also **'cunning of reason'; history and Philosophy of History; Objective Spirit; World Spirit**.

World Spirit (*der Weltgeist*) The many varieties of 'Spirit' in Hegel are a source of great confusion, and in particular there are many misconceptions surrounding his use of 'World Spirit'. Spirit refers simply to humanity and its consciousness, which is unique in that it is capable of self-reflection. Hegel argues, in fact, that all forms of Spirit are in one way or another aiming at self-consciousness, which is only truly achieved in Absolute Spirit (art, religion and philosophy). Human consciousness, however, does not just suddenly appear on the scene already actualized. In fact, Spirit must develop itself over time: the achievement of human self-understanding is a long process, and history is essentially the account of it. Thus, when Hegel looks at history he sees Spirit working within it as, in effect, its goal or final cause. When Hegel refers to Spirit as what moves history, he often terms it 'World Spirit' – but in fact there is little difference between the concepts of 'Spirit' and 'World Spirit'. Hegel is often misunderstood as claiming that there is some kind of hypostatized, ghostly 'spirit' – or God – acting in history to achieve its ends. When Hegel speaks this way, however, he speaks figuratively. All Hegel really claims is that there is an inner logic to history, and that it is the process of Spirit (or self-aware humanity) realizing itself. He writes in *The Lectures on the Philosophy of World History*: 'the history of the world is a rational process, the rational and necessary evolution of the World Spirit. This Spirit [is] the substance of history; its nature is always one and the same; and it discloses this nature in the existence of the world. (The World Spirit is the Absolute Spirit.)' (Nisbet, 29). Thus, for Hegel, what happens in history will usually turn out to be intelligible as directly or indirectly helping to achieve this end. It is in this sense only that he speaks of a 'World Spirit' immanent in history. See also **'cunning of reason'; history and Philosophy of History; Spirit; world-historical individuals**.

wrong (*das Unrecht*)   In Hegel's *Philosophy of Right*, it is through the concept of 'wrong' that the dialectic passes beyond the stage of abstract right, in which society is seen as existing for the narrowly conceived self-interest of individuals. Under abstract right, there are no duties save one: the duty to respect other people's rights; to let others alone. Still, when we interact and make contracts with one another, there are bound to be people who will feel free to break the rules, and this is essentially what Hegel means by wrong.

The most important form of wrong that he discusses is crime, which always implicitly or explicitly involves some form of coercion. Mugging is an obvious example of this: someone is forced at gunpoint or knifepoint to hand over their money. However, a confidence trickster also coerces his victims, though in a more subtle way. In getting someone to act on the basis of false information the con man is, in essence, compelling another person to act in a manner contrary to how he *would* act if he were in possession of the real truth. The individual who is 'conned' is thus made to act against reason, and against his own interests. When we coerce others Hegel says that we engage in a fundamental contradiction. We regard ourselves as persons who are free and possess rights, and we know that others in society are like us in this respect. When we coerce them, however, it is as if we willfully disregard this fact and choose to treat them as objects without rights or dignity. Coercion is thus a kind of denial of reality – and Hegel tells us that it is a negation. But *what* does it negate? The idea of wrong serves to point us towards something positive: universal principles of right or justice negated by the wrongdoer's actions. It is out of recognition of these principles, in fact, that we demand wrongdoers be punished.

However, punishing people in the name of right requires that we be able to function as impartial judges, able to set aside our individual desires or circumstances and to judge according to universal principles. But in the sphere of abstract right we follow the rules, and apply them, for exclusively selfish reasons: because it suits us to do so. Abstract Right thus cannot be self-sufficient because its self-maintenance requires a kind of impartiality – indeed, a *moral* standpoint – which it does not itself engender. The world of abstract right, in fact, provides us with no ethical guidance whatsoever, beyond telling us not to interfere with the 'rights' of others. With this realization, we make the transition to what Hegel calls 'Morality'. See also **abstract right**; **morality**; ***Philosophy of Right***; **punishment**.

— Z —

Zeitgeist Meaning literally 'spirit of the times', *Zeitgeist* is a term that has come to be associated with Hegel's philosophy of history, though he himself does not use it. In his *Lectures on the History of Philosophy* (1805, published posthumously), Hegel tells us that 'no man can overleap his own time, for the spirit of his time [*der Geist seiner Zeit*] is also his spirit' (LHP II, 96; Werke 19, 111). Similar statements occur elsewhere in Hegel, the most famous being in the Preface to *The Philosophy of Right*, where Hegel tells us that the idea of philosophy transcending its own time is as foolish as the idea that a man can leap over the statue of Rhodes. This is often misunderstood as an assertion of radical historicism (the belief that all claims, even philosophical ones, are true only for the time period in which they are asserted). In fact, Hegel believes that each time period and its unique spirit is a stage in the development of World Spirit itself; a particular, cultural step in humanity's long struggle to come to consciousness of itself. As this process is ongoing, individuals are themselves always expressions of their place in history and its limitations. Thus they can never step completely out of their time period in order to comprehend the world and themselves 'objectively'. However, Hegel believed that he was living at a time when history had reached a kind of consummation: when certain necessary cultural and philosophical forms had been run through and completed. The result is that it is now possible, Hegel claimed, to survey the entire course of history, understand its goal as human self-consciousness, and to argue that in fact that goal had been reached. Hegel did not exempt himself from the rule that one may not step outside one's time period – but he did claim that his time period was unique in that it made possible the achievement of a synoptic view of history and culture. See also **'cunning of reason'; history and Philosophy of History; Objective Spirit; 'owl of Minerva'; 'rose in the cross of the present'; world-historical individuals; World Spirit**.

Chronology

1770	Georg Wilhelm Friedrich Hegel is born on 27 August in Stuttgart.
1777	Hegel attends the Gymnasium Illustre, until 1788.
1783	Hegel's mother dies on 20 September.
1788	Hegel, along with Hölderlin (born 20 March 1770), enters the Protestant seminary at the University of Tübingen. Schelling (born 27 January 1775) enters two years later. The three become close friends.
1790	Hegel receives his master's degree.
1793	Hegel graduates from the seminary. He takes up a post as tutor to the children of Captain von Steiger in Berne.
1795	Hegel writes essays 'The Life of Jesus' and 'The Positivity of the Christian Religion'.
1797	In January, Hegel moves to Frankfurt am Main to become tutor to the Gogel family, a post secured for him by Hölderlin.
1798	Hegel's first publication appears, though anonymously: a translation, with commentary, of a pamphlet detailing the oppression of the French-speaking people of the Swiss canton of Vaud.
1799	Hegel's father dies on 14 January. Hegel composes 'The Spirit of Christianity and its Fate'.
1800	Hegel finishes his 'System-fragment'.
1801	Hegel relocates to Jena with the help of Schelling, who is Professor of Philosophy at the University. Hegel offers lectures as a *Privatdozent*. Hegel's first signed publication, *The Difference Between Fichte's and Schelling's Systems of Philosophy*, appears. Hegel writes his dissertation, *On the Orbits of the Planets*.
1802	Hegel and Schelling launch the *Critical Journal of Philosophy* (which ceases publication in 1803, when Schelling departs Jena). Hegel writes essays including 'Faith and Knowledge' and 'On Natural Law'.
1803	Hegel drafts an early version of his philosophic system.
1805	With the help of Goethe, Hegel is promoted to Professor Extraordinarius. For the first time, Hegel gives his Lectures on the History of Philosophy.

1806	Fathers a child with his landlady. In October he completes the manuscript of *The Phenomenology of Spirit* as Napoleon enters Jena.
1807	*The Phenomenology of Spirit* is published. On 5 February, Hegel's (illegitimate) son Ludwig is born. In March, Hegel relocates to Bamberg to edit a newspaper.
1808	Hegel relocates to Nuremberg to become rector of a Gymnasium.
1811	On 15 September Hegel marries Marie Helena Susanna von Tucher.
1812	Volume One of *The Science of Logic* (The Doctrine of Being) is published. On 27 June Hegel's daughter Susanna is born. On 8 August she dies.
1813	On 7 June Hegel's son Karl is born. The second volume of *The Science of Logic* (The Doctrine of Essence) is published.
1814	On 25 September Hegel's son Immanuel is born.
1816	Hegel takes up his new post as Professor of Philosophy at the University of Heidelberg. Volume Three of *The Science of Logic* (The Doctrine of the Concept) is published.
1817	The first edition of *The Encyclopedia of the Philosophical Sciences in Outline* is published. Hegel lectures for the first time on the material that would become *The Philosophy of Right*.
1818	Hegel lectures for the first time on aesthetics. He is invited to succeed Fichte (who died in 1814) at the University of Berlin.
1820	*The Philosophy of Right* is published.
1821	Hegel lectures on the Philosophy of Religion for the first time.
1822	Hegel lectures on the Philosophy of History for the first time. Travels to Holland.
1824	Hegel travels to Vienna.
1826	Hegel founds the *Yearbooks for Scientific Criticism*.
1827	Hegel visits Paris. The second edition of the *Encyclopedia* appears.
1830	Hegel becomes Rector of the University of Berlin. The third edition of the *Encyclopedia* appears.
1831	Hegel's son Ludwig dies on 28 August. On 14 November, Hegel dies.

Suggestions for Further Reading

For English translations of works by Hegel, consult the 'Abbreviations and Conventions' at the beginning of this book.

Hegel's posthumously published lecture courses are an ideal place for students to begin reading him, as they are written in a far more accessible style than the writings he published during his lifetime. The following inexpensive volumes contain excerpts from these courses:

G. W. F. Hegel, *Introduction to the Philosophy of History*, trans. Leo Rauch (Indianapolis, IN: Hackett Publishing, 1988).

G. W. F. Hegel, *On Art Religion, and the History of Philosophy: Introductory Lectures*, ed. J. Glenn Gray (Indianapolis, IN: Hackett Publishing, 1997; a reprint of the 1970 Harper Torchbooks edition).

General introductions to Hegel and reference volumes

J. N. Findlay, *Hegel: A Re-examination* (1958) (London: Routledge, 2004). This is without question the most popular and widely read introduction to Hegel in English. It has been reprinted many times and used copies are in plentiful supply. The book is generally quite readable and reliable, but it is not without its flaws. Findlay frequently fails to shed much light on important dialectical transitions in Hegel's system, and his treatment of Hegel's social and political thought is dismissive and obtuse. He also continually crosses swords with figures like Russell, Moore and Wittgenstein, which is a distraction and dates the book quite a bit.

Errol E. Harris, *The Spirit of Hegel* (Atlantic Highlands, NJ: Humanities Press, 1993). A marvellous collection of essays by one of the finest Hegelian philosophers writing in English. Topics range over the whole of Hegel's system. Definitely a challenge for beginning students, but worthwhile.

Stephen Houlgate, *An Introduction to Hegel: Freedom, Truth, and History* (New York: Wiley-Blackwell, 2005). In my judgement this is the best introduction to Hegel available in English – especially for undergraduates. Houlgate's explanations of Hegel's ideas are remarkably clear and reliable.

Michael Inwood, *A Hegel Dictionary* (Oxford: Blackwell Publishers, 1992). Inwood's *Dictionary* differs from the present volume in being geared more towards graduate students and professional scholars. Key terms in Hegel are explained with admirable clarity and precision, and many entries include an in-depth account of how the same terms were used by earlier philosophers. Inwood even discusses the etymology of many words, and readers can learn much from him about Hegel's German. This book is thus an extremely valuable resource for advanced students who want to deepen their understanding of Hegel's philosophical vocabulary.

G. R. G. Mure, *An Introduction to Hegel* (Oxford: Oxford University Press, 1940). Mure introduces us to Hegel by showing how his philosophy can be seen as transformation of Aristotelian ideas. Almost half of this classic book is devoted solely to Aristotle! Not an easy read, but worthwhile – both as an introduction to Hegel, and to Aristotle.

G. R. G. Mure, *The Philosophy of Hegel* (Oxford: Oxford University Press, 1965). A short, accessible overview of Hegel's system.

Terry Pinkard, *Hegel: A Biography* (Cambridge: Cambridge University Press, 2000). A long, readable account of Hegel's life and writings.

Ivan Soll, *An Introduction to Hegel's Metaphysics* (Chicago: University of Chicago Press, 1969). A very brief, very clear introduction to Hegel's system.

W. T. Stace, *The Philosophy of Hegel* (1924) (New York: Dover Publications, 1955). This once widely-read book has fallen out of favour in recent years, but it is not without its virtues (the most famous of which is the wonderful pull-out chart of Hegel's system).

On *The Phenomenology of Spirit*

Jean Hyppolite, *The Genesis and Structure of Hegel's Phenomenology of Spirit*, trans. Samuel Cherniak and John Heckman (Evanston, IL: Northwestern University Press, 1974). One of the classic studies of the *Phenomenology*; a very difficult text for those just beginning their study of Hegel, but rewarding for somewhat more advanced students.

Alexandre Kojève, *Introduction to the Reading of Hegel: Lectures on The Phenomenology of Spirit*, trans. James H. Nicholls, Jr. (Ithaca, NY: Cornell University Press, 1969). Both highly influential and controversial, Kojève's lectures on the *Phenomenology* are undeniably distorted by his Marxist convictions. Nevertheless, they are often brilliantly insightful, and exciting to read.

Donald Phillip Verene, *Hegel's Absolute: An Introduction to Reading The Phenomenology of Spirit* (Albany, NY: State University of New York Press, 2007). A very brief, but extremely valuable introduction to Hegel's most difficult work; ideal for those approaching the text for the first time.

Suggestions for Further Reading

Donald Phillip Verene, *Hegel's Recollection: A Study of Images in the Phenomenology of Spirit* (Albany, NY: State University of New York Press, 1985). This work argues that the use of metaphor and imagery in the *Phenomenology* is an integral part of Hegel's philosophic 'method'. An unusual approach to Hegel, well worth considering.

On Hegel's Logic and philosophical approach

Errol E. Harris, *An Interpretation of the Logic of Hegel* (Lanham, MD: University Press of America, 1983). By far the clearest introduction to Hegel's Logic available. Harris writes as a follower of Hegel, not merely as a commentator, and succeeds admirably in shedding light on some of the most difficult ideas in his philosophy.

William Maker, *Philosophy Without Foundations: Rethinking Hegel* (Albany: State University of New York Press, 1994). This work, like Winfield's *Overcoming Foundations* (see below), emphasizes the anti-foundational character of Hegel's thought, and shows how his philosophy constitutes a presuppositionless and self-grounding system.

G. R. G. Mure, *A Study of Hegel's Logic* (Oxford: Oxford University Press, 1950). Like Mure's other books on Hegel, this is not easy reading. However, next to Harris's commentary (see above) this is the best survey of the entirety of Hegel's Logic that I know of.

Richard Dien Winfield, *Overcoming Foundations: Studies in Systematic Philosophy* (New York: Columbia University Press, 1989).

On the Philosophy of Nature

Comparatively little has been published in English on Hegel's Philosophy of Nature. Perhaps the best place to begin is with M. J. Petry's annotated edition of the Philosophy of Nature itself: *Hegel's Philosophy of Nature*, 3 vols, trans. M. J. Petry (London: George Allen and Unwin, 1970). Hegel's frequent references to the science of his time are often baffling to twenty-first century readers. Petry sheds light on these passages, and much else.

The following works by Errol E. Harris are not commentaries on the text of the Philosophy of Nature. Instead, they attempt to show how Hegel's philosophy provides a framework for interpreting recent science, especially physics. (In short, they attempt to do for the science of today what Hegel did for the science of yesterday.) These works are readable and exciting, and they presuppose little background in science.

Errol E. Harris, *Cosmos and Anthropos: A Philosophical Interpretation of the Anthropic Cosmological Principle* (Atlantic Highlands, NJ: Humanities Press, 1991).

Errol E. Harris, *Cosmos and Theos: Ethical and Theological Implications of* the *Anthropic Cosmological Principle* (Atlantic Highlands, NJ: Humanities Press, 1992).

Errol E. Harris, *Formal, Transcendental, and Dialectical Thinking: Logic and Reality* (Albany, NY: State University of New York Press, 1987).

On Hegel's social and political thought ('Objective Spirit')

Lewis P. Hinchman, *Hegel's Critique of the Enlightenment* (Gainesville, FL: University of Florida Press, 1984). In the process of dealing with Hegel's treatment of the Enlightenment, Hinchman discusses much of Hegel's system, especially *The Philosophy of Right*. An extremely insightful treatment of Hegel's political thought, recommended for more advanced students.

W. H. Walsh, *Hegelian Ethics* (Bristol, UK: Thoemmes Press, 1998). A very brief (less than 100 pages), lucid introduction to Hegel's ethical thought, as set forth in *The Philosophy of Right*.

On Hegel's Philosophy of Art

William Desmond, *Art and the Absolute* (Albany, NY: State University of New York Press, 1986). Desmond's book argues for the central importance of the Philosophy of Art in Hegel's system, and relates it to later Continental thought.

Jack Kaminsky, *Hegel on Art* (Albany, NY: State University of New York Press, 1962). An excellent, accessible introduction to Hegel's Philosophy of Art.

On Hegel's Philosophy of Religion

Emile Fackenheim, *The Religious Dimension in Hegel's Thought* (Chicago: University of Chicago Press, 1967). A classic study; highly readable.

Walter Jaeschke, *Reason in Religion: The Foundations of Hegel's Philosophy of Religion*, trans. J. Michael Stewart and Peter C. Hodgson (Berkeley, CA: University of California Press, 1990). An exhaustive study of Hegel's Philosophy of Religion, covering his entire corpus. Recommended for more advanced students.

Glenn Alexander Magee, *Hegel and the Hermetic Tradition* (Ithaca, NY: Cornell University Press, 2001; revised paperback edition, 2008). My book argues for the influence of the Western mystical and esoteric traditions on Hegel's Philosophy of Religion, and, indeed, on his entire philosophy.

Endnotes

1. Eric Voegelin, 'On Hegel: A Study in Sorcery', in *The Collected Works of Eric Voegelin*, Vol. 12, Published Essays, ed. Ellis Sandoz (Baton Rouge: Louisiana State University Press, 1990), 228. Voegelin's metaphor plays on the fact that Hegel describes his Logic as a circle and his philosophy itself as a 'circle of circles'.
2. See Terry Pinkard, 'Hegel: A Life', in *The Cambridge Companion to Hegel and Nineteenth-Century Philosophy*, Frederick C. Beiser, ed. (Cambridge: Cambridge University Press, 2008), 17. Pinkard's article is a condensed version of his book-length *Hegel: A Biography* (Cambridge: Cambridge University Press, 2000). Both the book and the article offer highly readable, thoroughly researched accounts of Hegel's life, and the reader is hereby referred to them for more information. Like most commentators on Hegel, however, Pinkard has his own axes to grind. Among other things he consistently downplays the religious and socially conservative sides to Hegel's thought, and character.
3. In Germany a *Gymnasium* is a secondary school for university-bound students. The Hegel house at Eberhardstrasse 53 still exists and is now a tourist attraction: it contains a small museum devoted to Hegel's life and writings.
4. Pinkard, 'Hegel: A Life,' 21.
5. For more information see Pinkard, 'Hegel: A Life', 23–24.
6. *Langenscheidt's New College German Dictionary* (New York: Langenscheidt, 1995), 705.
7. Quoted in an explanatory endnote in Hegel, *Elements of the Philosophy of Right*, ed. Allen W. Wood, trans. H. B. Nisbet (Cambridge: Cambridge University Press, 1991), 390.
8. G. W. F. Hegel, *Natural Right*, trans. T. M. Knox (Philadelphia: University of Pennsylvania Press, 1975), 89; *Naturrecht*, in *Gesammelte Werke*, Vol. 4, ed. Harmut Buchner and Otto Pöggler (Hamburg: Felix Meiner Verlag, 1968), 446.
9. Jean Hyppolite, *The Genesis and Structure of Hegel's Phenomenology of Spirit*, trans. S. Cherniak and J. Heckman (Evanston: Northwestern University Press, 1974), 15; my emphasis.
10. I am excluding from consideration here early works by Hegel, including his early essays, as well as his posthumously published notes, and other minor works such as review essays.
11. The translation is by Donald Phillip Verene and appears in his *Hegel's Recollection* (Albany: State University of New York Press, 1985), 6; quoted by permission. The German original reads:

    Freundlos war der grosse Weltenmeister,
    Fühlte *Mangel* – darum schuf er Geister,

Selge Spiegel *seiner* Seligkeit! –
Fand das höchste Wesen schon kein gleiches,
Aus dem Kelch des ganzen Seelenreiches
Schäumt *ihm* – die Unendlichkeit.

12. Walter Dierauer, *Hölderlin und der Spekulative Pietismus Württembergs: Gemeinsame Anschauungshorizonte im Werk Oetingers und Hölderlins* (Zürich: Juris, 1986); Ulrich Gaier, *Der gesetzliche Kalkül: Hölderlin's Dichtungslehre* (Tübingen: Max Niemeyer, 1962); Priscilla A. Hayden-Roy, *'A Foretaste of Heaven': Friedrich Hölderlin in the Context of Württemberg Pietism* (Amsterdam: Rodopi B.V., 1994).
13. Alan M. Olson, *Hegel and the Spirit: Philosophy as Pneumatology* (Princeton: Princeton University Press, 1992), 58.
14. See Terry Pinkard, *Hegel: A Biography* (Cambridge: Cambridge University Press, 2000), 82.
15. See Errol E. Harris, *The Spirit of Hegel* (Atlantic Highlands, NJ: Humanities Press, 1993), 141.
16. The translation is by Richard D. McKirahan, Jr. in *A Presocratics Reader*, ed. Patricia Curd (Indianapolis: Hackett, 1996), 35.
17. *Intelligenzblatt der Jenaischen Allgemeinen Literaturzeitung*, 28 October 1807. Quoted in M. J. Petry, *Hegel's Philosophy of Subjective Spirit*, Vol. I (Dordrecht: D. Reidel, 1978), lxvii.
18. J. N. Findlay, *Hegel: A Re-Examination* (New York: Oxford University Press, 1958), 116.
19. Karl Rosenkranz, *G. W. F. Hegels Leben* (Berlin: Dunker and Humblot, 1944), 192.
20. Quoted in an explanatory endnote in Hegel, *Elements of the Philosophy of Right*, ed. Allen W. Wood, trans. H. B. Nisbet (Cambridge: Cambridge University Press, 1991), 390.
21. An admirably clear discussion of this point is to be found in Alexandre Kojève's *Introduction to the Reading of Hegel*, trans. James H. Nichols, Jr. (Ithaca: Cornell University Press, 1969), see especially pp. 41–44.
22. See Verene, *Hegel's Recollection*, 2–3.
23. 'Über die Hegelsche Lehre oder absolutes Wissen und moderner Pantheismus. Über Philosophie überhaupt und Hegels *Enzyklopädie der philosophischen Wissenschaften* insbesondere', (1829), in *Werke* 11, 466.
24. F. W. J. Schelling, *System of Transcendental Idealism*, trans. Peter Heath (Charlottesville: University of Virginia Press, 1978), 12.
25. Quoted in *Hegel: The Letters*, 32.
26. LHP 3, 288; not present in *Werke*, see *Sämtliche Werke*, Vol. 19, ed. Hermann Glockner (Stuttgart: Fromann, 1928), 377.
27. This interpretation is advanced by Verene in *Hegel's Recollection*, 92–93.
28. G. R. G. Mure's discussion of this matter is admirably clear. See his *The Philosophy of Hegel* (Oxford: Oxford University Press, 1965), 136.
29. See Jacob Klein, 'Leibniz, an Introduction', in *Jacob Klein: Lectures and Essays*, edited by Robert B. Williamson and Elliott Zuckerman (Annapolis: St John's College, 1985), 201.
30. Miller actually omits the crucial words 'of the whole' in his translation.

www.ingramcontent.com/pod-product-compliance
Lightning Source LLC
Chambersburg PA
CBHW052219300426
44115CB00011B/1746